THE MODAL FUTURE

It is commonly assumed that we conceive of the past and the future as symmetrical. In this book, Fabrizio Cariani develops a new theory of future-directed discourse and thought – one that shows our linguistic and philosophical conceptions of the past and future are, in fact, fundamentally different. Future thought and talk, Cariani suggests, are best understood in terms of a systematic analogy with counter-factual thought and talk, rather than as just mirror images of the past. Cariani makes this case by developing detailed formal semantic theories as well as by advancing less technical views about the nature of future-directed judgment and prediction. His book addresses, in a thought-provoking way, several important debates in contemporary philosophy, and his synthesis of parallel threads of research will benefit scholars in the philosophy of language, metaphysics, epistemology, linguistics, and cognitive science.

FABRIZIO CARIANI is Associate Professor of Philosophy at University of Maryland, College Park. He has published extensively in the areas of philosophy of language, epistemology, and logic. He is an editor for the journal *Philosopher's Imprint*.

T0370541

THE MODAL FUTURE

A Theory of Future-Directed Thought and Talk

FABRIZIO CARIANI

University of Maryland, College Park

Shaftesbury Road, Cambridge CB2 8EA, United Kingdom

One Liberty Plaza, 20th Floor, New York, NY 10006, USA

477 Williamstown Road, Port Melbourne, VIC 3207, Australia

314–321, 3rd Floor, Plot 3, Splendor Forum, Jasola District Centre, New Delhi – 110025, India

103 Penang Road, #05–06/07, Visioncrest Commercial, Singapore 238467

Cambridge University Press is part of Cambridge University Press & Assessment, a department of the University of Cambridge.

We share the University's mission to contribute to society through the pursuit of education, learning and research at the highest international levels of excellence.

www.cambridge.org
Information on this title: www.cambridge.org/9781108465472

DOI: 10.1017/9781108668514

© Fabrizio Cariani 2021

First published 2021
First paperback edition 2023

A catalogue record for this publication is available from the British Library

ISBN   978-1-108-47477-1   Hardback
ISBN   978-1-108-46547-2   Paperback

To my parents Patrizia and Walter and my brother Edoardo.

Contents

Figures

xii *List of Figures*

Preface

I would not have had the competence to write this book without sustained intellectual dealings with colleagues and mentors. John MacFarlane directed my PhD thesis in 2009. Although the thesis itself was about something else, it was John's work that got me started thinking about future discourse already back in 2004. Some of my 2004 discussions with (then-fellow-grad-student) Mike Caie still resonate in these pages. I didn't have much of a project, however, until I started discussing this material with Paolo Santorio a decade later in 2014. At this time, I had convinced myself that future discourse had a modal component, but I was struggling with how to square that with some very simple observations philosophers had been accumulating about the temporal aspect of its meaning. Paolo suggested the broad idea of mimicking Stalnaker's account of conditionals in the semantics of *will*, and then together we worked on making this work. This became "*Will* Done Better" – a paper we both regard as one of our respective bests, and one of the centerpieces of the theory in this book. Mike Caie also commented on an early version of "*Will* Done Better" at the Central APA in 2016. Meanwhile, at every conference I attended, I seemed to run into Simon Goldstein. I don't know anybody who enjoys talking philosophy as much as Simon does, which makes talking philosophy with him just as enjoyable. This project is the happy beneficiary of Simon's generosity with his time and his endless stream of thoughts.

I started giving talks about this project in the fall of 2014. There's a lot of audiences to thank, but here they are. Before joining forces with Santorio, I spoke on these subjects at the 2014 Philosophy of Language and Linguistics Conference in Dubrovnik; the Fourth Parma Workshop in Semantics; the University of Chicago, Linguistics and Philosophy Workshop; the nonstandard modals workshop at the University of Leeds (where Santorio and I started talking about collaborating); University of St. Andrews, Arché Center; and the Linguistics and Philosophy Working Group at the University of Michigan. In collaboration with Santorio,

I spoke at the 2015 meeting of the Australasian Association of Philosophy (I was heavily jet-lagged and had an audience of three – not my best performance!); the LENLS 12, Tokyo, Japan; the University of Chicago, Workshop on Nonveridical Expressions and Subjectivity in Language; the 2015 Amsterdam Colloquium; and the 2016 Central APA, Chicago. After wrapping up "*Will* Done Better," I started giving talks with an eye toward this book. For that period, I thank audiences at the New York Philosophy of Language Discussion Group; the 2016 meeting of the Italian Society for Analytic Philosophy; the philosophy colloquium at the University of Illinois, Chicago; an impromptu talk at King's College in London; the Hans Kamp seminar at the University of Texas at Austin (and specifically I thank Josh Dever for inviting me and flooding me with useful feedback over the course of two talks); a workshop on the Philosophy of Information at Shanghai University; the philosophy colloquium at the University of North Carolina, Chapel Hill; more philosophy colloquia, at Northern Illinois University, at the University of Maryland College Park, and at Tufts University; the final round of talks at a symposium on future-directed assertions at the 2019 Pacific Meeting of the APA in Vancouver (where David Boylan delivered incisive and helpful comments); the 2019 PRIN conference in Venice; the Logic of Conceivability group and the 2019 Amsterdam Colloquium; and the Jowett Society in Oxford, where I spoke on February 29, 2020. Three weeks later we couldn't fly across the Atlantic anymore, but I still managed to get valuable feedback at a virtual philosophy of language work-in-progress group, organized by Ginger Schultheis and Matt Mandelkern.

There are some specific individuals in these talks who made comments that impacted the way I thought about these topics. Other individuals were simply kind enough to listen to me talk and then point me in useful directions. I tried to keep a running tab of these comments. I am sure I inadvertently left someone out and I am sure some people have forgotten we talked because it's been so long. But here's the list: Maria Aloni, Sam Alxatib, Sara Aronowitz, David Beaver, Harjit Bhogal, Andrea Bianchi, Justin Bledin, Kyle Blumberg, Daniel Bonevac, David Boylan, Sam Carter, Lucas Champollion, Ivano Ciardelli, Sam Cumming, Josh Dever, Aaron Doliana, Kevin Dorst, Daniel Drucker, Julien Dutant, Kenny Easwaran, Branden Fitelson, Melissa Fusco, Anastasia Giannakidou, Michael Glanzberg, Sandy Goldberg, Jeremy Goodman, Valentine Hacquard, John Hawthorne, Ben Holguin, Jeff Horty, Nick Huggett, Megan Hyska, Hans Kamp, Magdalena Kaufmann, Stefan Kaufmann, Chris Kennedy, Jeff King, Justin Khoo, Peter Klecha, Arc Kocurek, Natasha Korotkova,

Angelika Kratzer, Steven Kuhn, Jennifer Lackey, Maria Lasonen-Aarnio, Harvey Lederman, Nicholas Leonard, Matt Mandelkern, Alda Mari, Dean McHugh, Eleonora Montuschi, Sebastiano Moruzzi, Sarah Moss, Shyam Nair, Dilip Ninan, Carlotta Pavese, Paul Portner, Geoff Pynn, Brian Rabern, Baron Reed, Jessica Rett, Georges Rey, Lance Rips, Gillian Russell, Alessio Santelli, Anders Schoubye, Ginger Schultheis, James Shaw, Patrick Shireff, Vesela Simeonova, Giuseppe Spolaore, Shawn Standefer, Isidora Stojanovic, Una Stojnic, Mack Sullivan, Eric Swanson, Rich Thomason, Mike Titelbaum, Patrick Todd, Stephen Torre, Alexis Wellwood, Malte Willer, Alexander Williams, Robbie Williams, Alex Worsnip, Seth Yalcin, Igor Yanovich, Zhuoye Zhao, Sandro Zucchi. What can I say? If I failed, it's not because my interlocutors lacked in distinction, sharpness, or goodwill.

Three graduate seminars I taught at Northwestern were critical in shaping and sharpening my views on these topics. These were "Future Contingents" (Fall 2015), "Counterfactuals and Probability" (Spring 2018), and "The Modal Future" (Fall 2019). I want to thank the students in these seminars for their contributions: Andrés Abugattas, Beth Barker, John Beverley, Gretchen Ellefson, Nathaly Garcia, Andy Hull, Nate Lauffer, Whitney Lilly, Matthew Myers, Carry Osborne, Spencer Paulson, Kathryn Pogin, Ben Reuveni, Daniel Skibra, and Jon Vandenburgh. Additionally, John Beverley and Nate Lauffer also served as RAs, assisting me in preparing the final manuscript. In the nick of time, two virtual reading groups pointed out typos and some important mistakes (their members are already thanked in the previous paragraph).

Some of the research for this book happened concurrently with, and was presented with the support of, my New Directions Fellowship from the Mellon Foundation. While the New Directions helped me acquire new skills that are not very much on display here, themes from what I was learning have made their way through much of the book, and especially in Part V. I am grateful for the time away from teaching that the New Directions support afforded me.

At some point in 2016, I mentioned to my dentist, Dr. Leonard, that I was working on a book. He must keep a diary with interesting facts about his patients, because at every visit thereafter he'd ask me how far along my book was. The answer wasn't always the one *I* wanted to hear or utter. Anyway, 10% of what spurred me to finish the book is so I didn't have to feel like a fraud when talking to Dr. Leonard. He's getting a free copy.

I am also grateful to Hilary Gaskin in her role as philosophy editor at Cambridge University Press for her relentless professionalism and clear-headed stewardship of the project, as well as to Hal Churchman for his work as editorial assistant. I am grateful to Jill Hobbs for her expert copyediting work, which greatly improved the systematicity and clarity of my writing.

I started thinking about future thought and talk in the summer of 2014 – when my older daughter, Iris, was just weeks old. In 2018, our family welcomed another girl to the family, Vera. The personal story of the composition of this book is the story of my learning how to reconcile my work obligations with my desire to be around my family. The thing I will remember the most from this time is the baseline of happiness and gratitude that these girls, as well as my spouse Angeline, have filled my life with.

The book is dedicated to my parents, Patrizia and Walter, and to my brother, Edoardo. My becoming a researcher on the other side of the Atlantic depended in large part on their support, guidance, and companionship.

we consider some other asymmetries between past and future: I can try to rig Shiny's toss so that it lands heads, but I cannot rig Bright's toss. Admittedly, it may not be entirely clear what these intuitions amount to, but there is no denying that we have them.

It is not just that there are two perspectives, symmetric and asymmetric, with respect to one type of fact. There are several independent dimensions along which we might consider whether past and future are symmetric. The apparent asymmetry in openness of the future is one such dimension, but we can easily produce others without leaving the domain of metaphysics. Do laws of nature discriminate between past and future or are they symmetric? Do past individuals and events have the same ontological status as future individuals and events? These questions are largely independent of each other: One can consistently believe, say, that past and future are ontologically symmetric, and that the laws of nature are asymmetric. In cases where there are entailments and exclusions between answers, they are subtle and require careful scrutiny.

The crucial observation that sparks this book is that some dimensions of potential asymmetry arise outside the domain of metaphysics. Specifically, there are important asymmetries that pertain to how we think and talk about the future. The story of Shiny and Bright illustrated some respects in which belief formation and evidence might be asymmetric in this way. Here are some others: Does our linguistic system treat past and future as mirror images of each other? Do we bring to bear the same cognitive resources in thinking about the past as we do in thinking about the future?

These linguistic, cognitive, and epistemological questions are the central points of focus in this book. I argue that there are important cognitive and linguistic asymmetries between past and future. Moreover, I argue that these linguistic and cognitive asymmetries are largely independent of the traditional metaphysical symmetries.[1] Even if we were to accept that past and future are symmetric in every metaphysical respect, we would still have to accept that they are not symmetric in terms of how we think and talk about them. As in the metaphysical case, most of these questions are not automatically settled by one's stance on the others. But even so, my answers to the linguistic and cognitive symmetry questions impose constraints on the answer to the metaphysical ones. A lot of the interest of what is to come, I hope, will consist in exploring the connecting threads.

---

[1] I am fascinated, however, by attempts such as Albert's (2000, chapter 6) idea that we can explain some central asymmetries of knowledge in terms of fundamental physical facts. The level of analysis of the present book is very different from Albert's discussion, but some of the same questions drive my inquiry.

The overarching theme of the book is the thesis that thought and talk about the future are *modal*. The linguistic aspect of this thesis is that the meanings and content of future-directed claims, such as *the water will boil*, are best understood in terms of a fundamental parallel with counterfactual claims, such as *the water would have boiled if you had turned on the stove*. My defense of this claim builds on work I did with Paolo Santorio (Cariani and Santorio, 2017, 2018), as well as on a strong tradition in linguistics. The contrasting view, which I reject, understands future-directed thought and talk as being an extended parallel with past-directed thought and talk.

However, my research with Santorio is not merely a replication of the extant insights from linguistics. We found that nearly all of the developments of the modal future hypothesis in linguistics were problematic, often for reasons that are clearly developed in the parallel philosophy literature. Broadly speaking, these problems emerge from methodological blindspots in both semantics and epistemology, and ultimately from a lack of integration between them. As I view it, semantics – our best body of theories of linguistic meaning – is part of a philosophically integrated theory of information and inquiry. As such, semantics is subject to cognitive and epistemological constraints: When we compare semantic theories, we must keep an eye on how they interface with cognitive and epistemological matters. Conversely, choosing the best theory of rational credence and rational action might depend on questions of semantics. Because this integrated view is somewhat heretical, let me consider some powerful illustrations of these dependencies.

An underappreciated passage in Stalnaker's seminal discussion of counterfactual conditionals illustrates how semantics might be subject to epistemological constraints. Here is Stalnaker:

> [M]any counterfactuals seem to be synthetic, and contingent, statements about unrealized possibilities. But contingent statements must be capable of confirmation by empirical evidence, and the investigator can gather evidence only in the actual world. How are conditionals which are both empirical and contrary-to-fact possible at all? How do we learn about possible worlds, and where are the facts (or counterfacts) which make counterfactuals true? (Stalnaker, 1968, pp. 29–30)

Stalnaker's solution to this problem involves modeling the semantics of counterfactuals in terms of similarity to the actual world. When one acquires evidence that bears on which world is actual, one also acquires evidence that bears on which worlds are *similar* to the actual world. What matters to my present point is not so much Stalnaker's particular solution, but the methodology behind it. He is saying that an adequate semantics for counterfactuals should speak, to some degree, to epistemological questions, and hence that epistemology constrains semantics.

There are also constraints that run in the opposite direction. I offer two examples. Consider first the Bayesian epistemologist's assumption that rational agents ought to assign credence 1 to all logical truths. Under this assumption, semantics evidently constrains the theory of rational credence. There would be a tension between claiming that A is a logical truth and claiming that it is rational to assign intermediate credence to its content. Now, that Bayesian assumption is itself controversial. Strictly, speaking, probability theory only requires that rational agents assign credence 1 to Boolean tautologies (a modest subset of the set of all logical truths). Some theorists (Garber, 1983) even leverage the difference between Boolean tautologies and necessary truths more generally into a Bayesian solution to the problem of logical omniscience. However, the fact that the assumption is disputed does not disarm the argument: It is hard to find a plausible philosophical stance from which it's okay to require rational agents to assign credence 1 to tautologies, while allowing them to have intermediate credence in other kinds of *logical* truths. (This is compatible with relying on Garber's approach when it comes to uncertainty about mathematical truths, if those are nonlogical, or about other kinds of necessary truths.)

As a second example, consider principles that connect beliefs about chance and subjective credences, such as Lewis's (1986b) *Principal Principle*. According to the Principal Principle, one's credence in chancy propositions ought to align with one's credences about what the chances are. It is standard to think that the bearers of chance are propositions, not sentences. It would be implausible to claim that some sentence failed to express a proposition, but it still made sense to say that it had an objective chance.[2] At the same time, our intuitions about the chance of propositions are mediated by their linguistic forms. When I reflect on my credence that the coin will land heads, I think about the chances of a proposition through the medium of a sentence that expresses it. Semantic verdicts about which propositions are expressed by a sentence are of direct relevance to the theory of rational credence.

---

[2] Nonfactualists about conditionals tend to make this kind of move for subjective credence. They claim that there are senses of "credence" in which we can meaningfully have credence in sentences that do not have truth-conditions. For instance, they claim that the subjective credence in a conditional merely registers its degree of acceptability, which needn't be equal to its probability of truth. I submit that this kind of view is a nonstarter for objective chance.

These reflections support a two-way interaction between semantics and epistemology. That relation might in fact be three-way: A similar case can be made for the relation between semantics and cognition, but I'll save it for later in the book.

In calling the belief in these connections "heretical," I do not mean to suggest that I am alone in advocating this integrated approach. Though there is plenty of pushback, there is a growing movement in this direction.[3] But I went ahead with this sermon on behalf of theoretical integration, because I have not yet seen anyone else commit it to print, and because conversations suggest to me that there is fundamental disagreement between us integrationists and large groups of semanticists and epistemologists.

As a result of this broad perspective, the inquiry in this book is unapologetically interdisciplinary. This is fitting to the topic. As my students would put it, philosophers have puzzled about the semantic status of future-talk literally for millennia. Research on this topic grew enormously during the Middle Ages, where it got connected to questions concerning divine omniscience (Normore, 1982; Øhrstrøm, 2009). Many centuries later, it received a further jolt as part of the development of modern logic in the twentieth century (Prior, 1957, 1967, 1976; Łukasiewicz, 1970; Thomason, 1970). At the same time, the study of tense and aspect, and more generally of the devices that language recruits to allow us to talk about nonpresent events and states, is also a prominent area of research in both syntax and semantics. Given the level of specialization within each of these literature threads, it is unsurprising that the philosophical track and the linguistic track have proceeded in relative isolation from each other. Moreover, even when we do not altogether ignore each other (which fortunately happens less and less), it can be difficult for the two-way interaction between philosophy and linguistics to proceed smoothly, given our different canons, assumptions, argumentative standards, and backgrounds. An important part of the project of this book is to reach a view about future discourse that is as much as possible informed by *both* philosophical and linguistic theorizing, mending inconsistencies between the traditions when they arise.

---

[3] It is impossible to compile an exhaustive list. This integrated approach seems transparent to me in the works of Robert Stalnaker. But here are some recent works that have influenced me, from authors whom I claim as fellow-travelers (and hopefully they agree with the characterization): Boylan (in press a, b); Goldstein (in press a); Lassiter (2011, 2017); Mandelkern (2018); Mandelkern et al. (2017); Moss (2013, 2015, 2018); Todd and Rabern (in press), Santorio (2017, in press); and Schulz (2014, 2017).

When I started writing this book, the mission I gave to myself was to write "Lewis's *Counterfactuals* but for future discourse." At some point, that model broke. *Counterfactuals* begins with a bang: The first chapter tells us all the fundamentals of Lewis's theory. In the present case, before I could start developing my own proposal, I needed to set up my opponents and, more importantly, to introduce some foundational material.

Accordingly, Part I of the book develops one of my main polemical target, the *symmetric paradigm*. This is the view that the meanings of future and past tenses are mirror images of each other. Chapter 1 sets up the view, and Chapter 2 summarizes some important research that shows how the linguistic thesis that future- and past-directed discourse are symmetric might be available to someone who thought that future and past are *metaphysically asymmetric*. In essence, part I is a very opinionated review of the literature: It is the background I normally would presuppose in a specialist article, except this time I get to tell that background story in my preferred way. Readers who are familiar with the relevant literature might just skim it to get a sense of the notation I use and to take note of those places where my terminology and framework are not canonical.

Part II runs through the themes of Cariani and Santorio (2018) at a more deliberate pace. Chapter 3 introduces the linguistic case for the thesis that predictive expressions, such as *will*, are modals. Chapter 4 reproduces the key arguments we relied on in Cariani and Santorio (2018) against the thesis that if *will* is a modal, it must be a *quantificational* modal. Chapter 5 introduces the theory that Santorio and myself advocated to make sense of the idea that there are non-quantificational modals. I refer to this theory as *selection semantics*, because the formal presentation of the theory appeals to selection functions, roughly in analogy with Stalnaker's model of theoretic analysis of conditionals.

There are many ways of developing the selection semantics insight, and many bells and whistles we might add to the basic presentation of the theory. Part III goes beyond the theory of Cariani and Santorio (2018) in three respects. Chapter 6 discusses how *will* interacts semantically with other modals and specifically with possibility modals. Along the way, it fixes some problems with the basic semantics of Chapter 5. Chapter 7 adds on a different module to the account of Cariani and Santorio (2018). In that work, we largely punted on the question of why, if predictive expressions are modal, they help us make claims about the future. In this chapter, I develop a semantic framework inspired by Condoravdi's work on the future orientation of modals (Condoravdi, 2002). The elevator pitch for this view is that sentences such as *she will win* get to be about the future in the same way in which sentences such as *she might win* get to be about the future. Chapter 8 targets the interaction between *if* and *will*. Here I discuss what sorts of truth-conditions my theory predicts for *will*-conditionals as well as how the theory might be generalized beyond those.

Part IV shifts gears, turning to the pragmatics of future discourse. There is a long-standing concern that the idea that the future is open might be in conflict with the claim that it is normatively permissible to make assertions about the future. Some theorists even suggest that people never make assertions about the future. According to them, people engage in an assertion-like speech act that goes by the name of "prediction." Chapter 9 clears the ground by developing a comprehensive theory of the speech act of prediction and of its relation to assertion. It immediately follows from this discussion that some predictions also are assertions about the future. Chapter 9 also works as a self-standing discussion and indeed it is an expansion and reelaboration of Cariani (2020). With that work in place, Chapter 10 moves on to the apparent conflict between the idea that the future is open and the observation that future contingents are generally assertible. These conflicts are sometimes referred to as the "assertion problem." I argue that there are many versions of the assertion problem – and so that the label "assertion problem" is a misnomer. I go on to develop a few of them in detail. In Chapter 11, I argue that addressing the assertion problem might force us to revise the way we think about what it is for the future to be open. There are non-epistemic ways of thinking about the openness of the future that can defuse the standard problems connecting openness and the norms of assertion. More specifically I argue that, despite some bad press, a *Thin Red Line* metaphysics might be our best chance of making objective sense of the idea that the future is open while also making sense of future-directed discourse. In this chapter I endorse, for the sake of argument, the contention that it is metaphysically indeterminate which world is actual, although it is determinate that there is an actual world (Hirsch, 2006; Barnes and Cameron, 2009, 2011). The chapter aims to contribute a model of linguistic context to go with it.

Part V drops the theme of the openness of the future and moves on to future cognition and future epistemology. Chapter 12 discusses the cognitive faculties that people seem to recruit in making judgments about the future. Several theorists have suggested that a distinctive mechanism by which we make counterfactual judgments is "mental simulation" (see Kahneman and Tversky, 1982; for a recent discussion in the philosophy literature, see Williamson, 2008). In this chapter, I consider what that claim of distinctness might amount to and how it might generalize to future-directed discourse. I observe an important limitation of that extension: Future-directed judgments rely just as much on imaginative faculties such as mental simulation as they do on our inferential ones. I conclude that what is special about future-directed judgments is that they create the default expectation that they are based on indirect evidence, in a sense the chapter makes more precise. This idea is applied in Chapter 13 to some puzzles about the future stemming from the work of Ninan (2014, unpublished manuscript). Ninan's striking puzzle suggests that future-directed knowledge seems to be cheaper than past-directed knowledge. Chapter 13 explores what this debate looks like from the perspective of my theory of future-directed content and judgment, along the way developing an account of one of the key pieces of evidence for the modality of *will*, from Chapter 3.

There are a few paths through the book that involve less commitment than reading it from cover to cover. Part III is the most specialized – and in fact the most technically specialized – part of the book; there is a coherent sub-book that just omits it. At the opposite end, there is a sub-book in formal semantics that runs from Part I to Part III. Chapters 9, 12, and 13 are self-standing, as is the combination of Chapters 10 and 11 and Part II taken as a whole.

PART I

Background

CHAPTER I

The Symmetric Paradigm

1.1 The Symmetric Paradigm

From grade school to the higher reaches of tense logic, a fundamental paradigm prevails. Human languages offer up the ability to talk about past events, present ones, and future ones. According to the paradigm, in many human languages, this is implemented by a system of tenses with three broad categories: past, present, and future. With some exceptions and complications, these tenses line up with the temporal location of the appropriate events.[1]

The insight that past and future tenses have symmetric meanings is central to research frameworks that build on the classical framework for the logic of tense (Prior, 1957, 1967, 1969). The symmetric paradigm reverberates in many theoretical decisions concerning the syntax, the semantics, and logic of discourse about the future. When Prior (1967, p. 35) provides a series of postulates for "the logic of futurity," he immediately proceeds to lay down "a series of analogous postulates … to give the logic of pastness." Fast forward fifty years, and we find that von Fintel and Heim (2011) take as a starting point an approach on which the semantic entries for future and past tense (lifted from tense logic) look like "mirror images of each other, though they are of different syntactic categories" (p. 72).

This chapter develops the core idea of the symmetric paradigm. Eventually, I will critique this idea, with an eye toward developing my own, nonsymmetric account of future discourse. But before any cards are on the table, I want to clarify that my critique of the symmetric paradigm is limited in scope. Even if it turned out that the meanings of the expressions we use to talk about the future – the *predictive expressions*, as I will say – are of an entirely different sort from the meanings of the expressions we recruit to talk about the past, there is nothing inherently objectionable

---

[1]   While some languages, such as Mandarin Chinese, lack tense markers, it is nevertheless possible to characterize their devices of temporal reference symmetrically (Bittner, 2014).

about designing a system of *logic* with symmetric tenses. This is because studying the logic of tensed statements need not be part of a model of the meaning of tense in natural language. A formal temporal logic could be part of an attempt to regiment certain philosophical arguments and to clearly display their structural features. Alternatively, its purpose could be to state and compare rules for automated temporal reasoning – the kind of rules that we might want to instill in a computer carrying out reasoning tasks involving temporally structured information.[2]

A formal framework only becomes exposed to empirical evidence, and to the sort of argumentation I will build against the symmetric paradigm, if it is embedded in a theory with the ambition of predicting linguistic phenomena. This is the case for natural language semantics. These explanatory ambitions include developing a model of temporal discourse that systematizes and explains our judgments of acceptability (or unacceptability) of various speech acts in context as well as our judgments about the acceptability (or unacceptability) of various inference patterns.

With that said, even if Prior himself might not have had natural language applications on his mind, the interpretation of the tense logic framework as a module in a theory of meaning has nonetheless been influential. For example, simple tense logic is the default model of tense that is developed in two of the most influential textbooks in natural language semantics (Dowty et al., 1981, and in the notes in von Fintel and Heim, 2011) as well as in Richard Montague's influential essay "Pragmatics" (which can now be found in Montague, 1974, pp. 95–119). Even those who have objected to this application of tense logic have often landed on symmetric analyses (we will see some examples in due course).

Our first task, then, is to develop with more precision the hypothesis that the tenses of a natural language such as English are semantically symmetric. To do so, I spell out in detail the behavior of the simplest tense operators of tense logic. Once the symmetry assumption is spotted in this context, it is easy to also identify it in a variety of alternative, more complex frameworks.

1.2   Symmetric Semantics

Consider a toy language capable of expressing temporally structured information. The core feature of the sort of language I have in mind is that basic tensed sentences are the product of composing a temporal operator

---

[2]   See, e.g., Goldblatt (2006), §7.3 on the logic of concurrency.

with a tenseless sentence-like object. Thus the sentence *she passed* might be the result of composing a tense operator (something with the meaning of *in the past*) and a tenseless core (*she pass*). (Note that in giving examples of such tenseless cores, I will omit gender and number features.) It is a substantive empirical assumption, though one that seems initially plausible for many languages, that natural language sentences have this kind of linguistic structure. At any rate, I will accept this assumption for the sake of illustration.

The basic building blocks of the toy language are *sentence radicals*. Radicals are tenseless descriptions of events (*Bea run*) or states (*Al be happy*). I will not explore the inner structure of tense radicals, assuming instead that they are directly interpretable for truth and that if they are not in the scope of a tense operator, they default to a present interpretation. So *Al be happy* describes a state of happiness by Al that happens at the time at which it is uttered. (As the semantic development approaches something closer to English, in Chapter 7, I will require that radicals always combine with tense before being even interpretable for truth or falsity.) In addition to radicals, our toy language contains Boolean connectives (*and, or, not,* etc.) and the temporal operators *was* and *will.*

In this language, one can say things with obvious English analogues such as

> *will(Bea run) and not was (al be happy)*

The temporal operators of the toy language have meanings that roughly translate as *at some point in the past* and *at some point in the future.*

We can already read off these informal glosses the expectation that the meanings of *was* and *will* should be symmetric. This expectation is borne out upon development of standard techniques of model-theoretic semantics.[3]

The first thing we need toward that development are, of course, models. Think of models as abstract objects that depict the features of reality that are needed to capture the semantic properties of the expressions of the language. To use Etchemendy's (1990, chapter 2) terminology, this means that models are understood *representationally.* That is to say, models are simplified representations of temporally structured worlds. Under this conception, two different models represent two different ways a temporally

---

[3] A word about notation: When ignoring what happens at a sub-sentential level, I generalize over sentences and sentence radicals of this language by means of variables such as A, B, C, etc. In these cases, I will only be concerned with connectives and temporal operators as means of composition of sentence radicals.

structured world could be – fixing the meanings of our words.[4] Needless to say, much as our toy language does not aim to represent all the complexities of a natural language, these models incorporate substantial idealizations. They do not aim to represent all the complexity of our world and they do not aim to be completely accurate representations of those features that they do represent. With these clarifications in mind, define:

Definition 1.1   A *model* $\mathcal{M}$ is a triple $\langle \mathcal{T}, <, v \rangle$ with $\mathcal{T}$ a set of times; $<$ a linear order on $\mathcal{T}$; and v a valuation function.

A linear order on a set S is a transitive, antisymmetric, and total relation on S. The valuation function v maps each sentence radical of the target language $\mathcal{L}$ to a truth-value relative to a time. So if Bea does run at t_0, we have $v(Bea\ run, t_0) = 1$. The possible truth-values in our interpretation schema are 1, for true, and 0, for false.

Suppose that our toy language contains exactly four radicals

Bea run, Al run, Bea be happy, Al be happy

Figure 1.1 diagrams the structure of a simple model and possible assignments to sentence radicals by the valuation function. In these simplified settings, we can diagram the valuation function at each point by a sequence of four 0's and 1's, where a 1 in the nth place of the sequence means that the nth radical (in the preceding list) is true at the given time, and a 0 means that it is false. In the model diagrammed by Figure 1.1, *Bea* and *Al* are both running and happy at t_2; they both stop running at t_3, but only *Al* is happy then, and he stays happy for one more tick of the clock. After that, the world ends.

Models have two jobs: to contribute to a theory of the truth-conditions of sentences of the language and to contribute to an account of logical entailment. However, models (as just characterized) are not enough to state the truth-conditions for the sentences that are of interest. The question whether *Bea be happy* is true in the model of Figure 1.1 is ill posed: Bea is happy at some but not all times. To determine whether the radical *Bea*

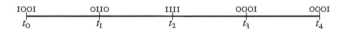

Figure 1.1   Valuation function for a model with four radicals

---

[4]   Representational models contrast with "interpretational models," which represent different ways in which we might interpret the nonlogical fragment of the language fixing what the world is like.

be happy is true, one must take the perspective of a particular point in the temporal development of the model.[5] Speaking formally, the compositional semantics for this language centers not on a definition of truth in a model $\mathcal{M}$ but on a definition of truth at a *point of evaluation*. In the semantics for the toy language, a point of evaluation consists of a model together with a time that is drawn from the stock of times of that model.

Given a model $\mathcal{M}$ and a time t that belongs to the model's stock of times, truth-values (again, 1 for true and 0 for false) can be assigned to all sentences of the language. The double brackets $[\![\cdot]\!]$ denote the interpretation function. This function inputs an expression and a point of evaluation and outputs the semantic value at a point of evaluation. Since points of evaluation are pairs consisting of a model and a time, I will write $[\![\cdot]\!]^{\mathcal{M},t}$. As our points of evaluation change, so will the parameters in the double-bracket notation. Unless it is important to remind the reader that everything is relativized to a model, I omit the $\mathcal{M}$ superscript.

The assignment starts with sentence radicals (this language's equivalent of "atomic sentences") that are interpreted directly by the valuation function. Suppose we want to evaluate the semantic value of *Bea run* at t_1 in model $\mathcal{M}$. First, extract the model's valuation function $v_{\mathcal{M}}$, and then check what the valuation function assigns to *Bea run* at t_1. In the model of Figure 1.1, this is 0, so we write $[\![Bea\ run]\!]^{t_1} = 0$.

The pattern of propagation is determined by the *lexical entries* of the various expressions that are used to generate complex sentences. For sentential connectives, adopt standard Boolean entries.

$[\![A\ and\ B]\!]^t = min([\![A]\!]^t, [\![B]\!]^t)$
$[\![A\ or\ B]\!]^t = max([\![A]\!]^t, [\![B]\!]^t)$
$[\![not\ A]\!]^t = 1 - [\![A]\!]^t$

A conjunction is true just in case both its conjuncts are true; a disjunction is true if even one disjunct is; and negations flip truth-values around.

Now for the queen of the entries. The goal is to assign semantic values to *was* and *will* that capture the symmetric approach to truth-conditions of past and future claims. To this end, say that *was(Bea run)* is true at t if there is a prior time at which Bea runs; on the future side, say *will(Bea run)* is true at t if there is a future time at which Bea runs. Figure 1.2 illustrates the idea.

---

[5] This parallels one of the standard moves to interpret models for modal logic: In that context, the points at which we evaluate atomic sentences are possible worlds. If the worlds in a model disagree on the truth-value of some sentence A, and for whatever reason it matters to fix that truth-value, we can designate a world in the model as actual.

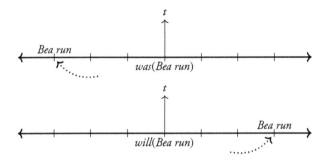

Figure 1.2   Temporal shift for symmetric semantics

More formally, and more generally, we can state the following pair of lexical entries:

LINEAR SYMMETRIC SEMANTICS

a. $[\![\mathit{was}(A)]\!]^t = 1$ iff $\exists u < t$, $[\![A]\!]^u = 1$
b. $[\![\mathit{will}(A)]\!]^t = 1$ iff $\exists u > t$, $[\![A]\!]^u = 1$

These entries complete the definition of truth at a model/time pair for our toy language.

From the model-theoretic perspective, a near-classical way to define entailment is as preservation of truth at a point of evaluation (a pair $\langle \mathcal{M}, t\rangle$). An argument with premises $A_1, \ldots, A_n$ and conclusion C is valid (written $A_1, \ldots, A_n \models C$) just in case there is no model $\mathcal{M}$ and time $t \in \mathcal{T}_{\mathcal{M}}$ such that all the A's are true at $\langle \mathcal{M}, t\rangle$ but C is not. It is invalid otherwise (in which case, we write $A_1, \ldots, A_n \not\models C$).

The system of logic resulting from this interpretation of temporal language has been studied in A. N. Prior's seminal work (Prior, 1957, 1967, 1969) and, later, in the context of the explosion of model theoretic techniques for modal logic (Rescher and Urquhart, 1971; Burgess, 1979). The appendix to this chapter reviews a sound and complete axiomatization of (a slight refinement on) this consequence relation.

At a less formal level, it is important to understand the proper interpretation of verdicts about validity and invalidity in this system. Here are four sample patterns, a valid one and three invalid ones.

(1)   a. $\mathit{will}(\mathit{will}(A)) \models \mathit{will}(A)$
       b. $A \not\models \mathit{will}(A)$
       c. $A \not\models \mathit{will}(\mathit{was}(A))$
       d. $A \not\models \mathit{was}(\mathit{will}(A))$

It is tempting to assess these verdicts by considering parallel inferences in English and evaluating whether they sound valid. It is remarkable, however, that the inferences in (1) do not have immediate, natural-sounding translations. Consider (1-d). The tempting thought is to view this as a theoretical prediction about the invalidity of an inference that in English we might put as follows:

I am happy

It was the case at some point in the past that I was going to be happy

The problem is that the English inference features additional material that is not exactly semantically inert: *was going to* is not precisely the same as *will*. Another problem is that, as I will show shortly, even holding fixed the semantics, we can change the validities by imposing constraints on the class of models. For this reason, we need to be careful in making judgments about the acceptability of this inference as evidence for or against the semantics.

It is possible to justify the verdicts in (1) by appealing to intuitions of a different sort. We might have intuitions about whether these inferences should come out valid *given the informal glosses for the tense operators.* To illustrate with (1-a), we might reason that if at some future point, there is a further future point at which **A** is true, then it has to be true that at the origin point there is a future point at which **A** is true. As for (1-b), it is clearly invalid under the informal glosses we have been operating with: The present truth of **A** at some point in time is not enough to establish the truth of **A** at a later point. While these judgments cannot be used to address the *empirical adequacy* of the symmetric semantics, they can help us investigate whether the formalism is a correct implementation of its informal design specifications.

In addition, the semantics can illuminate correspondences between logical validities and the temporal reality they represent. Consider again (1-c) and (1-d). As we think through the meanings of the symmetric tense operators, we might intuit (1-c) and (1-d) as valid. Surprisingly, the current semantics invalidates them both. Consider evaluating *Al be happy* at the last time t^* of a finite model. Because this is the last time in the model, every sentence of the form *will* **A** is false at t^*. After all, if there is no time after t^*, there is no time after t^* at which **A** is true. As a result, both *will(Al be happy)* and *will not(Al be happy)* are false. To enforce the validity of (1-c) and (1-d), we could constrain time to have no endpoints toward the future, which validates (1-c), or toward the past, which validates (1-d). The familiar point here is that, given the standard tense logic entries, there is a correspondence between the metaphysical assumption that timelines are infinite and the validity of (1-c) and (1-d).

Alternatively, we could adopt a more pragmatic perspective: In any context in which speakers can convince themselves that they are not evaluating from the temporal edge of the world, these schemas will preserve truth. So in practice, we might be warranted in treating them as valid inferences even if they are not valid in full generality. This perspective might be bolstered by noting that the following are valid entailments in this system.

(2)   a.   **A**, *will*($\top$) $\models$ *will*(*was*(**A**))
        b.   **A**, *was*($\top$) $\models$ *was*(*will*(**A**))

(Here $\top$ stands in for an arbitrary tautology.) We might take this to mean that the inferences (1-c) and (1-d) should be acceptable (again, given an informal gloss on the temporal operators) whenever it is presupposed that there is a future (by implicitly accepting *will*($\top$)) or that there is a past (by implicitly accepting *was*($\top$)).

1.3   The Symmetric Paradigm Contextualized

The semantic analysis I provided in Section 1.2 exemplifies but does not exhaust the symmetric paradigm. Much pioneering work in tense logic was not explicitly addressed to the semantic analysis of natural language. And it is misleading to take Prior's work as directly providing a semantic analysis of English tenses (Ogihara, 2007, pp. 393–397).[6] Moreover, the empirical hypothesis that natural language tenses might work like tense logic operators quickly found a rival approach – namely, the view that instead they work as object-language referential devices (Partee, 1973; Dowty, 1982; see King, 2003, chapter 6 for an extensive overview).

The essence of the symmetric paradigm is not a specific semantic assumption, however. Instead, it is the general idea that the semantics of

---

[6] Ogihara discusses the tricky case of theorists such as Montague. Unlike Prior, Montague is clearly concerned with providing a model of the semantic functioning of the natural language tense system. However, Montague's methodology involves translating from English to an intermediate language like the toy language of Section 1.2. It seems possible to argue that it is not a problem if the intermediate translation language is *too* expressive. A more significant problem is that, even when natural language tenses do stack, the truth-conditions are generally not what is predicted by the tense operator account.

future and past tenses ought to be mirror images of each other. Even as the semantics of tense has become more nuanced and expressive, the symmetric paradigm has maintained some of its shine and theoretical grip. In this section, I consider some simple ways of refining our understanding of the semantics of tense while sticking to the central tenets of the symmetric paradigm.

One way in which the operators of tense logic are at best coarse approximations of natural language tenses is that not every future moment can matter to our evaluation of future claims and not every past moment can matter to our evaluation of past claims. Ordinarily, as speakers, we restrict attention to certain specific points in time. Sometimes we do that by explicitly restricting the relevant temporal range. If I say *I cooked dinner*, I arguably do not speak truly if I cooked dinner once in 1995. In practice, I must be talking about some restricted interval of time that is easily identifiable by my conversational partners. This suggests that temporal talk has a context-sensitive dimension that is absent from my initial formulation of the symmetric clauses. What is more, these salient intervals are not controlled only by the linguistic context. They can be explicitly restricted or modified.

(3) a. Last May, Isabella visited Canada
     b. In 1984, Los Angeles hosted the Olympics

We cannot correctly analyze these phrases if English past tense just meant *at some point in the past* and if it did not compositionally interact with these restricting expressions.

There is a natural way to enrich the symmetric semantics to provide it with this kind of flexibility. Suppose that instead of a time, the points of evaluation also keep track of a time interval.[7]

Definition 1.2 An *interval* $\mathcal{I}$ is a set of times satisfying the property that for any two times t and v both in $\mathcal{I}$, if $t \leq u \leq v$, then $u \in \mathcal{I}$.

More succinctly, intervals are *convex* sets of times (with respect to the temporal precedence ordering).[8]

This modification allows a distinction (as in Figure 1.3) between those cases in which **A** occurs within the designated range I and those in which

---

[7] The idea of using intervals in the semantics comes from Bennett and Partee (1972), and has been widely applied in many subsequent frameworks (Dowty, 1982; Condoravdi, 2002).

[8] Proponents of intervals in temporal semantics commonly stipulate that the set of times has the cardinality of the continuum (this is the approach of Bennett and Partee, 1972, p. 69). Definition 1.2 is neutral on matters of cardinality.

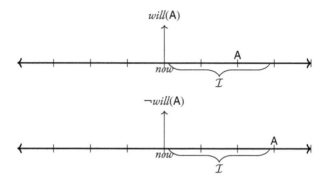

Figure 1.3   Linear symmetric semantics with intervals

A occurs only outside this range. Formulating a semantics along these lines requires a different approach to the semantics for sentence radicals. But the point I want to make here is that even moving to this sort of system allows for a symmetric analysis of tense operators. Say that an interval $\mathcal{I}_1$ precedes a $\mathcal{I}_2$ ($\mathcal{I}_1 < \mathcal{I}_2$) iff every point in $\mathcal{I}_1$ precedes every point in $\mathcal{I}_2$.

LINEAR SYMMETRIC SEMANTICS WITH INTERVALS

a. $[\![was(\text{A})]\!]^{\mathcal{I}} = 1$ iff $\exists \mathcal{I}^* < \mathcal{I}, [\![\text{A}]\!]^{\mathcal{I}^*} = 1$
b. $[\![will(\text{A})]\!]^{\mathcal{I}} = 1$ iff $\exists \mathcal{I}^* > \mathcal{I}, [\![\text{A}]\!]^{\mathcal{I}^*} = 1$

Informally, *it will rain* is true at an interval iff *it rains* is true at a later point in that interval. As noted, one would have to explain what it means for a radical to be true relative to an interval. The idea we will implement (in Chapter 7) for radicals such as *it rains* is that this is true relative to $\mathcal{I}$ iff there is a raining event that occurs entirely within $\mathcal{I}$.

Once we have intervals in the semantics, we can add some tweaks to the framework and formulate clauses for phrases such as *in 1984*. Assume that in addition to the interval in the index, there is a background interval $\mathcal{J}$. The initial value of $\mathcal{J}$ might be unrestricted – that is, $\mathcal{J}$ might be the full history of the world. Tweak the clauses for *was* and *will* so that they quantify over the intersection of $\mathcal{I}$ and $\mathcal{J}$. Then interpret *in 1984* as restricting the background interval to 1984.

A few extra tweaks are needed to model temporal indexicals such as *yesterday* – specifically, some explicit representation of the context of utterance. One option is to add an abstract representation of context to our point of evaluations. The standard, Kaplanian way to add context is to let c be a parameter that records all the elements of context that are relevant to the interpretation of indexicals, and evaluate at points of the form $\langle \mathcal{M}, c, \mathcal{I}, t \rangle$. Then *yesterday* would set the background interval $\mathcal{J}$ to the day preceding the day of the context c and set t to some time within that day.

The addition of a context coordinate allows us to define some new concepts. As I mentioned, part of the job of semantics is to make predictions about the acceptability conditions of utterances in context. An important tool in that enterprise is a definition of truth at a context. The standard, Kaplanian approach to this stage of the theory is to stipulate that the parameters that go beyond the model and the context get their initial value assigned by the context of utterance. For example, one might say that $t_{\mathcal{M},c}$ (more often written here as t_c) is the time at which context c occurs (in model $\mathcal{M}$). In a setting with intervals, one would typically conceive of $\mathcal{I}_{\mathcal{M},c}$ as a very narrow interval including only the moment of utterance. It is important to emphasize that this is an *initial* value: Tense operators might shift these parameters away from their initial values.

Having established these determination facts, we can characterize the relevant concept of truth at a context:

TRUTH AT A CONTEXT (WITH MODELS)

A is true in c (relative to $\mathcal{M}$) iff $[\![A]\!]^{\mathcal{M},c} = 1$ iff $[\![A]\!]^{\mathcal{M},c,\mathcal{I}_{\mathcal{M},c}} = 1$

As usual, omitting models improves legibility, so it's worth looking at that characterization again without them:

TRUTH AT A CONTEXT (WITHOUT MODELS)

A is true in c iff $[\![A]\!]^c = 1$ iff $[\![A]\!]^{c,\mathcal{I}_c} = 1$

Adding context is an indispensable first move if our goal is to draw up a semantics for *yesterday*. The basic idea here might would be this: Past tense shifts the interval away from $\mathcal{I}_c$ to some prior interval $\mathcal{I}^*$ of evaluation, as demanded by the linear symmetric semantics with intervals. Then *yesterday* restricts that past interval to the day that precedes the day of the context of utterance. Fully implementing this idea and making sure it plays well with the many other desiderata that govern a theory of tense is beyond the scope of this discussion.

From a linguistic point of view, these variants of the linear symmetric semantics do not go nearly far enough. In her classic paper "Some Structural Analogies between Tenses and Pronouns" (1973), Barbara Partee (1973) argues that tenses behave in a way that seems importantly similar to pronouns. Partee notes examples like this:

(4)   Sheila had a party last Friday and Sam sang a song

Example (4) illustrates that the time of the singing is anchored onto the time of the party. This anaphoric relationship is not explicable in a rigid system according to which tenses are existential quantifiers. By contrast, if tenses are allowed to perform pronoun-like reference to temporal points or intervals, we can make clearer sense of the temporal relationship between the two conjuncts of (4). This referential account is compatible with the view that tenses might sometimes also involve quantificational truth-conditions. In particular, if *was* and *will* actually are object language quantifiers, there might be anaphoric relations between their domains. The referential account is also perfectly compatible with a symmetric approach to the meanings of predictive expressions, though it must be noted here that Partee herself has already blazed the trail for the modal revolution in the semantics of the future (Partee, 1973, pp. 601–602).

1.4   Temporal Ontology and Symmetric Semantics

We have latched onto a core idea for a symmetric semantics of future and past, and developed a model theoretic treatment to go with it. I want to close this chapter on a different, more foundational note. How do these abstract model theories connect to the temporal reality that languages (even primitive ones like the one I set up) are meant to describe?

One way to approach this problem is by thinking about what our semantics tells us about truth-conditions. Our most general notion of truth is relativized to a model and a context. But the concept of truth that matters to "truth-conditional" semantics is not relativized to a model. It would be desirable to get rid of that relativization to models so that we could truly say that we have characterized the truth-conditions of some class of sentences. To bridge this gap, we must connect the set theoretic objects we call "models" with the temporal reality they represent.

In our specific application, we need to get clearer about how a temporally structured world might fix the parameters that define an abstract model. I will refer to this task as elaborating the *fit* of the representational models to reality.

Linear models, such as the ones introduced in Definition 1.1, naturally fit a metaphysics that treats past and future symmetrically. Metaphysical symmetry, as I understand it, is the requirement that future and past be alike in terms of ontology and structure. The ontology part of the requirement rules out, among other things, metaphysical views that deny future ontology (i.e., the existence of future objects and events) but do not deny past ontology. This is the *growing block* doctrine (Broad, 1923; Tooley, 1997; Briggs and Forbes, 2012). As for the structure part, it is the requirement that whatever structural constraints govern the temporal precedence relation must apply when the relation is reversed. For example, structural symmetry requires that if reality does not branch toward the past, it should not branch toward the future. This rules out the *branching time metaphysics*, which posits that reality branches toward the future but not toward the past (see Chapter 2).[9]

Although the requirements of ontological and structural symmetry are non-trivial, they do not pin down a unique conception of the nature of temporal reality. Fundamentally different conceptions of the nature of time are consistent with both requirements. A prototypical symmetric theory is the standard version of the *block universe* theory. According to this metaphysical conception, past, present, and future are all equally real; there is no objective present moment and no branching.[10] Another type of theory that is ontologically and structurally symmetrical is the *moving spotlight* theory, which adds to the block universe an objectively distinguished moment – an objective present. Even *presentism* – the view that only the present is real – could be developed so as to satisfy the two symmetry requirements.

Among these theories, the simplest fit with symmetric semantics is offered by the eternalist theories, which accept both future and past ontology (such as the block universe theory and the moving spotlight theory). Let us focus our presentation on these theories. What needs to be explained

---

[9] This asymmetry is structural as opposed to ontological in the sense that a branching time metaphysician need not say that there is a difference in ontological status between future object and events and past objects and events.

[10] The "no branching" condition is not definitional of the block universe theory – it is merely typical of its standard versions. There is nothing in principle that prevents us from thinking that the universe is a block *and* that it branches. A block universe theorist believes that the block is tree-like, as long as there is no privileged point on the block. This point is made in many places, including by Cameron (2015), who is not himself a block theorist.

is how, given a future-directed sentence in a given context, a theorist might use the abstract model theory to evaluate that sentence as true or false in that context. Suppose, for definiteness, that the temporal structure of w is as an ordering of instantaneous *moments* without endpoints in either direction. Roughly speaking, moments are instantaneous snapshots of a world, three-dimensional Euclidean spaces characterizing a "frozen frame" of reality.[11]

For each point in time, moments settle the totality of categorical nontemporal facts that hold at that time. For example, a moment should settle whether Alaa is sick in her bed, whether she is asleep, whether she is a student, whether she is within one mile of her favorite ice-cream shop, and so on. It should not settle whether Carl has had a haircut on one of the previous three days, or whether he will walk to guitar lessons within the next hour, and so on.

Under this conception, an event of utterance can fix all the parameters that go in the abstract stipulation of a model. To illustrate this, consider our simplest linear models: triples of the form $\langle \mathcal{T}, <, v \rangle$, consisting of a set of times, an ordering over it, and a valuation function. Consider an utterance event e of some future-directed sentence s; e must take place in a unique, temporally structured world w. Suppose for simplicity that w is a countably infinite succession of moments with no endpoints in either direction. Then we can choose $\mathcal{T}$ as the set of integers and $<$ as the less-than relation over $\mathcal{T}$. As a result, there is a one-to-one correspondence between $\mathcal{T}$ and the moments in w. Moreover, there is a one-to-one correspondence that respects the order of the moments in w. Call this order-preserving correspondence h.

Finally, set up the valuation function corresponding to w. Recall that we assumed that moments settle all the categorical tenseless facts at each time in world w. With that understanding, let v map a time $t \in \mathcal{T}$ and a sentence radical A to 1 if A holds at $h(x)$ in w, where $h(t)$ is the image of time t under the one-to-one correspondence between the points in $\mathcal{T}$ and the moments in w.

The moral of this exercise is that truth-conditional semanticists aiming to tell a complete story about the truth-conditions of temporal discourse must step outside the shell of the model theory and work carefully on how their model theory might connect with the underlying metaphysics.

---

[11] The terminology and the conception of "moments" comes from Belnap (1992), who views this – correctly in my view – as an idealization that substantively simplifies the semantics.

Appendix: The Logic *K$_t$*

To state the logic of standard tense operators correctly, we must rework some of our key definitions to better fit the standard approach in the semantics of modal logic.

Definition 1.3 (Temporal frames and models)

(i) A *simple temporal frame* is a pair $\langle \mathcal{T}, < \rangle$ with $\mathcal{T}$ a set of times and $<$ a linear order on $\mathcal{T}$.
(ii) A *simple temporal model* $\mathcal{M}$ is a triple $\langle \mathcal{T}, <, v \rangle$ with $\mathcal{T}$ a set of times; $<$ a linear order on $\mathcal{T}$; and v a valuation function.
(iii) Given a frame $\mathcal{F} = \langle \mathcal{T}, < \rangle$ and a model $\mathcal{M} = \langle \mathcal{T}', <', v \rangle$, say that $\mathcal{M}$ is *based* on $\mathcal{F}$ iff $\mathcal{T} = \mathcal{T}'$ and the orders $<$ and $<'$ are also identical.

Definition 1.4 (Validity)

(i) A is valid in model $\mathcal{M}$ iff for every $t \in \mathcal{T}_{\mathcal{M}}$, $[\![A]\!]^{\mathcal{M},t} = 1$.
(ii) A is valid in a frame $\mathcal{F}$ iff A is valid in every model $\mathcal{M}$ that is based on $\mathcal{F}$.
(iii) A is valid in the class of simple temporal frames iff A is valid in every simple temporal frame.

When A is valid in the class of simple temporal frames, write $\models_{STF}$ A.

To axiomatize the class of valid sentences, it helps to consider the universal duals of *will* and *was*. So let

- $\triangleright A =_{df} \neg will \neg A$
- $\triangleleft A =_{df} \neg was \neg A$

The intuitive interpretations of these operators are, respectively, *always in the future* and *always in the past*. The resulting logic *K$_t$* is presented here axiomatically. Start with standard axioms for classical sentential logic, and add the following axiom schemas:

K$_\triangleright$. $\triangleright(A \supset B) \supset (\triangleright A \supset \triangleright B)$
K$_\triangleleft$. $\triangleleft(A \supset B) \supset (\triangleleft A \supset \triangleleft B)$
FB. $A \supset (\triangleright \ was \ A)$
BF. $A \supset (\triangleleft \ will \ A)$

Let '$\vdash_{K_t}$' denote the property of theoremhood in this system. The theorems of *K$_t$* are the class of sentences defined recursively by starting with all the instances of all the axioms and by closing under the following rules:

MP. if $\vdash_{K_t}$ A and $\vdash_{K_t}$ A $\supset$ B then $\vdash_{K_t}$ B

NEC$_\rhd$ if $\vdash_{K_t}$ A, then $\vdash_{K_t}$ $\rhd$A

NEC$_\lhd$ if $\vdash_{K_t}$ A, then $\vdash_{K_t}$ $\lhd$A

This logic is sound and complete with respect to the class of *simple temporal frames*.

Theorem 1.5 *The logic K_t characterizes the class of simple temporal frames, i.e.,*

$$\vdash_{K_t} A \text{ iff } \vDash_{STF} A$$

CHAPTER 2

Symmetric Semantics in an Asymmetric World

In a scene from *Back to the Future II*, scientist Emmett "Doc" Brown explains to Marty McFly (the movie's protagonist) that they ended in an alternate, dystopian version of 1985. At the heart of Dr. Brown's explanation is the drawing of a branching diagram (as in Figure 2.1): two timelines branching from each other at some point that lies in the past with respect to 1985.

Somehow, Brown says, he and McFly landed on the wrong branch: a world in which a spoiled and abusive hotel and casino owner has accumulated massive amounts of power and wealth. Brown's metaphysical explanation of how he and McFly moved between branches is confusing and unlikely to be instructive to the metaphysician. No matter how wild your hair looks, you cannot just draw a branching diagram and expect to have clearly conveyed a metaphysical view of the future. We'll try to do better, at least as far as the relationship between branching timelines and semantics is concerned.

This chapter has two main goals. The first is to establish that symmetric semantics does not require the underlying metaphysics to be symmetric. It is consistent to believe that future and past talk are semantically symmetric while also believing that future and past are metaphysically asymmetric in the sense that, given a point in time, there are many timelines stretching toward the future, but only one timeline going toward the past.

Original 1985   Dystopian 1985

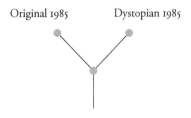

Figure 2.1   Temporal branching

The technical result I will reproduce here involves *branching models*. These model-theoretic entities are designed to fit a world endowed with a "branching metaphysics" (see Section 2.1). A classic paper by Thomason (1970) shows how symmetric semantics can be used on branching models. I will develop a Thomason-style formalism within the formal setup I have been developing. The second goal of this chapter is to argue that branching models and branching time metaphysics are not inextricably linked. Once we distinguish among the main possible interpretations of branching models, we can wrestle the branching models away from the branching time metaphysicians. Once it's all said and done, we will need to acknowledge a three-way distinction between (i) the metaphysical idea of a branching *world*; (ii) the model-theoretic idea of branching *models*, or branching *structures*; and (iii) the presentational aid of branching *diagrams*.

2.1 Branching Metaphysics

Branching time metaphysics has it that our temporal reality branches toward the future – but not backward. The strongest version of this view takes the idea of branching about as literally as one can, as Lewis highlighted in a memorable quote (Lewis is emphatically not a proponent of the view):

> In branching, worlds are like Siamese twins. There is one initial spatiotemporal segment; it is continued by two different futures – different both numerically and qualitatively – and so there are two overlapping worlds. One world consists of the initial segment plus one of its futures; the other world consists of the identical initial segment plus the other future. (Lewis, 1986a, p. 206)

The world that contains me and my surroundings, *my world*, might have two continuations. In one continuation, this radioactive atom decays within ten thousand hours; in the other, it does not. According to the branching metaphysics, no objective feature of reality makes it the case that one of these two continuations is privileged over the other. Neither is the *unique* continuation of my world at the original time.

The standard interpretation of this branching world idea is eternalist and *B*-theoretic. It is eternalist in positing the timeless existence of past, present, and future events. It is *B*-theoretic in declining to posit that any one point on this eternal structure is privileged.[1] In other words, the standard version

---

[1] I am partial to Ross Cameron's (2015) way of drawing the distinction between the *A*-theory and the *B*-theory. According to Cameron, to be an *A*-theorist is to think (i) that there is a privileged point

of branching metaphysics is the view that reality is atemporally structured as a forward branching tree with no privileged present. What speakers refer to as "the present" or "now" is just whatever point on the tree they find themselves at.[2]

Proponents of branching time metaphysics believe that it can help us understand the sense in which the future is open. Here is a programmatic statement by Belnap, Perloff, and Xu:

> The theory is based on a picture of moments as ordered into a treelike structure, with forward branching representing the openness or indeterminacy of the future and the absence of backward branching representing the determinacy of the past. (Belnap et al., 2001, p. 30)

I will not discuss "openness" until much later in this book (in Chapter 11), but I will put some cards on the table right away. I very much doubt that branching time metaphysics is a good model of the openness of the future (see Williams, 2008a; Torre, 2011; Cameron, 2015; and Chapter 10 of this book for some reasons to doubt this). In turn, one of the key questions to be considered is whether the *technical* innovations of branching time semantics are separable from the branching time metaphysics.

2.2 Branching Models

The key result concerning branching metaphysics is that symmetric semantics does not require symmetric metaphysics. This result is neither novel nor mine. The idea of a system of branching possibilities as an option for semantic evaluation was first outlined in a famous letter that seventeen-year-old Saul Kripke sent to A. N. Prior:

> Now in an indetermined system, we perhaps should not regard time as a linear series, as you have done. Given the present moment, there are several possibilities for what the next moment may be like – and for each possible next moment, there are several possibilities for the next moment after that. Thus the situation takes the form, not of a linear sequence, but of a "tree" …

---

of time and (ii) that that privileged point *moves*. This is not necessarily the most *canonical* way of drawing that distinction, but it is the one that will be most helpful here.

[2] *A*-theoretic conceptions of branching time are also possible and worthy of investigation. For example, one might have the view that as the objective present "travels" along the tree (whatever that might mean), branches that are no longer options on the objective present's path lose their status as objective possibilities. In this book, "branching time metaphysics" always refers to the *B*-theoretic versions.

The whole tree then represents the entire set of possibilities for present and future; and every point determines a subtree consisting of its own present and future. (Kripke, 1958)

Kripke's point is that a broad commitment to an "indeterministic" metaphysics should lead to a model theory that uses nonlinear, branching structures (as opposed to the linear models of Chapter 1).

Thomason (1970, 1984) further developed Kripke's and Prior's insights by applying the method of supervaluations to the tree-like structures described by Kripke. Thomason's work shows that if we draw the right distinctions, we can match symmetric semantics with branching metaphysics. I will present Thomason's framework in two stages – first by characterizing branching models, and then by showing how to apply supervaluational techniques to them.

To define branching structures, we need the auxiliary concept of a *branching order*. A relation $<$ is a *branching order* on a set P of points iff $<$ is a partial order of P (i.e., a transitive, irreflexive, and anti-symmetric relation over P) with the following additional property:

BRANCHING PROPERTY.

For any $x, y, z \in P$, if $x \leq z$ and $y \leq z$, then either $x \leq y$ or $y \leq x$.

Informally, branching orders are partial orders in which any two points x and y that precede a common point z are comparable. The job of the branching property is to rule out backward branching while allowing forward branching. If you imagine landing at an arbitrary point of a branching order and "turning back" toward the past, you would see a linear sequence of points.

Tree-like diagrams, such as the *Back to the Future II* diagram in Figure 2.1, exhibit the branching property. I replicated the structure of that diagram in Figure 2.2. (In all branching diagrams in this book, the "future" direction is up.)

Figure 2.2   Forward branching

Figure 2.3   Backward branching

Not every partial order is a branching order. The branching property excludes structures like the one in Figure 2.3, where *a* and *b* both precede *c*, without themselves being comparable.

Given the concept of a branching order, we can say that a branching *model* is a set of points arranged in a branching, tree-like structure.

Definition 2.1   A *branching model* is a triple $\langle S, <, v \rangle$ with S a non-empty set of points; $<$ a branching order on S; and v a valuation function.

As usual, we write $S_{\mathcal{M}}$ to denote the set of points in $\mathcal{M}$ and similarly for the other coordinates of $\mathcal{M}$. It is natural to interpret the points in a branching model as model-theoretic analogues of "moments" as characterized in Section 1.4. These points represent temporal "slices" of reality, and their key feature is they settle all the tenseless facts. In other words, moments, and thus points in a model, must settle whether Bea is happy but they needn't settle whether Bea was happy three days prior. As a result of this requirement, given a language $\mathcal{L}$, and a branching model for it, the valuation function $v(\cdot, \cdot)$ can input any moment in the model and any sentence radical in the language and map them to a truth-value.[3]

Branching models are partially representable by branching diagrams like the one in Figure 2.2.[4] After all, branching diagrams can represent all the information encoded in a branching model *minus* the valuation function. (In the logician's lingo, branching diagrams represent the *frames* on which branching models are built.) More complex branching diagrams, corresponding to more complex branching models, might look like the one in Figure 2.4.

---

[3] This is somewhat different from how I defined valuation functions in the context of linear models in Chapter 1. There, I assumed that v maps a radical and a *time* to a truth-value. Now I assume that v maps a radical and a *moment* to a truth-value. In general, as we change our points of evaluation going forward, we might have to adjust the exact understanding of valuation functions that is best for each model.

[4] Linear models are special cases of branching models – namely, those branching models in which the order $<$ is total.

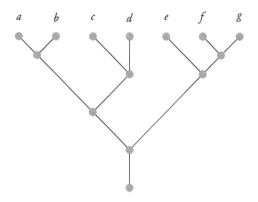

Figure 2.4   Branching diagram

Although our characterization of branching models does not deploy the notion of a possible world, possible worlds can be defined within branching models.[5]

Definition 2.2 (Possible worlds in branching models, also known as *histories*)

- A *linear path* in a branching model M is any set of points from M that are linearly ordered by the temporal precedence relation of M.
- A *world* in M is a linear path through M that is maximal, in the sense that it cannot be extended with other points of M, without making it nonlinear (with respect to the relation $<_M$).

Informally, worlds are linear paths through a branching structure that cannot be extended by adding an extra node drawn from the model without breaking one of the linearity assumptions. For example, in Figure 2.4, any linear path from the origin to one of the endpoints labeled a to g is a world. Note that if every world has an endpoint, there will be a one-to-one correspondence between worlds and their terminal points.

The upshot is that even if branching models do not contain worlds as *primitives*, we are entitled to assume that they *determine* worlds.[6]

---

[5]   What I am calling *worlds* are usually called *histories* in the literature on branching time. I think there is a sensible reason for this: In a branching setting, the word "world" might be taken to mean the individual timeline or, alternatively, it might be taken to refer to the entire tree. Using "histories" for the former helps eliminate this ambiguity. Nonetheless, I have opted here for the terminology that prevails in the semantics literature outside of the branching time camp.

[6]   Further questions might be pushed about branching models: Can there be multiple, disconnected trees? Or do we require that any two worlds have at least one point of overlap (in which case there

The price of the move from linear models to branching models is the loss of the notion of a time in a model. In the linear setting, it is common to assume that each point in the model corresponds to a point in time. However, in the branching setting, nothing guarantees that two points that do not belong to the same world can be compared in terms of their temporal location. For instance, nothing settles that the terminal nodes in Figure 2.4 happen at the same time or at a different time. Even worse, it might not make conceptual sense to suppose that there is a unified temporal "clock" for worlds on different branches. It might be that nothing determines that time t in world c is the same as time t' in world e.

The idealization involved here goes beyond the standard (in model theoretic semantics) pretense that the world is (broadly speaking) Newtonian. The Newtonian idealization enables us to talk about slicing up possible worlds into three-dimensional moments, populated with absolutely simultaneous events. But we need something beyond this to compare times on different timelines: We need some basis for saying that moments on *different* branches (and thus moments that are not related by the temporal precedence relation) are (or are not) simultaneous.

Hard as that might be, when it comes to designing a model for future-directed language, it is enormously convenient to posit such a unified clock. Actually, "convenient" is not the right word; "indispensable" would be better. Everyone who accepts any kind of possible world semantics for modals already spotted themselves some way of picking out the same time across different worlds. Without it, they would not be able to make sense of such basic sentences as *it could rain tomorrow or it could be sunny*. It is impossible to make sense of the modals in such sentences without some concept of cross-world simultaneity. If the semantic function of *tomorrow* is to restrict an interval of evaluation, we need to be able to perform that restriction on those possible worlds where tomorrow is sunny and those where tomorrow is rainy. This *might* be a special case of the more general problem of trans-world identity. But even so, it requires careful thought. The only attempt I know to make conceptual sense of cross-world

can be only one tree)? Standard assumptions about the metaphysics of worlds intuitively suggest the multiple-trees picture. For example, if two worlds have different gravitational constants for the entire duration of their respective histories, then they presumably do not ever overlap. It seems possible that such pairs of worlds could exist and so it seems possible that a complete picture of the multiverse might contain constellations of disconnected trees. However, at this point, we do not have much to give us intellectual traction on these questions; moreover, we will not consider modal operators that can shift our evaluation from one tree to another. For these reasons, I set aside the possibility of models with multiple, disconnected trees and focus instead on simple, *single-tree* models.

simultaneity is the extensive discussion in Tulenheimo (2015). The rest of us have been enjoying the benefits of theft over honest toil.

In the interest of modularity, I shall give theft another go-around, and will add cross-world simultaneity relations to our models without further theorizing about them. A simple-minded way of doing so is to revise our definition of a branching model by adding another coordinate to the model itself (Belnap et al., 2001, p. 35).

Definition 2.3 R is a cross-world simultaneity relation on a branching model $\mathcal{M}$ iff

- R is a reflexive, symmetric and transitive on the set of points of $\mathcal{M}$ and
- For any x, y with xRy and $x \neq y$, then $\neg(x < y)$ and $\neg(y < x)$, and
- For any x, y with $x < y$ and any x', y' on the same branch with xRx' and yRy', we must have $x' < y'$.

Definition 2.4 (Branching model, revised)   A *branching model* is a quadruple $\langle \mathcal{S}, <, R, v \rangle$ with $\mathcal{S}$ a non-empty set of points; $<$ a branching order on $\mathcal{S}$; R a cross-world simultaneity relation on $\langle \mathcal{S}, <, v \rangle$; and v a valuation function.

A cross-world simultaneity relation on a branching model $\mathcal{M}$ partitions the points in $\mathcal{M}$. Every point in $\mathcal{M}$ belongs to exactly one partition cell. Moreover, the partitioning happens in such a way that points that are related by the simultaneity relation are never on the same branch. In mathematical parlance, the cells of the partition generated by R are the equivalence classes.[7] With a step of abstraction, we can think of times as equivalence classes of points under R.[8]

TIMES. The set $\mathcal{T}_\mathcal{M}$ of times in branching model $\mathcal{M}$ with respect to R is

$$\{\sigma \subseteq \mathcal{S}_\mathcal{M} \mid \exists s \in \mathcal{S}_\mathcal{M}(\sigma = \{x \in \mathcal{S}_\mathcal{M} \mid sRx\})\}$$

This identifies times with sets of points that are related by the cross-world simultaneity relation.

The ordering on nodes can be lifted to an ordering on times. Specifically, given two times $t, u \in \mathcal{T}$, we say

ORDERING ON TIMES. $t <_\mathcal{T} u$ iff $\exists n \in t, \exists m \in u(n < m)$

---

[7]   The equivalence classes from some set D generated by an equivalence relation R are in general sets of the form $\{x \in D \mid \exists z \in D(xRz)\}$.

[8]   Here, too, I am somewhat at variance with the terminology of Belnap et al. (2001), who call these *instants*.

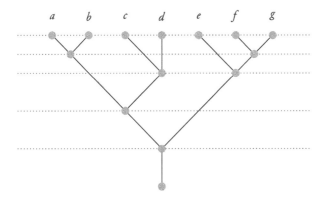

Figure 2.5   Branching diagram with cross-world simultaneity

Informally, time t precedes time u iff the points that belong to t precede the points that belong to u.

To visualize these concepts, and to give them some informal explanation, consider adding a set of times (generated by a simultaneity relation) to Figure 2.5.

Each of the dotted lines represents a time. Note that an arbitrary branching model does not uniquely fix a partition of the model's points in times. There might be multiple ways of setting up cross-world simultaneity. For example, a different simultaneity relation from the one in Figure 2.5 might shift the final chunk of worlds e, f, and g so that they might occupy an "earlier" position.

Having times around is good enough for some of our intended applications. Unfortunately, it is not enough for all of them. Indeed, analyzing frame adverbials such as *tomorrow* and *in three days* demands even more than a relation of cross-world simultaneity. It demands a *temporal metric* – for example, a function from times to real numbers. The job of this function would be to represent the distance between times. We'll spot ourselves such enrichments of our model as they become needed.

2.3   Symmetric Semantics on Branching Models

How might one appeal to the linear symmetric semantics within a branching framework? After all, any one utterance presumably takes place at some point on the tree. At nearly all of these points, there will be a unique way of backtracking, and many ways of going forward.

The central conceptual insight we need to introduce is that the semantic evaluation of sentences might be usefully split in two separate modules. The first module consists of a recursive definition of truth relative to a point of evaluation. If we are careful to evaluate sentences against symmetric points of evaluation, we should be able to use the symmetric clauses. What is distinctive of a branching model is the fact that multiple points of evaluation might be associated with any one point in the tree. To resolve this indeterminacy, Thomason (1970) advocates supervaluating over the relevant class of points.

Let us go through this development step-by-step. Start by adding a world coordinate to the points of evaluation $\langle \mathcal{M}, w, t \rangle$. Recall that in branching models, neither worlds nor times are primitive components of the model, but since they can both be defined, they can figure in the points of evaluation. Next, lift the basic semantic entries from Chapter 1 to this new set of points of evaluation:

OCKHAMIST SYMMETRIC SEMANTICS

$$[\![\mathit{was}(\mathrm{A})]\!]^{w,t} = 1 \text{ iff } \exists u, u < t, [\![\mathrm{A}]\!]^{w,u} = 1$$
$$[\![\mathit{will}(\mathrm{A})]\!]^{w,t} = 1 \text{ iff } \exists u, u > t, [\![\mathrm{A}]\!]^{w,u} = 1$$

These are essentially the same linear entries we saw in Chapter 1. The only remarkable addition is the appearance of a world parameter among the coordinates of evaluation.

At first blush, that might seem puzzling. Unlike the time coordinate, the world coordinate is not being read or operated on by anything in this entry. It would then seem that adding possible worlds to the points of evaluation is an idle operation. This appearance is misleading: Keeping track of the world of evaluation allows us to locate the node that results from shifting the initial node forward into the future. Consider again a very basic model, as diagrammed in Figure 2.6.

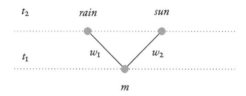

Figure 2.6   Basic binary branching model

Consider evaluating the sentence *it will rain* at $\langle w_1, t_1 \rangle$. Note that there are two ways of picking out the origin point, moment m: We could think of it as the first time in world 1 or as the first time in world 2. More precisely, the moment determined by the pair $\langle w_1, t_1 \rangle$ is identical to the moment determined by the pair $\langle w_2, t_1 \rangle$. This means that if we did not keep track of which world we are evaluating from – if we thought of moment m as an unstructured lump – the semantic engine would not know how to go forward in time. Because of that, the linear semantic entries would not work. By adding worlds to the points of evaluation, we give the semantic engine a determinate path for forward shift.

The Ockhamist symmetric semantics can also be formulated without appealing to times (and hence without implicitly appealing to simultaneity relations). Indeed, this is Thomason's preferred formulation. Times can be removed by speaking directly in terms of nodes on the branching model. In this variant analysis, points of evaluation consist of model $\mathcal{M}$ (suppressed in the notation, as usual), world w, and node n drawn from the set $\mathcal{S}$ of points of $\mathcal{M}$.

OCKHAMIST SYMMETRIC SEMANTICS (NODE-BASED)

a. $[\![was(\mathrm{A})]\!]^{w,n} = 1$ iff $\exists m \in \mathcal{S}_\mathcal{M}, m < n, [\![\mathrm{A}]\!]^{w,m} = 1$
b. $[\![will(\mathrm{A})]\!]^{w,n} = 1$ iff $\exists m \in \mathcal{S}_\mathcal{M}, m > n, [\![\mathrm{A}]\!]^{w,m} = 1$

If times are available, these ways of picking out points of evaluation are equivalent. For any point of the form $\langle w, n \rangle$, there is a corresponding point of the form $\langle w, t \rangle$ – just pick t to be the time at which n happens – and vice versa.

To illustrate this correspondence with an example, consider evaluating A at the world that terminates in f (call it w_f) and the node marked as 'n' in Figure 2.7.

Given times, we could pick out $\langle w_f, n \rangle$ as $\langle w_f, t^* \rangle$. Conversely, we could pick out $\langle w_f, t^* \rangle$ as $\langle w_f, n \rangle$.[9] This should convince us that the two semantic theories are indeed equivalent.

---

[9] One superficial difference would be that, when running the truth-conditions of tensed claims, we would get shifted along the order on times (not along the order on nodes). However, since the order on times is derived from the order on worlds, we get equivalent truth-conditions. The only real advantage of the node-based semantics is that it can be formulated wholly independently of simultaneity relations.

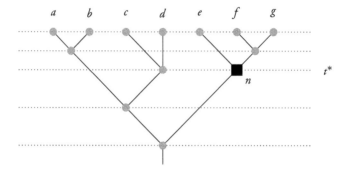

Figure 2.7   Node-based diagram

This completes my presentation of the *first* module in Thomason's framework. To see why we might need more modules in addition to this, let us go back to Thomason's own presentation:

> [T]his account is not above criticism. It says that more is needed to assign a truth-value to a formula at a time α than a model structure and assignment of truth-values to formulas not involving tense operators. Besides these a possible future for α must be specified, for on this view statements in the future tense do not in general take a truth-value at α unless a possible future for α is given. (Thomason, 1970, p. 270)

In other words, if the Ockhamist semantics were the end of the story, we would have to say one of two implausible things. Consider again the diagram in Figure 2.7, and specifically the node marked as 'n'. We would like to be able to say that sentences like *it will rain* have whatever truth-value they have relative to moments, such as n. But the Ockhamist semantics doesn't allow us to say just that. A point of evaluation also requires specifying a possible world, and three worlds go through that node: w_e, w_f, and w_g. We need to make a choice here. One option is to say that one of these worlds is privileged – that one of them truly is the actual world. While that is likely to have been Ockham's actual view, it appears to conflict with the branching theorist's idea that neither future is objectively privileged. The alternative is the head-spinning view that the sentence *it will rain* could be true or false at moment m depending on whether m is conceptualized as lying on w_1 or as lying on w_2. Unfortunately, it's hard to understand what that could possibly mean.

Thomason's solution to these problems is to add a second module to the semantics, whose job it is to "supervaluate" over the possible futures.

In addition to the recursive notion of truth to which the Ockhamist semantics contributes, there is a further nonrecursively defined concept of truth that resolves the mismatch between what reality offers at a given moment (a bundle of worlds) and what the recursive semantics needs (a unique world).

More formally, let worlds($\cdot$) be a function that given a moment m outputs all the worlds that go through m. For instance, in Figure 2.7, worlds(n) = $\{w_e, w_f, w_g\}$. The key move is to say that A is true as uttered in situation at moment m and model $\mathcal{M}$ if it is true at $\langle \mathcal{M}, w, m \rangle$ given every choice w of world in worlds(m). Since this is a supervaluationist theory, it requires a separate clause for falsehood.

BRANCHING SUPERVALUATIONISM

> A is true at $\langle \mathcal{M}, m \rangle$ iff for every world $w \in$ worlds(m), $[\![A]\!]^{\mathcal{M},w,m} = 1$.
>
> A is false at $\langle \mathcal{M}, m \rangle$ iff for every world $w \in$ worlds(m), $[\![A]\!]^{\mathcal{M},w,m} = 0$.

It is thanks to this supervaluational step that we can avoid having to fix one world as the privileged world of m.

Thomason (1970) is primarily focused on characterizing an adequate notion of logical entailment that would fit with a commitment to branching metaphysics. However, much like Prior's work on tense logic, these logical developments traveled quickly from logic to philosophy of language. Much as we did in Chapter 1, we can integrate the supervaluationist technique with a Kaplan-style framework for context sensitivity (Kaplan, 1989b). The result of this work will be a characterization of truth relative to a context of utterance.

However, in doing so we must attend to the metaphysics of context. Kaplan distinguishes between situations of utterance and contexts – the former being concrete events, the latter being abstract representations of those concrete events. For him, a situation of utterance s determines an abstract context c: c records the time, the speaker, the location, etc., of utterance s. Standard representations of context also assign it a world parameter, recording the world at which the utterance takes place.

The branching theorist's concern reemerges here: There might not be a unique world at which the utterance takes place. If I utter *it will rain* at moment n in the diagram in Figure 2.7, that utterance is simultaneously on worlds w_e, w_f, and w_g. Contexts determine bundles of worlds, not single worlds. Here, too, the supervaluationist machinery comes to the rescue.

Let worlds(c) denote the worlds that go through the moment corresponding to context c. Then, restate supervaluationism as a proposal about how to define truth at a context (superseding the previous characterization from Section 1.3).

CONTEXTUALIST BRANCHING SUPERVALUATIONISM

A is true in c iff for every world $w \in$ worlds(c), $[\![A]\!]^{\mathcal{M}_c,w,m_c} = 1$.

A is false in c iff for every world $w \in$ worlds(c), $[\![A]\!]^{\mathcal{M}_c,w,m_c} = 0$.

MacFarlane (2003, 2014) has a useful name for theoretical modules like this: *postsemantics*. The job of the postsemantics is to interface between the compositional semantics – what he calls *semantics proper* – and the pragmatics.

Viewing the postsemantics as a module tacked onto the semantics opens up the possibility that there might be alternatives to supervaluationism. MacFarlane's development of relativism adds one more postsemantic option to the menu of eligible approaches (MacFarlane, 2003, 2005, 2014). MacFarlane's preferred postsemantics involves a truth predicate with two contextual relativizations.

BRANCHING RELATIVISM

A is true as uttered in context c_U and assessed in context c_A iff for every world $w \in$ worlds(c_A), $[\![A]\!]^{\mathcal{M}_{c_U},w,m_{c_U}} = 1$.

A is false as uttered in context c_U and assessed in context c_A iff for every world $w \in$ worlds(c_A), $[\![A]\!]^{\mathcal{M}_{c_U},w,m_{c_U}} = 0$.

While the relativist and supervaluationist postsemantic theories differ in many critical predictions, they agree in that both permit the use of symmetric clauses for the meanings of temporal operators.[10] Like supervaluationism, the relativist postsemantics allows the use of symmetric clauses for tense operators against the background of a branching metaphysics.

Taking stock, we have reached our promised result and our intermediate conclusion: An asymmetric conception of temporal reality can be combined with a symmetric analysis of the meanings of *will* and *was*.

[10] The discussion in MacFarlane (2014) makes this a bit harder to identify than in his prior work. This is because the 2014 book focuses on the temporal indexical *tomorrow*, as opposed to *will*. However, MacFarlane relies on a Ockhamist treatment of *tomorrow* in which it plays two roles.

This combination is possible if the asymmetry is dealt with in the post-semantics – for example, by supervaluating or by adopting the relativist postsemantics.

2.4 Ways of Being an Ockhamist

I have used the label "Ockhamist" to refer to a kind of symmetric semantic analysis – one that uses points of evaluation of the form $\langle \mathcal{M}, w, t \rangle$, with w being the world of evaluation and t being quantified over by the tense operators. The point of this short and boring book-keeping section is to note that the literature features two non-equivalent views, both of which are dubbed "Ockhamism."

Theorists who draw a sharp line between semantics and postsemantics use "Ockhamist" as I did here, to refer to a certain kind of compositional semantic entry.[11] Outside of such contexts, "Ockhamism" tends to refer to a more general thesis with more distinctively metaphysical implications. This thesis is even sometimes viewed as *incompatible* with a supervaluationist system (Rosenkranz, 2012). A recent example of this type of formulation is offered by Todd (2016), who writes, "As a first approximation, what the Ockhamist *will* presupposes is that there exists what we might call *the unique actual future*." Todd (who is well aware of the distinction between the two ways of appropriating Ockham) characterizes Ockhamism as the thesis that whether something *will* happen is a matter of whether it does happen in the future. The thesis, though vaguely stated, aims to be in the first place a *metaphysical* thesis. By contrast, the first way of characterizing Ockhamism is semantic.

The two concepts are independent. A metaphysical Ockhamist doesn't have to adopt a semantic Ockhamist's semantics, and vice versa. There is no reason why this terminological disagreement ought to be settled by anything other than personal preference. With that said, I find it more useful to use the label in the first sense, and I will continue to do so below. However, insofar as what we call "Ockhamism" has to share some content with something Ockham may actually have defended, the latter,

---

[11] To be more precise, Thomason (1970, section 6) says that the supervaluationist system agrees with the validities of Prior's Ockhamist system. Thomason (1984), and Malpass and Wawer (2012), and MacFarlane (2014) speak exactly as I did here.

more metaphysically laden thesis is more likely to be right. For summaries and discussion of Ockham's actual views, see Normore (1982, pp. 370–373) and Øhrstrøm (2009, section 1).

2.5   Interpreting Branching Models

Let us wrap up this chapter with a tour of the main metaphysical interpretations behind branching models and branching diagrams. Branching models are natural ingredients for a semantic theory based on branching time metaphysics. However, I argue that, understood as modeling tools, their interpretation is relatively neutral: They can combine with very different metaphysical outlooks, including some symmetric metaphysical theories.

Broadly speaking, branching structures represent systems of related possibilities that are endowed with temporal structure. They are composed of two main ingredients: nodes and edges. Focus on the nodes first. We interpreted the nodes as analogous to three-dimensional frames in the four-dimensional movie reel of the world.

There are two importantly different ways of making sense of this nodes-as-frames analogy. We might think of nodes in a branching structure as standing for temporal slices of a concrete world. If a concrete world is a spatiotemporally continuous lump of matter, say that a *world slice* is the result of "slicing" that lump of matter at a particular time – an instantaneous section of a world.[12]

Assuming that the nodes in a branching model are world slices yields a *concretist* picture of the system of worlds we are trying to diagram. Concretists about possible worlds (such as Lewis, 1986a) believe that there is a plurality of concrete worlds. In Lewis's version, which is incompatible with branching, each world is a spatiotemporally continuous four-dimensional manifold in its own right. While Lewis famously maintained that distinct worlds are spatiotemporally disconnected from each other, most branching time theorists reject this notion and believe instead that different worlds are spatiotemporally connected, in virtue of their sharing of parts (see, e.g., Belnap, 2012, p. 15).

---

[12]   Once again, this kind of talk presupposes that we can talk about what our world is like at a fixed point in time. We should acknowledge that in light of relativity theory, this absolute notion of a world at a point in time might be incorrect. Researchers in the branching time tradition have made several initial attempts to shed the Newtonian underpinnings of their background metaphysics (Weiner and Belnap, 2006; Belnap, 2007).

By contrast, the talk of world slices will not be useful to those who believe that the only concrete world is the actual one. Consider, for instance, *ersatzism* – the view that possible worlds are real but abstract. Ersatzists distinguish two senses of "possible world": In one sense, worlds are abstract objects (what kind of abstract object varies according to the kind of ersatzism, but they must all exist in the actual world); in the other, they are concrete lumps of matter. A typical view among ersatzists is that of the many abstract worlds, exactly one corresponds to the lump of matter that constitutes *our* world. (The exact nature of the correspondence varies according to which version of ersatzism is at stake.) This world is said to be *actualized*.

What should an ersatzist say about branching structures? In particular, how should they understand nonactual instants (say, ones in which you are asleep and a dragon is watching you sleep)? Despite the variety of ersatzist views, I think there is a relatively uniform answer which each particular ersatzist can decline in their preferred way. Ersatzists tend to agree there is no concrete moment in which a dragon is watching you sleep, but deny that this has any impact on whether they can use branching models and diagrams. Instead, they would prefer to interpret nodes in a diagram (and points in a branching model) as representing abstract objects.[13]

To mark the difference between the two interpretations of nodes, we will say that under their abstract interpretation, nodes represent *world frames* (as opposed to *world slices*). World frames are to world slices as ersatz worlds are to possible worlds. For illustration, consider the "linguistic" variety of ersatzism. In its standard formulation, this view identifies worlds with maximally consistent sets of sentences. But in our theoretical context, ersatzists might go for a variant of their view, according to which world frames are identified with maximally consistent sets of sentence radicals and negations of sentence radicals. Similarly, consider those ersatzists who think that worlds are properties a world might have. For them, world frames will be properties a world slice might have. And so on for the various versions of ersatzism.

Having distinguished between these two interpretations of nodes, let us go back to the branching models. Unlike nodes, the edges of a branching model do not directly represent constituents of our world. Instead, they represent the structure in which world frames (or slices, as the case

---

[13] For analyses that treat times as abstract objects, see Zalta (1987), Bourne (2006), Crisp, (2007), Briggs and Forbes (2012).

might be) are arranged. The standard interpretation is that nodes that are connected by an edge represent different moments on the same temporally structured world.

If the nodes of a branching model represent world slices – i.e., concrete parts of a world – then sharing of nodes must be sharing of concrete parts. This is a key tenet of branching time metaphysics that was captured by Lewis's Siamese twins metaphor. However, proponents of the branching time metaphysics sometimes emphasize a related, but less metaphysically loaded conception.

> Central to the idea of indeterminism is this: At a given moment in the history of the world there are a variety of ways in which affairs might carry on. Before the toss of the coin there are two things that could happen, either Heads up or Tails up. This possibility is not merely epistemic, but *in re*. (Belnap and Green, 1994, p. 365)

Set aside the talk of indeterminism, which in my view is not entirely appropriate here.[14] Belnap and Green are gesturing toward a thesis that on the face of it need have nothing to do with sharing of parts between worlds.

PARITY. Fixing a world slice, there are many possible ways in which that slice's future might unfold that are objectively on a par.

Suppose I am speaking of some polonium atom, Bob. I say, "Bob will decay within the next three days." Any metaphysical theory that satisfies PARITY, together with some assumptions about radioactive decay, will claim that at the time of my utterance, reality does not privilege the futures in which Bob does decay within three days over the futures in which Bob does not.

Those who deny PARITY maintain that there is a (linearly structured) world that is determinately designated as actual. The leading concretist development of this idea is *divergence* metaphysics, which is Lewis's (1973, 1986a) preferred version of concretism. According to it, our world is a (non-branching) four-dimensional manifold, one of many possible concrete manifolds.

---

[14] Indeterminism is the claim that the current state of the world plus the laws of nature fail to determine the state of the world at some later time. Branching metaphysics is compatible with determinism provided that the laws of nature say that, given that the history is such-and-such, there are two, or more, continuations. For discussion of this point within the metaphysics literature, see Barnes and Cameron (2009) and Torre (2011).

Divergence metaphysics need not prevent us from using branching diagrams or branching models, as long as we gloss them differently. The divergence theorist can hold that sharing of nodes is not literally sharing of parts. Instead, it is best understood as duplication. Under this conception, when two worlds in the diagram share a node, they agree in all matters of particular fact at that point in time.

The important metaphysical insight is that sharing a node in this sense is perfectly compatible with denying PARITY. Even if two worlds verify the same matters of particular fact up to a point in time, there is no implication that they share constituents and no obstacle to the idea that an individual event is located in one, but not the other, of two branching worlds. Although nothing prevents divergence metaphysicians from deploying branching diagrams and models in accounting for future talk, they should hasten to add that from the point of view of an individual located in a particular world, the model and its associated diagram are *missing* the crucial information about which world that individual is located in.

So far, I have considered how two concretist conceptions of possible worlds might view branching diagrams and branching models. Let us move on and consider what an ersatzist might say. To start, ersatzism can come in variaties that uphold, as well as ones that deny, the parity thesis. To get a parity-violating version of ersatzism, imagine a theorist who thinks that among the many merely possible timelines, exactly one is actualized and that it is determinate which timeline it is. The tree identifies a plurality of ways the world could be, but exactly one is distinguished as the actual timeline.

This possibility illustrates an important fact: Sharing of nodes in a branching diagram represents overlap, but is not enough to yield the parity thesis. Temporally structured ersatz worlds can share initial segments without significant metaphysical consequences. If two ersatz worlds share a segment, this segment must be composed of abstract objects, so what they share is an initial sequence of abstract objects. This sort of sharing does not entail anything metaphysically significant about PARITY. Suppose, for an analogy, that I deface a score of Beethoven's Moonlight Sonata. Armed with white-out, I erase the last chord, a C major, and replace it with an F minor (sorry, Beethoven!). I happily call the result "Cariani's Moonlight Sonata." There is nothing metaphysically controversial in saying that the two Moonlight Sonatas share an initial segment of bars (almost all of them, in fact).

Back to the case of possible worlds. The ersatzist I have been describing agrees there is a feature of reality that privileges one world over the other worlds that overlap with it. That feature applies exclusively to the concrete, actualized world. A representation of this feature is missing from branching diagrams and branching models. But it could be added to them, just as we added cross-world simultaneity relations. The broader lesson is that sharing of nodes only counts as settling the PARITY question if nodes are interpreted as world slices.

Importantly, there are also versions of ersatzism that endorse PARITY. These all share the idea that the concrete lump of matter does not settle which of the abstract worlds is actualized. Here is an illustration by Barnes and Cameron:

> Think about the open future as follows: for every time at our world w, there is a set of possible worlds that represents the potential ways w could be atemporally given its history and current state. That is, for any arbitrary time t at w, there are a set of worlds that are duplicates of w up to t and represent the ways w could possibly be atemporally, given its history up until t. Call this set {Futures}. At the beginning of w's history, {Futures} is very large; it gets smaller as w moves through time. Each change in w has the effect of removing worlds from {Futures} making certain ways a world could be (atemporally) no longer compatible with the way w is now. At the last instant of w's life, perhaps, {Futures} will have been whittled down to a single possible world: the possible atemporal state of which w which is *actualized*. (Barnes and Cameron, 2009, p. 295)

One view along these lines, though not the one Barnes and Cameron prefer, would claim that the reason why {Futures} shrinks is that what is instantiated at any given time is an initial segment of a complete world and that the set of instantiated times keeps increasing as time passes. This is a version of the *growing block* theory. Figure 2.8 diagrams the actualized block as the solid segment starting at the origin and extending out to the rectangular node. In this scenario, the dotted worlds (*a–d*) are not possible completions of the actualized timeline, while worlds e, f, g are still in the running.

Another kind of view claims that even though it is determinate that a lump of matter corresponding to past, present, and future is instantiated, it is indeterminate which is actually instantiated (Cameron, 2015). I do not aim to settle the score between these conceptions. I am slightly more bullish than Cameron (2015, chapter 5) about the prospects for integrating the growing block metaphysics with a sensible semantics for future talk, but I won't tackle these issues of temporal ontology head on.

What matters to the present discussion is that we can populate our map of metaphysical options with a fourth family of views: ersatzist views that endorse PARITY.

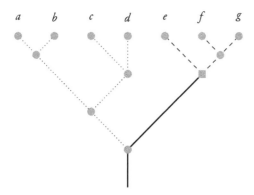

Figure 2.8   Branching diagrams for non-eternalists

The more general conclusion I want to draw is that branching diagrams and branching models are not for the sole use of concretist branching time metaphysics. Many kinds of theorists can deploy them as long as they appropriately change their conception of what it means for the model, or for the diagram, to fit some metaphysical conception of the worlds. Viewed from the opposite end, branching diagrams and branching models are not, by themselves, a transparent guide to the underlying metaphysics.

PART II

The Road to Selection Semantics

CHAPTER 3

The Modal Challenge

The key idea of the symmetric paradigm is that *will* and *was* have structurally symmetric meanings – the only difference is that in one case we go forward in time and in the other case we go backward. Although I noted some work in linguistics semantics in setting up the symmetric paradigm, much research in linguistics has challenged this hypothesis. It is a prominent hypothesis among semanticists that *will* but not *was* is a modal expression.[1] The *modal hypothesis* (about English) is the view that modality distinguishes English predictive expressions like *will* and *gonna* from past-tense markers like *was*. Modal hypotheses come in various local flavors: Its English version is independent of parallel theses about Italian or Welsh, or Mandarin or Japanese. This chapter sets out the master argument for the modal hypothesis – in the first instance about English, but without losing sight of similar questions about other languages.

As in Cariani and Santorio (2018), I will rely heavily on a compelling battery of arguments for the modal hypothesis by Peter Klecha (2014). Before diving into those arguments, however, we need to have an operative understanding of what it means to claim that some expression is a modal (Section 3.1). After considering a couple warm-up arguments (Sections 3.2–3.3), I get to Klecha's main arguments (Sections 3.4–3.5).

---

[1] For discussion of modal views, see Enç (1996), Condoravdi (2002, 2003), Kaufmann (2005), Portner (2009), Copley (2009), Klecha (2014), Giannakidou and Mari (2015, 2017), Kratzer (2021), and Cariani and Santorio (2018). The point isn't recent, either: The classification of *will* as a modal was endorsed decades ago by Partee (1973). In the philosophical literature, the position that *will* is a modal is virtually only represented in the context of what Prior called Peircean semantics (see Section 4.1). Malpass and Wawer (2012, section 7.2) propose a disjunctive hybrid of non-modal truth-conditions and Peircean truth-conditions. For defenses in linguistics of the opposing view (i.e., that *will* is not a modal), see Comrie (1989), Kissine (2008), and to some extent von Stechow (1995).

3.1   What Is a Modal?

If there is a modal hypothesis that is to be opposed to the symmetric paradigm, we need some kind of grip on what makes an expression a modal, and it better be that the semantic analyses of the symmetric paradigm count as non-modal.

Modality is in the first instance a linguistic category, and a hard one to define at that. It is symptomatic of this difficulty that an important, comprehensive book on the field (Portner, 2009) sketches the countours of the category in very tentative terms:

> I am not too comfortable defining modality, but a definition provides a useful place to start: modality is the linguistic phenomenon whereby grammar allows one to say things about, or on the basis of, situations which need not be real. (Portner, 2009, p. 1)

Part of the difficulty is that the category of modality has many manifestations and it is not tied to any particular syntactic category.

To make things more complicated, there are inequivalent ways of drawing the boundary of modality – some of which are not helpful to get at the relevant distinctions. In some quarters, the modal expressions of a language are identified with those expressions that express concepts of possibility and necessity. In my view, this is best understood as a sufficient but not necessary criterion. For many expressions, it is not obvious that a quantificational semantics is most appropriate. For example, recent literature has highlighted the advantages of measure theoretic accounts of probability operators (Yalcin 2010; Lassiter 2011, 2017; Swanson 2011; Moss 2015, 2018) over their quantificational rivals. According to these accounts, *probably* is neither a necessity operator nor a possibility operator.

Another common thought is that modality has something to do with "displacement" and "displaced evaluation" (von Fintel and Heim, 2011, pp. 1–2). Displacement is the feature of human languages that allows their speakers to make claims that are not about what is present to them (Hockett et al., 1960). The problem here is that merely talking about displacement won't exactly draw the distinction we need. The symmetric operators of tense logic (Chapter 1) are devices of displaced evaluation, since they introduce displacement with respect to time. However in the relevant sense they do not count as modals. What we would like is a way of drawing the distinction such that the English *must* counts as a modal, but the operators of tense logic do not.

We might try to fuse together Portner's insight with the idea of displacement. More precisely, we might suppose that an expression *e* is modal when it gives rise to "worldly" displacement: The semantic rules governing *e* intervene on a possible world coordinate of evaluation. This is quite vague, but perhaps it can be illustrated by contrasting two lexical entries:

MODAL. $[\![\textit{necessarily } A]\!]^{w,t} = \forall v[wRv \rightarrow [\![A]\!]^{v,t} = 1]$

NON-MODAL. $[\![\textit{was } A]\!]^{w,t} = \exists u < t[\![A]\!]^{w,u} = 1$

In these semantic clauses, *w* and *t* appear as evaluation coordinates for every expression in our target language. Non-modal entries may need to read the world coordinate of the point of evaluation, but unlike the modal entries, they do not *intervene* on them. The modals are those expressions whose meanings intervene on world coordinates – in this example, by quantifying over them.

This principle of worldly displacement correctly classifies as modals the canonical expressions you'd expect (*must*, *might*, etc.), provided that they are given some standard quantificational semantics. The principle also sorts as modals some non-quantificational expressions. A simple example could be the actuality operator of two-dimensional modal logic. This operator sets the world of evaluation to the world of the context.[2] Other expressions that are correctly classified as modals by this rule are Lewis's (1973) variably strict counterfactual conditional operator and Stalnaker's (1968) similarity-based conditional operator. As noted earlier, the principle also classifies the operators of tense logic as non-modal, as desired. Although these shift a parameter of evaluation, they do not intervene on the world parameter.

I am not quite ready to sign off on the principle of worldly displacement as a fully adequate characterization of the class of modal expression. For one thing, I am willing to count probability operators (e.g., *probably*) as modals. But, according to the measure-theoretic semantic theories mentioned earlier, these operators do not intervene on possible worlds. Moreover, the characterization won't work correctly for certain dynamic theories of modality, such as the update semantics of Veltman (1996). These limits should prompt us to qualify endorsement for a characterization in terms of worldy displacement.

---

[2] Note, however, that it is unclear that the English word *actually* has this meaning (see, e.g., Yalcin, 2015).

We can fall back on a weaker position that is still sufficient to carry our discussion. Much like the idea that modals express concepts of possibility and necessity, worldly displacement is a sufficient, though perhaps not necessary condition to count an expression as a modal (given a semantic analysis for that expression). Because possibility and necessity operators are all devices of worldly displacement, this sufficient condition is strictly more permissive than the one in terms of possibility and necessity. For the expressions that are not well modeled in terms of worldly displacement, there needs to be some independent case to classify them as modals. That means that we still have reason to classify *must* as a modal and to classify the operators of tense logic as non-modal.

What makes an expression a modal is its semantic entry. In particular, endorsement or rejection of supervaluationist techniques (or any other postsemantic device) is irrelevant to the question whether some expression *e* is a modal. The supervaluationist techniques discussed in Chapter 2 give us no more right to sort *will* as a modal than to sort as any other expression of the language, such as the name *Paris*, as modal.

With these clarifications out of the way, we are ready to tackle the arguments for the modal hypothesis. At the core of these arguments is the idea that predictive expressions, such as *will*, share many important features with bona fide modal expressions, such as *must* and *would*. In fact, that they have more in common with these than they do with past-tense markers. The arguments I present in support of this thesis are not deductive. Ultimately, the hypothesis that predictive expressions are modals is supported by an inference to the best explanation. The more constructive chapters to come are also parts of that inference to the best explanation, since they are essential in supporting the idea that the modal analysis can be developed clearly and coherently.

3.2 The Argument from Common Morphology

Several linguists have noted (Abusch, 1997, 1998; Condoravdi, 2002; Kaufmann, 2005) that *will* shares morphology with the modal *would*. In particular, *will* and *would* have in common a modal morpheme, often represented as WOLL: *will* is PRESENT + WOLL; *would* is PAST + WOLL. The assumption of common morphology allows us to explain otherwise puzzling semantic facts. For example, it explains why we can replace *will* with *would* in indirect reports of past utterances of *will*-sentences. Suppose that Clara says:

(1)   I will make this three-point shot.

After she makes the shot, we can report her utterance by saying:

(2)   Clara said she would make the three-point shot.

A possible reason for concern here is that the morphological relationship between *will* and *would* (in particular, the fact that *would* is the past tense of *will*) does appear to be a localized historical accident of English. In the introduction, I resolved to not let the philosophical argument depend on peculiarities of specific languages. That argument might appear to go against this point, since this morphological connection is indeed local to English. Worse yet, it is local to a specific predictive expression of English: To point out the obvious, *gonna* does not share any morphological elements with *would*.

   In response, I want to distinguish between the morphological/historical fact that *would* starts out as the past tense of *will* from the availability of reports such as (2). The observation that one can use expressions like *would* to report past utterances of predictive expressions does generalizes to other languages. Consider Italian translations of (1) and (2):

(3)   Segnerò   questo tiro da tre.
       I make will this   shot for three.

(4)   Clara ha detto che   avrebbe   segnato quel tiro da tre.
       Clara said   that she would have made   that shot for three.

(4) shows that, from Tuesday's point of view, we report the future tense in (3) with the "future in the past" construction exploiting the conditional verbal mood.

   This is interesting because it suggests, that even without the common morphological history between *will* and *would*, we see similar phenomena involving the Italian analogues of *will*-sentences and *would*-sentences. For instance, we can use (6) to report on an earlier utterance of (5):

(5)   Se guarisce,   verrà   al lavoro domani.
       If she is healed, she will come to work tomorrow.

(6)   Se fosse   guarita, Clara sarebbe   venuta al lavoro.
       If she had healed, Clara would have come   to work.

   These considerations about Italian do not just extend the argument to another language. They also reinforce the argument for English: The fact that this relationship between *will* and *would* is replicated in different languages suggests that it is unlikely that the reporting facts about English are local historical accidents. In fact, we don't need to leave the English language to appreciate a similar point. (2) could just as well report (1) as it could report an utterance by Clara of *I am going to make this three-point shot.*

3.3 The Argument from Present-Directed Uses

The materials for our next argument are presented in Palmer (1987), Enç (1996), and Huddleston and Pullum (2002, p. 188). The key observation is that *will* has non-future-directed modal uses, as in:

(7)   The laundry will be done by now.

The meaning of (7) is roughly similar, though not identical, to the meaning of:

(8)   The laundry must be done by now.

Furthermore, present-directed *will* seems to be playing a somewhat similar cognitive role to some uses of *must*: To accept (7) and (8) is to be in an epistemic state that settles that the laundry is done. Moreover, like *must*, *will* has evidential requirements.[3] Both (7) and (8) are somewhat infelicitous if uttered when one is staring right at the washed clothes in the washing machine.

It need not follow from these considerations that *will* and *must* have exactly the same meaning. One difference, noted in Huddleston and Pullum (2002), is that *must* figures more naturally in explanation contexts. Contrast:

(9)   a.   Ed's late – he must have overslept.
       b.   *Ed's late – he will have overslept.

The argument, then, is this: *Will* has uses that seem naturally understood as expressing a modality of sorts. The modal hypothesis would nicely unify these uses with the predictive ones. By contrast, if *will* was not a modal, we would have one of two options: either postulate a secondary modal sense

---

[3] For a comprehensive study of the evidentiality of *will*, see Winans (2016). While I do not agree with every aspect of her discussion, Winans forcefully drives home a very important point: Although there are connections between the evidential requirements of *will* and those of *must*, there are also important differences and we cannot simply assimilate the former to the latter.

just to account for these readings or hypothesize that in the special cases in which *will* gets these uses, a covert modal is added.[4]

It is important to remark that this behavior is not limited to *will*. It is shared with other predictive expressions, such as *going to*. Suppose I am cooking fish in the oven. I hear my timer go off. I can plausibly say:

(10) a.   The fish is going to be ready now.
      b.   The fish is not going to be ready yet.

Finally, we note that this behavior extends to languages like Italian that have tense morphology.

(11)   Il   pesce sarà   pronto a   quest'ora.
       The fish   will be ready   by this time.

In fact, far from lacking this potential, the Italian future tense allows for another present-directed reading of the "future tense" that seems not to exist in English (Giannakidou and Mari, 2015). Suppose we are inquiring about the whereabout of our friend Carlo – perhaps someone asked "Dove è Carlo?" ("Where Is Carlo?").

(12)   Sarà   andato a fare la spesa.
       He will have   gone shopping.

There is no parallel way of using past-tense markers to express this kind of modality.

In later chapters, as we transition to building a positive modal theory, we will need to explain what keeps together these present-directed and future-directed uses of predictive expressions. The early moral is that the symmetric paradigm cannot quite explain this asymmetry in the behavior of future and past without ad hoc stipulations. If we can do better within a modal system, that will be a point in favor of the modal analysis.

---

[4] Some even think that *will* can trigger deontic and generic readings in sentences like these:

(i)   You will do the homework your teacher assigns (or else you do not get to go to the trip).

(ii)   Cars by this manufacturer will break down after 50,000 miles.

If so, that would strengthen the contention that *will* has modal uses. However, it is not clear that these deontic and generic flavors are due to the contribution of *will*. After all, *cars by this manufacturer break down after 50,000 miles* sounds equivalent to (ii). This would suggest that the modality does not come from *will*. Be that as it may, it is clear that *will* has present-directed epistemic uses.

Although this argument does make trouble for a flat-footed non-modal analyses of *will*, it is possible to have a view of *will* according to which it is non-modal but also carries evidential requirements. Whether this is possible turns on some vexing questions in semantics concerning the proper conception of modality, the proper conception of evidentiality, and the relationship between modality and evidentiality. I write on the assumption that there is a fairly tight connection between these two. But conversation with Natasha Korotkova convinced me that this assumption is more like an unreflective choice of party affiliation than anything else. Korotkova (2016) argues that we cannot automatically trace evidential constraints to modal features. And, to repeat, this opens up the possibility that *will* and *must* might have similar evidential contributions, regardless of whether *will* is a modal. Ultimately, I believe that the most convincing diagnostic for the modality of *will* is the argument from modal subordination discussed in Section 3.4.

3.4   The Argument from Modal Subordination

Future-directed *will* can occur in the consequents of conditionals. Consider this example:

(13)   If Katie travels to Berkeley, she will shop at Amoeba Records.

We interpret the prediction in (13) as somehow restricted to those worlds in which Katie travels to Berkeley. The modal hypothesis makes easy work of this observation. For example, in Kratzer's (1991a) influential framework for modal semantics, the job of conditional antecedents is to restrict the domain of worlds against which modals are evaluated. If *will* were a modal, the function of the antecedent of (13) is to restrict its domain, which is as expected in (13).

As Klecha (2014) notes, however, the mere existence of these conditional predictions fails to establish that *will* is a modal because a modal analysis of *will* is not required to handle (13). Even if *will* were not a modal, a standard Kratzerian framework for the analysis of conditionals would still make available an alternative construal on which the conditional antecedent restricts a covert (i.e., unpronounced) necessity modal, as in:

(14)   If Katie travels to Berkeley, [MUST] she will shop at Amoeba.

The worry here is that the antecedent *If Katie travels to Berkeley* might instead restrict this covert operator. If this move is allowed, the claim that conditional antecedents can give rise to restricted predictions does not favor a modal analysis over its non-modal rivals.[5]

However, following the lead of Klecha (2014), and ultimately that of Roberts (1989), we can improve on that first stab. Klecha presents a version of this argument that leverages the same general feature – the possibility of restricting a modal base in *will* – but uses a different kind of restricting device. Specifically, Klecha notes that predictive *will* can inherit its restrictions in cases of modal subordination. Consider these discourses:

(15) a. If Katie travels to Berkeley, she will shop at Amoeba Records. She <u>will</u> buy a boxed set and a dozen used LPs.
      b. Please do not throw paper towels in the toilet. It <u>will</u> clog and overflow. [6]

In (15-a), the prediction that Katie will buy boxed sets and LPs is not made unconditionally. We would like to say that the underlined *will* inherits its restriction from the conditional antecedent of (15-a). We interpret the second sentence of (15-a) roughly as *if Katie travels to Berkeley, she will buy a boxed set and a dozen used LPs.* This is an instance of the phenomenon of modal subordination (Roberts, 1989). A modally subordinated expression inherits constraints on the assignments to its evaluation parameters from previous stretches of the discourse. However, for the second sentence of (15-a) to be modally subordinated, it must contain a modal. Moreover, there

---

[5]   This is not to say that these considerations are entirely inconclusive. For one thing, they constrain the available of options for a number of theorists. They impose particularly sharp constraints on certain kinds of supervaluationist and relativist theories. Depending on which semantics they choose for the conditional, supervaluationists and relativists might end up with an implausible interpretation of predictive conditionals like (13). For example, MacFarlane (2014, p. 267) adopts a semantics in which conditionals are either true at every world or false at every world. This introduces a bizarre asymmetry between bare predictive sentences and conditional ones: *The coin will land heads* is predicted to be neither true nor false, but *if you flip it, the coin will land heads* has to be either true at every world or false at every world. It is hard to see what explains these asymmetries. These difficulties might not be insurmountable, however. After all, one can integrate the supervaluationist/relativist machinery with a different account of conditionals. The point remains that supervaluationism and relativism constrain the eligible accounts of conditionals in ways that are not usually noted by their defenders.

[6]   Thanks to Ram Neta for bringing this kind of example to my attention by posting a photo of a sign with a discourse similar to this on social media. What is especially striking about this example is that it shows modal subordination working across different clause types.

is no reason to assume that a covert modal is present here. If so, the modal must be the underlined *will*.

Interestingly, (15-b) shows that this can also happen across clause types. The declarative clause at the end of the discourse is subordinated to propositional material that is extracted from the imperative clause at the beginning of the discourse.

I note incidentally that although Klecha was the first to claim that availability for modal subordination was diagnostic of modality, Roberts (1989) had already noted examples of modal subordination with *will*. Indeed, the very first set of examples of Roberts (1989) includes these pairs:

(16)   a.   If Edna forgets to fill the birdfeeder, she will feel very bad.
       b.   The birds will get hungry.

(17)   a.   If John bought a book, he'll be home reading it by now.
       b.   # It's a murder mystery.

(18)   a.   If John bought a book, he'll be home reading it by now.
       b.   It'll be a murder mystery.

These subordinated readings are available in other languages. Here are some Italian judgments:

(19)   Se Katie viene a Roma vorrà   mangiare davanti al
       If Katie comes to Rome she will want to eat   in front of
       Colosseo;   David la   porterà altrove.
       the Coliseum; David her will take elsewhere.

Klecha's argument (and Roberts' original data) cleanly distinguishes the hypothesis that *will* is just a marker of tense (with a meaning that is symmetric to the meaning of *was*) from the hypothesis that it is a modal. If *will* was a tense marker, we should expect *will* and corresponding past-tense expressions to behave in symmetric ways – but they do not. As Klecha notes, the discourse in (15-a) contrasts with:

(20)   a.   If Katie traveled to Berkeley, she shopped at Amoeba Records.
       b.   # She bought a boxed set and a dozen used records.

(21)   Se Katie é venuta a Roma, ha voluto   mangiare davanti al
       If Katie came   to Rome, she wanted to eat   in front of
       Colosseo.   # David l'ha portata altrove.
       the Coliseum; # David her took   elsewhere.

Informants either reject (20-b) as ill formed, or do not take the second sentence to inherit its restriction from the conditional antecedent in the first.

Since the cases of subordination across clause types will play an important dialectical role, I want to pause and explore what the situation vis-á-vis past tense looks like for them. The subordination from imperative to declarative in (15-b) might not look like the best test case. When designing a contrasting case with past tense, one might worry that imperatives automatically force subordinated material to be in the future. To sidestep this issue, we can consider a small paradigm involving subordination with material from questions. Suppose I am reading the story of Cinderella to my daughter, but we have to stop before the end. Contrast these commentaries she might make:

(22)   a.   Does she stay at the ball past midnight? The carriage will turn into a pumpkin!
       b.   Did she stay at the ball past midnight? # The carriage turned into a pumpkin!
       c.   Did she stay at the ball past midnight? The carriage must have turned into a pumpkin!

Once again, *will* and *must* can be subordinated to material emerging from the question. Past tense cannot.

Acknowledging the data about (20-b) and (22-b) is also important to fend off a possible challenge to the argument. Recall that the first stab at the argument failed because modals can occur covertly in the consequents of conditionals. Perhaps they can occur covertly at the beginnings of clauses in discourse, so that (15-a) really looks more like:

(23)   If Katie travels to Berkeley, she will shop at Amoeba Records. [MUST] She <u>will</u> buy a boxed set and a dozen used LPs.

If what gets restricted is the covert MUST, then there is no pressure to assume that *will*, as it occurs in (23), is a modal. One problem with this suggestion is that it fails to predict why the past tense in (20-b) does not tolerate this kind of restriction. If the covert modals can show up at the top of the second sentence of the future-directed discourse in (23), they should also be allowed to show up at the top of past-directed discourses like (20-b). Similarly, this argument fails to predict the difference between (22-b) and (22-c).

In several discussions, I encountered some pushback on some elements of this argument. First, there are some cases of past-directed modal subordination that appear to go through. Here are a couple examples from Goldstein and Hawthorne (private correspondence; I have also received similar examples from Nate Lauffer):

(24)   If he went to the park yesterday, he had a sandwich. He had a beer, too.

(25)   If the supplies arrived yesterday, it was late in the day. But it was before 11 PM.

These cases do invite a conditional reading of the second sentence in each discourse. I do not think, however, that these are examples of modal subordination and it behooves me to say why. Two elements of these sentences interfere. The first is that some of the additional material might introduce anaphoric relations – perhaps *too* in (24). The examples of modal subordination involving *will* did not seem to require such anaphoric material. The second interfering element is that one can get subordination-like effects by treating the second sentence as a second conjunct in the conditional. Since the period in the discourse is not pronounced, it can be difficult to think about what counts as two separate sentences, as opposed to a slightly drawn-out way of uttering one sentence. But the case of (25) seems like a clear example of this sort of thing. This challenge would be more compelling if there were cases of putative modal subordination occurring across distinct clause types as in (15-b).

Taking stock, the outline of the argument from restricting behavior is this: Predictive expressions seem to allow restricted interpretations that are typical of modals – specifically, they seem to allow for modal subordination. Past-tense markers do not allow this. So we have evidence that predictive expressions, but not past-tense markers, have one of the hallmarks of modality.

3.5   The Argument from Acquaintance Inferences

Klecha (2014) offers one more argument for the modal hypothesis. This argument involves the relation between *will* and predicates of personal taste. Bare applications of predicates of personal taste invite inferences to the effect that the speaker has had the relevant experience. Call this the *acquaintance inference*.[7]

---

[7]   There is a growing literature on what generates and what suppresses the acquaintance inference. For an incomplete list of references see Pearson (2013), Ninan (2014), Kennedy and Willer (2016),

(26) a. That tomato juice is disgusting.   (# but I have not tried it)
     b. This movie is great.   (# but I have not seen it)

Klecha notes important facts about the distribution of this inference – in particular, about how the inference is triggered (or suppressed) in more complex sentences. First, past tense invites the acquaintance inference.

(27) a. That tomato juice was disgusting. (# but I have not tried it)
     b. This movie was great.   (# but I have not seen it)

Second, modals suppress acquaintance inferences, thus allowing speakers to flawlessly deny that they had the relevant experience.

(28) a. That tomato juice must (/might/should) be disgusting (but I have not tried it).
     b. This movie must (/might/should) be great (but I have not seen it).

Third, and crucial, predictive *will* lines up with the modals in suppressing acquaintance inferences:

(29) a. That tomato juice will (/is going to) be disgusting (but I have not tried it).
     b. This movie will (/is going to) be great (but I have not seen it).

If *will* is a modal, this behavior is easily explained. If *will* were just a mere tense marker, we expect it to behave similarly to past tense. However, (27-a)–(27-b) refute this prediction.

It has been informally suggested to me that the explanation for these asymmetries might involve the fact that regardless of the correct metaphysics, we treat the past as settled and the future as open. I am not sure about how to explain the preceding data on the basis of this observation. There is one version of this reply that I find clear enough to evaluate: Perhaps the acquaintance inference is only to the conclusion that *it is (historically) possible* that I had the experience. In the case of sentences about the past, if I have not had the experience, then it is not possible

Anand and Korotkova (2018), and references therein. In addition to Klecha, the discussion in Ninan (2014) is the most directly relevant to questions concerning the semantics of the future.

that I have had it. In the case of sentences about the future, the fact that I have not had the experience is compatible with the possibility that I will have it.

If this is the correct representation of the objection, my reply is that it incorrectly predicts that (30) is defective.

(30)   That tomato juice will be disgusting and there is no possibility that I will ever try it.

But it is pretty clear that (30) is both a felicitous sentence and, depending on the contents of the tomato juice, a sensible thought.

Perhaps unsurprisingly, the acquaintance inference paradigm is entirely reproducible in Italian. Here are translations of (26-a), (27-a), (28-a), and (29-a):

(31)   a.   Quel succo di pomodoro é disgustoso   (# ma non l'ho
              assaggiato)
        b.   Quel succo di pomodoro potrebbe essere disgustoso (ma non
              l'ho assaggiato)
        c.   Quel succo di pomodoro sará digustoso   (ma non l'ho
              assaggiato)
        d.   Quel succo di pomodoro era disgustoso   (# ma non l'ho
              assaggiato)

They repeat the same pattern of acceptance and non-acceptance we saw earlier, with simple present and past tense triggering acquaintance inferences, while modals and *will* suppress them.

As with the argument from present-directed uses, we must add an important caveat. Anand and Korotkova (2018) argue that suppression of the acquaintance inference is diagnostic of evidentiality. If we have a background view on which evidentiality and modality are tightly linked, then it will be diagnostic of modality as well. But against the alternative view that evidentiality and modality float free of each other, we cannot deduce that *will* is a modal from the observation that it imposes certain evidential requirements.

This is strictly speaking correct, but there is a looser interpretation of Klecha's argument on which the argument carries more force than these considerations suggest. Even if modality and evidentiality are distinct categories, they are plausibly related at least in the sense that many modals have distinctive evidential contributions. Insofar as the evidential behavior of *will* is similar enough to the evidential behavior of *must*, that similarity suggests, at least abductively, that they might be similar to together in other important respects.

3.6   Morals and Distinctions

Taken together, these arguments strongly suggest that future-directed talk has a modal character that outstrips what can be captured by the classical symmetric paradigm. But we ought to be careful in stressing what sorts of argument I have endorsed here. In particular, there is one type of argument for the modal hypothesis that I prefer not to rely on. Bonomi and Del Prete, in an unpublished manuscript, argue that there is a difference between future claims that are settled by presently available evidence and future claims that can only be settled by evidence and facts that only the future can yield. As an example of the first, they consider a January 2008 utterance of

(32)   The next Olympics will be in Beijing.

As an example of the latter, they consider an utterance of (33) in a context in which a fair die is about to be tossed.

(33)   The die will come up six.

They claim that (32) is a modal claim and means something like *all of the possibilities that are compatible with the evidence are ones in which the Olympics are in Beijing*. By contrast, (33) is non-modal because it constrains only one possibility, whichever possibility is actual.

Bonomi and Del Prete maintain that these differences point toward a *lexical* ambiguity in future-tense markers, with a modal tense marker reserved for the first sort of reading and a non-modal tense marker reserved for the second. None of the arguments I have made in this section supports a distinction of this sort or a rigid link between the type of evidence that can support a claim and its status as modal. While these links provide useful heuristics for generalizations about how we form certain judgments, they are not reliable guides for semantic categorization. According to the approach I prefer, there is a single lexical analysis for *will*, and many different kinds of evidence that may support propositions expressed by sentences involving it.

Bonomi and Del Prete are not alone in pursuing this line of argument. In the massive *Cambridge Grammar of the English Language*, Huddleston and Pullum (2002) write:

> There is a close intrinsic connection between futurity and modality: our knowledge of the future is inevitably much more limited than our knowledge about the past and the present, and what we say about the future will typically be perceived as having the character of prediction rather than an unqualified factual assertion.

By the time I am done with my book, I will have disagreed with this passage twice over. First, I reject the idea that there is a path from the type of evidence to modal classification. Second, I argue (in Chapter 9) that many predictions *are* in fact assertions.

CHAPTER 4

Modality without Quantification

Suppose we accept that predictive expressions are modals. What sorts of modals are they? Theorists in the model-theoretic tradition view ordinary modals like *must* and *may* as expressing universal and existential quantification, respectively, over some domain of worlds or, in some cases, some related but more complex quantificational constraints. What kind of quantificational force does *will* have?

The answer I will defend is *none*: *Will* is a modal but not a quantificational modal. I have originally developed this idea in my collaboration with Paolo Santorio.[1] We argue that *will* and *would* are best understood as selecting a world out of a modal domain. The direct inspiration for this idea is Stalnaker's selection semantics for conditionals. This denial that *will* has quantificational force distinguishes us from the vast majority of theorists who endorse the modal hypothesis, since they generally accept some kind of quantificational account.

This chapter presents some of the key considerations for avoiding quantificational theories of future talk. The basic argumentative strategy is to note that there are many respects in which *will* and *would* behave differently from other modals. Here is a bit of argumentative canapé: Huddleston and Pullum (2002, p. 190) observe that *will* sometimes behaves as if it had a "minimal degree of modality." By this, they mean is that it behaves as if the only displacement it operates is temporal. In support of this, they offer the example

(1)   It will soon be too dark to play any more.

---

[1]   Cariani and Santorio (2018); see also Kratzer (2021), who, in passing and independently, sketches the same view. While much of the present chapter relies on arguments that were previously available in the literature, I will flag a few places in which Santorio and I have taken somewhat original stances. It goes without saying that credit for these ideas is shared equally between us. This is even more true of Chapter 5, which presents a theory that was generated in an entirely collaborative fashion.

The invited reasoning here is this: (1) is entirely about the world in which it is uttered. Suppose Topher utters (1) while we are playing a hard-fought tennis match. Now suppose that we cannot even finish the next game. Then what Topher said was true and we do not need to inspect the goings-on in non-actual worlds to establish that. Alternatively, if it turns out we still have tons of time before darkness sets in, (1) is false. If so, the goings-on in non-actual worlds must be irrelevant to its truth-conditions. And if that is true, it is hard to reconcile this particular use of *will* with a quantificational modal analysis.

4.1 Quantificational Theories

The main quantificational theories are refinements of what Prior called the "Peircean" semantics (Prior, 1967, pp. 132–136). According to this theory, *it will rain* is true if and only if it rains at some future time in each of the worlds that are objectively possible at the time of utterance. Peircean truth-conditions for *will* can be stated more precisely against the background of branching models. At one point in developing that framework, we spotted ourselves a function `worlds` that inputs a context and outputs a set of worlds. Let us modify this to a function `worlds*` that inputs a model, a world w and a time t and outputs all the worlds in the model that agree with w up to t.

With this notational tool, we can say:

PEIRCEAN SEMANTICS.

$$[\![will(\mathsf{A})]\!]^{w,t} = 1 \text{ iff } \forall v \in \text{worlds*}(\mathcal{M}, w, t) \; \exists j > t, [\![\mathsf{A}]\!]^{v,j} = 1$$

Informally: *It will rain* is true (relative to a model, a world, and a time) if and only if it rains in the future of each of the worlds that are historically possible at the input time.

It is important not to confuse the Peircean semantics with the supervaluationist postsemantics. As I emphasized in Chapter 3, adopting a supervaluationist postsemantics is entirely orthogonal to adopting a modal analysis of *will*. The latter is a lexical hypothesis – a claim about what a bit of language means. Supervaluationism is not a thesis about the meanings of some lexical items.

A distinctive, and problematic, implication of Peirceanism is that if a proposition **A** is contingent, in the sense of being true at some possible futures and false at others, then *will* **A** must be false. Imagine a situation

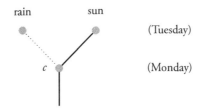

Figure 4.1   Basic binary branching model

corresponding to the very simple branching diagram in Figure 4.1. Suppose that in context *c*, located on Monday, I utter *it will rain*. Then the Peircean predicts that what I said in *c* is false.

This distinctive implication is problematic because it reveals that the Peircean truth-conditions are too demanding. Sure, it is possible that it will not rain – but that's not enough to conclude that it is false that it will rain. Indeed, Prior suggests in passing that the Peircean analysis might be thought of as modeling the meaning of *will inevitably* as opposed to the meaning of *will*. (In the rest of the book, I occasionally introduce operators such as *will inevitably* or *it is settled that*, implicitly assuming that they are governed by a Peircean semantics.)

The linguistic literature features proposals in the quantificational mold that avoid this problem by weakening the Peircean truth-conditions. Just like the Peircean account, these proposals take *will* to be a universal quantifier. However, they depart from naïve Peirceanism by taking *will* to have an additional restriction. In Kratzer's sense, they analyze *will* as a doubly relative modal, by taking it to quantify over a subset of the set of objectively possible futures. The different proposals diverge in how they construe this set. Kaufmann's (2005) truth-conditions for *will* A are that **A** holds at a future time in all the most *likely* worlds. Kaufmann uses a local measure of likelihood: Worlds are ranked by their individual probability, rather than by, say, the probabilities of some partitions they belong to.[2] Copley (2009) proposes instead that the truth-conditions for *will* A are that **A** must hold at a future time in all the most *normal* worlds. (Copley's official view also adds a homogeneity requirement I will discuss shortly.) Giannakidou and Mari (2017) treat *will* as an epistemic modal, quantifying over knowledge states.

---

[2]   This, in itself, has some strange consequences I will not elaborate on: *Will* A may be true even if the proposition that A, i.e., **A**, is less likely than its negation $\bar{\mathbf{A}}$, provided that the most likely A-world is more likely than the most likely $\bar{\mathbf{A}}$-world.

4.2   Universal Analyses and Retrospective Evaluations

Analyses that treat *will* as a doubly relativized universal quantifier tend to face an immediate problem (which some of them are able to sidestep), and then a host of more complex problems. Although the immediate problem is quite general, I start by considering it within the more local context of Kaufmann's proposal.

Suppose that on Monday, I utter *it will rain tomorrow*. Based on Monday's conditions, with a storm approaching town – and due to hit sometime on Tuesday – rain within the evaluation interval is indeed the most likely outcome. This probability, we are supposing, is not merely epistemic, but a matter of high objective chance. Of course, the likely – and even the *objectively* likely – does not have to happen. Due to a fortuitous confluence of events, on Tuesday it does not rain. Thinking back about my utterance, I am tempted to say that I was mistaken, or that what I said was wrong. But it is unclear how the doubly relative account might handle this judgment. After all, what I said was that it rains in the futures that were most likely at the time of utterance. And *that* seems true.

This problem has a more general form. It is part of a more general dilemma for quantificational views that attempt to abide by the PARITY thesis of Chapter 2. (Recall that this thesis states that, fixing a situation of utterance, there are many ways the future might be that are objectively on a par.) Either the domain for *will* is the set **H** of all the objectively possible futures or it is a proper subset of **H**. If it is the former, we have the overly demanding Peircean theory. If it is the latter, then there should be a world v that is objectively possible but not in **H**. But consider an utterance at t_0 of *it will be the case that* A, where A will indeed be the case (at some future point) in every world in **H** but it will never be the case in v. Then when we retroactively assess the original utterance at a later time in v, we are forced to say that the utterance was true even though it sounds false.

Some may view it as unfair that I am using retrospective evaluations as criteria for theory choice since retrospective evaluations present thorny complications for many (perhaps all) accounts of future-talk. For example, MacFarlane (2003, 2008, 2014) has argued that only a relativist postsemantics can help correctly model retrospective evaluations. But a relativist postsemantics is available as a modification for *each* of the purely semantic theories considered earlier.[3] In the next sections, then, I consider other

---

[3]   Some quantificational views avoid this problem. These views guarantee that the world containing the actual future is in the domain of quantification. An example is Giannakidou and Mari's (2017) thesis that *will* quantifies over all the futures that are compatible with the knowledge that is available at the time of utterance. If there is any future point from which we can retrospectively evaluate an

objections against sophisticated quantificational views that do not involve retrospective evaluation.

4.3 Prior's Bet Objection

The sophisticated quantificational views improve on Peirceanism by restricting the domain of quantification so that not all possible futures count. This weakens truth-conditions so that some future contingents can come out true. But the problem with the Peircean semantics is not just that it imposes truth-conditions for future contingents that are too demanding. More generally, it does not fit coherently with how we think and talk about the future. An old objection by Prior is a good way of driving home this point:

> [Peircean semantics] is grossly at variance with the ways in which even non-determinists ordinarily appraise or assign truth-values to predictions, bets and guesses. Suppose at the beginning of a race I bet you that Phar Lap will win, and then he does win, and I come to claim my bet. You might then ask me, "Why, do you think this victory was unpreventable when you made your bet?" I admit that I don't, so you say, "Well then I'm not paying up then – when you said Phar Lap would win, what you said wasn't true …. So I'm sticking to the money. And I must admit that if anyone treated a bet of mine like that I would feel aggrieved." (Prior, 1976, p. 100)

This objection is forceful regardless of whether we take the quantification to be over all possible futures or over some designated subset. Consider, again, the sophisticated quantificational view according to which we quantify universally over the most likely worlds. Suppose also that, in whatever sense of probability that might be relevant, Phar Lap is unlikely to win. Then the claim that Phar Lap will win is predicted false, even if, as the future unfolds, Phar Lap defeats odds (and opponents) to win the race. Should Prior expect his friend to pay up? If Prior's friend denied payment on the grounds that Prior's original assertion was false, Prior would be justified in feeling swindled. It is easy to see that this problem is shared by quantificational views that set the domain in a different way. The problem only depends on the fact that *will* A (i) is predicted false if at the time of utterance, the rule for setting the domain lets in ¬A-worlds, and (ii) should not be predicted false if at the time at which the outcome of the bet is being discussed, A has become settled.

---

utterance of *it will rain tomorrow*, it must have been compatible with what we know at the time of utterance, and so it could not possibly have been ruled out by the quantificational account.

4.4   The Zero Credence Problem

Assume that the set of objectively possible futures is not homogeneous with respect to coin tosses. In some futures, the coin lands heads; in others, it lands tails. Finally, assume you know that the particular toss you are about to execute will be fair. That is, you know that the objective chance that the coin will land heads is one half. What credences are you rationally allowed to assign to the proposition expressed by *this coin will land heads* in this kind of context? Quantificational theories give an answer that conflicts with both ordinary intuition and with some plausible verdicts from Bayesian epistemology. I take this to be evidence against the quantificational theories.[4]

Chance-credence principles, such as Lewis's (1986b) *Principal Principle*, require rational agents to have credences that cohere with their beliefs about the chances. While this is not the place for an extended discussion of the Principal Principle, it is the place for some concise remarks about its proper interpretation.[5] Lewis (1986b) provides two formulations of the Principal Principle and claims that they are equivalent. Infamously, the first formulation does, and the second formulation does *not*, make use of the concept of admissible evidence. Meacham (2010) makes a compelling case that the second formulation from Lewis (1986b) is superior to the first formulation as well as to some folk statements found in the literature. My interpretation of the Principal Principle here closely follows Meacham's.

Let us start by introducing some auxiliary concepts. Let $\mathbf{H}_{w,t}$ be a proposition that is true in world v iff v and w are duplicates up to time t. One can think of $\mathbf{H}_{w,t}$ as a complete characterization of the history of w up to t. Let $\mathbf{T}_w$ be a proposition capturing the complete theory of chance of world w, i.e., a statement, for each moment in w, of all of the chance facts at that moment. Call conjunctions of the form $\mathbf{H}_{w,t}$ & $\mathbf{T}_w$ *chance-grounding claims* (CGCs). Note that each CGC fixes a chance function $ch_{w,t}$ – i.e., the chance function that $\mathbf{T}_w$ thinks is appropriate in world w at time t. Finally, let c_0 be an agent's *initial* credence function. With these concepts we can state the Principal Principle as the following constraint:

$$c_0(\mathbf{A} \mid \mathbf{H}_{w,t} \ \& \ \mathbf{T}_w) = ch_{w,t}(\mathbf{A})$$

Although this principle directly constrains an agent's *initial* credence function, it also indirectly constrains their later credences, since anything that the agent learns, and thus conditionalizes on, is equivalent to a disjunction of conjunctions of the form $\mathbf{H}_{w,t}$ & $\mathbf{T}_w$ (for some appropriate choices of w and t).[6]

To see this, consider an agent who acquires a single piece of evidence $\mathbf{E}$ – namely, that the coin that is about to be flipped is fair. By conditionalization, their posterior credence equals their initial credence conditional on $\mathbf{E}$.

$$c_1([\![\textit{will}(\text{heads})]\!]) = c_0([\![\textit{will}(\text{heads})]\!] \mid \mathbf{E})$$

To use the Principal Principle, we must reformulate $\mathbf{E}$. Fortunately, the claim that the coin is fair in world w at some time t is equivalent to a disjunction of all the conjunctions of the form $\mathbf{H}_{w,t}$ & $\mathbf{T}_w$ according to which the coin in question is fair at w in t. Call the set of such conjunctions **fair**. Then, the agent's rational credence at this later time is mandated to be the weighted average of the chances according to each CGC, weighted by the probability of that CGC.

$$c_0([\![\textit{will}(\text{heads})]\!] \mid \mathbf{E})$$
$$= \sum_{(\mathbf{H}_{w,t}\ \&\ \mathbf{T}_w) \in \mathbf{fair}} ch_{w,t}([\![\textit{will}(\text{heads})]\!]) \cdot c_0(\mathbf{H}_{w,t}\ \&\ \mathbf{T}_w \mid \mathbf{E})$$

In the example, all the CGCs agree that $[\![\textit{will}(\text{heads})]\!]$ has chance 0.5. So the term on the right in the equation simplifies to 0.5. It follows that, no matter the weights, the probability that the coin will land heads ought to be 0.5.

I argue that no quantificational theory can agree with the intuitively compelling constraint provided by the Principal Principle. Instead, such views invariably predict that the probability of such claims is allowed to be much lower than one half. In fact, it is quite clearly allowed to be zero.

Consider first the answer of a flat-footed Peircean. Under plausible assumptions, Peirceanism requires you to assign *zero* credence to the proposition that the coin will land heads. Any other assignment, I will argue, would be impermissible. All it takes to derive this verdict is a basic assumption about the relationship between truth in a world and

---

[6] The Principal Principle is not the only chance-credence principle worth entertaining. There is a compelling argument that it ought to be weakened, as noted by Hall (1994) and Lewis (1994). These authors advocate the *New Principle*. The reasons that motivate the transition from the Principal Principle to the New Principle need not concern us here, as the argument in the text will go through without substantial alternation with the New Principle in place of the Principal Principle.

subjective probability. Suppose that the *world-profile* of a sentence A in context c is the following set:

$$\{w \mid [\![A]\!]^{w,t_c} = 1\}$$

In the possible-worlds frameworks, this set is the proposition expressed by A. But the argument does not require the full set of idealizations associated with the possible-worlds framework. What the argument requires is this sufficient condition:

EMPTINESS.

> If a sentence A, as uttered in context c, has an empty world-profile, then it is rationally permissible to ascribe to its content a very low credence (zero or near-zero).

Indeed, the world-profile of *this coin will land heads*, as uttered in the kind of contexts we are imagining, must be empty. For each world w in which the coin is fair, there is a world that is historically possible from w's perspective in which the coin does not land heads. That world could be w itself, or it could be some other world that duplicates w up to the time of utterance. Given EMPTINESS, it is rationally permissible to assign credence zero to the content of *the coin will land heads*. By parallel reasoning, it is also rationally permissible to assign credence zero to the content of *the coin will not land heads*. For each world w in which the coin is fair, there is a world that is historically possible from w's perspective in which the coin *does* land heads. Moreover, someone who adopted these credences also ought to assign full credence (i.e., 1) to the wide-scope negations of these claims. For example, one should assign credence 1 to *it is not the case that the coin will land heads*. All of these facts are individually in conflict with the constraints emerging from the Principal Principle.

 That does it for naïve Peirceanism. What about the more sophisticated quantificational views? The three doubly relative accounts I have considered all share a general shape that makes them vulnerable to similar objections. Start, again, with Kaufmann. Recall that Kaufmann's domain consists of all the most likely worlds. Suppose that when we order worlds in terms of their probability, we end up with a tie at the top between a heads-world w_{heads} and a tails-world w_{tails}. This seems plausible given that the coin toss is fair. Now if we are certain that w_{heads} and w_{tails} are among the most likely worlds, Kaufmann's account seems to entail that the world profile of *the coin will land heads* should also be empty. And so again, it should be rationally permissible to assign these claims probability zero.

4.5   Scope with Negation

Another problem for quantificational views stems from the fact that nega-tion and *will* can appear in two possible scope configurations: *will* (*not* A) and *not* (*will* A). For quantificational modals, whether universal or exis-tential, the relative scope with negation makes a real truth-conditional difference. Here are some examples with epistemic and deontic flavors:

(2)   a.   She must not have passed
       b.   It is not the case that she must have passed

(3)   a.   She must not enter
       b.   It is not the case that she must enter

In both cases, we detect scope interactions between *must* and negation. For example, (3-b) merely says that she does not have to enter, whereas (3-a) says there is a requirement preventing her from entering.

   Suppose that *doubt* lexicalizes negation, so it means something like *believe not* and note the gap between:

(4)   a.   I believe she must not pass.
       b.   I doubt that she must pass.

Similar inequivalences can be detected with quantifiers:

(5)   a.   No student must have passed her class.
       b.   Every student must have failed her class.

The problem is that *will* does not behave in this way at all (MacFarlane, 2014; Schoubye and Rabern, 2017; Cariani and Santorio, 2018). A sentence like *it will not rain* does not have two readings corresponding to two possible scope configurations. The scope configurations are possible only in the superficial sense that *will* could, in principle, occupy certain positions rel-ative to negation. These different positions would impact truth-conditions if *will* indeed had a quantificational meaning. Intuitively, however, they do not impact the truth-conditions at all.

(6)   a.   She will not enter.
       b.   It is not the case that she will enter.

(7)   a.   I believe she will not pass.
       b.   I doubt that she will pass.

(8)   a.   No student who takes my class will pass it.
       b.   Every student who takes my class will fail it.

These pairs straightforwardly sound equivalent, and any theory that fails to deliver their equivalence must be rejected.[7] This includes nearly all versions of the quantificational theory.

These considerations provide some support for:

NEGATION SWAP. *will not* A is equivalent to *not will* A

In the terminology of Cariani and Santorio (2018), *will* is "scopeless" with respect to negation. A consequence of this equivalence is the intuitive validity of strengthened versions of the law of excluded middle. The classical law of excluded middle is the following schema:

A ∨ *not* A,

This schema is part of classical logic, which I am happy to take on board here. The classical schema has instances of the form:

will A ∨ *not will* A

Given NEGATION SWAP and the assumption that logical equivalents may be substituted for each other in disjunction contexts, the classical law of excluded middle is equivalent to:

WILL EXCLUDED MIDDLE (WEM). *will* A ∨ *will not* A is a logical truth.

Note that this differs from the classical law of excluded middle only in the relative scope of *will* and negation in the second disjunct.

In addition to the arguments in support of the semantic scopelessness of *will*, there is strong, direct intuitive support for WEM. Here is Thomason (1970, p. 267):

> It will or it won't has the force of tautology. It is invariably true to say things such as *either it will rain tomorrow or it won't*, even in cases where there is no more justification for saying that it will than for saying that it won't rain.

If Thomason's point needed anything else in the way of support, consider how reflexive it is for us, upon learning that there is a 70% chance that it will rain tomorrow, to allocate the remaining 30% to the proposition that it will not rain. This would not be expected unless WEM was a logical truth.

---

7   There is an important literature concerning the significance of pairs like the one in (8) in supporting the principle of conditional excluded middle. See Higginbotham (1986), von Fintel and Iatridou (2002), Leslie (2009), Klinedinst (2011), and Kratzer (2021). This literature is highly relevant here since, as I am about to argue, the fact that negation and *will* do not enter in significant scope relations is evidence for a parallel excluded middle principle for *will*.

In conversation, and later in Todd (2020), I have encountered a worry whose upshot would be that branching theorists might be able to reject this argument. Those who advance these arguments are motivated roughly by the following reasoning: "If there are multiple futures with equal claim to be my future, then the truth-value of *will* A (and *will* ¬A) cannot privilege one over the others. But if it does not privilege one over the others, then they can either both be true or both be not true. And if both are not true, then their disjunction cannot be true." We should resist this line of thought. For one thing, the possibility of a supervaluationist approach shows that the reasoning falters at the last step. For another, semantic theory is anchored to and evaluated against certain empirical judgments. To the extent that we can do so consistently, we must make sense of strongly held judgments of acceptability of sentences in context or of strong inference patterns – at least insofar as there is no way of explaining away why we are systematically disposed to make these judgments. Thomason's judgments in support of the validity of WEM are as strong as any of the judgments that semanticists typically base their theories on.

4.6 Homogeneity

Recent linguistic literature has provided a way out of the argument made in Section 4.5. Copley (2009, pp. 52–53), who is well aware of these issues concerning scope with negation, extends work by von Fintel (1997) on homogeneity presuppositions. To understand the mechanics of her account, start with an observation about plural definites. The disjunction in (9) sounds tautological:

(9)   Either the girls are at camp or they are not at camp

This strong inclination to accept (9) would persist even in contexts in which we would reject both disjuncts.

(10)   a.   The girls are at camp.
        b.   The girls are not at camp.

What is more, we could reject the disjuncts and accept (9) even if we were not ignorant about any aspect of the situation. Say that there are two relevant girls, Arya and Sansa, and suppose that we know everything there is to know about their location: We know that Arya is at camp, but Sansa is at the beach. In this epistemic situation, we would reject (10-a) – Sansa is not at camp, after all. And we would reject (10-b), because Arya is at camp. Neither disjunct is assertible, and yet (9) seems true.

What explains this pattern of judgment? Here is a picture: It is sufficient for the truth of (10-a) if all the relevant girls are at camp; it is sufficient for the truth of (10-b) if none of them are; but if some but not all are at camp, something that would be required for (10-a) and (10-b) to be true is violated. This is the phenomenon of *homogeneity*. The truth of a plural definite *the F's are G's* seems to imply that the *F*'s are uniformly *G*'s or uniformly not *G*'s. To make the account more specific and predictive, Copley follows von Fintel in modeling homogeneity as a presupposition.[8] The reason why the disjunction in (9) sounds tautological is that *if its presuppositions are satisfied*, (9) cannot fail to be true. This way of modeling logical validity is called *Strawson validity*.[9]

The next idea in this approach is to apply the homogeneity account to *will*. A good starting point is von Fintel's (1997) attempt to make it work for *will*-conditionals like:

(11)   a.   If I strike this match, it will light.
        b.   If I strike this match, it won't light.

The idea is that (11-a) is true [and (11-b) is false] if all the relevant worlds in which I strike the match are ones in which it lights. (11-a) is false [and (11-b) is true] if all the relevant worlds in which I strike the match are ones in which it does not light. For both conditionals to even be defined, either all the relevant worlds in which the match is struck must be worlds in which it lights or all the relevant worlds in which the match is struck must be worlds in which it does not light.

The same general idea might be applied to *will* and to predictive expressions more generally. In the specific case of *will*, we could take it to be a universal quantifier over a domain of worlds, with the presupposition that all the worlds in its domain have to be homogeneous with respect to

---

[8]   In more recent literature, some authors who accept homogeneity phenomena as genuine have rejected their presuppositional construal (Križ, 2015). The critical arguments in this section do depend somewhat on the presuppositional understanding of homogeneity. The alternative project is to develop a trivalent account of homogeneity and accompany it with an appropriate theory of credence. This is very much a project in progress at the time of this writing. Instead of trying to chase every trivalent way of thinking about homogeneity and how it might be combined with an account of credence, I will assign a proper comparison between this framework and mine as homework for future research.

[9]   It is so called because of its connection to some ideas of Strawson's (1952). For discussions of Strawson entailment, see von Fintel (1997, 1999) and Cariani and Goldstein (in press).

its prejacent. If entailment is modeled as Strawson entailment, these ideas can successfully account for WEM.

Let us reserve *Q&H* as a label for views that combine quantificational structure with homogeneity presuppositions. There is much to recommend *Q&H*, but I have three reasons to resist it. First, the claim that *will* involves a homogeneity presupposition is highly stipulative. There is no specific test for presupposition that makes it plausible that predictive modals presuppose that the future is homogeneous with respect to their prejacents. Second, even if *Q&H* successfully captures the scope data about the interaction with negation, it does not capture the relevant facts about credence. Suppose that you are certain that the objectively possible futures are equally distributed between heads worlds and tails worlds. Then should be plausible for you to have some intermediate credence – plausibly 1/2 – in the claim that the coin will land heads. But according to *Q&H*, the credence I should assign to this claim is whatever credence I should assign to contents of sentences whose presuppositions are violated.

So let us think about these contents. The claim is that these two credence assignments should be similar:

> My credence in the content of *the coin will land heads* when the domain of quantification contains some heads worlds and some tails worlds (and I am certain of this).

> My credence in the content of *the girls are at camp* when some of the relevant girls are at camp and some of the relevant girls are on vacation (and I am certain of this).

The problem is that these cases are not parallel. In the future contingents case, my credence can span the entire interval from 0 to 1 depending on what else I believe about the coin. In the case of plural definites, my credence in the content of *the girls are at camp* is 0 (or nearby), because my credence in **A** is my credence that **A** is true, and I am certain (or at any rate highly confident) that the content *the girls are at camp* is not true.

Going beyond homogeneity presuppositions, consider some other examples of beliefs in contents of sentences with violated presuppositions. What credence should you have in *Diana restrung her racquet* if Diana does not own a racquet? What credence should you have in *the king of France is bald* if there is no king of France? While I do not know of any attempts at a general theory of credence assignment under presupposition failure, it seems that we have two options: Either these credences are undefined or they equal 0. We might be pushed toward the undefined choice if we think that, just as satisfaction of presuppositions might be a necessary condition for the interpretation function to be defined, it is also a necessary conditions for an agent's credence function to be defined. We might be pushed toward 0 if we think that, to have any positive credence, an agent in **A** must believe that it is possible that **A** is true. Neither option is serviceable when it comes to future claims: It is a fundamental fact about future claims that we can have intermediate credences about them.

Relatedly, *Q&H* does not have the resources to handle embeddings of *will* under epistemic operators:

(12)   It is possible that Riya will study medicine and it is possible that she will study architecture.

Claims like (12) are precisely meant to express the fact that the relevant worlds are not homogeneous with respect to what Riya will study. But it is not clear how this might be captured by the homogeneity account. Note in particular how our judgments about (12) differ from our judgments about (13) as uttered in a context in which it is known that half the girls are at camp and half on vacation.

(13)   It is possible that the girls are at camp and it is possible that the girls are on vacation.

On balance, then, while there is much to recommend the *Q&H* picture, it would also be desirable if we could develop an account with all the benefits of that picture and none of its drawbacks. Chapter 5 develops one such account.

4.7   Neg-Raising to the Rescue?

Another kind of response to the negation arguments comes from independent contributions by Winans (2016) and Todd (2020).

Todd is no fan of quantificational modal theories, but he nonetheless thinks that *will* is not scopeless and, therefore, that the principle I called NEGATION SWAP is invalid. According to him, *will* A means that A is true in the actual future. If "the actual future" is a non-referring definite description, as Todd thinks it should be in a branching setting, then *will* A is false for any A. [See Todd, 2016; Schoubye and Rabern (2017) point out that by Todd's reasoning, future necessities must also be false.] This also means that *will not* A is false, for any A. If so, *not will* A is always true. Scopelessness fails. There are some real problems for Todd's view (Schoubye and Rabern, 2017), and this is not the place to rehash them. However, part of Todd's project (2020) is to narrowly address the scopelessness concern, independently of the overarching conception of future discourse that leads to it.

In this connection, Todd proposes that future-directed *will* is a neg-raiser. Neg-raising is the phenomenon whereby *I don't believe it's raining* ends up conveying the meaning of *I believe it's not raining*. Similarly, *It's not the case that it will rain* might by the same mechanisms express the same content as *It will not rain*. Todd does not try to give a theory of neg-raising, and he shouldn't be required to do so, as long as there is a plausible claim that general features of neg-raising are enough to carry his argument.

As noted, this is also the thesis of prior work by Winans (2016, especially chapter 6). I referenced this work earlier for the nuanced study of the evidential features of predictive expressions. But it's also part of the view that the *will* excluded middle is to be accounted for in terms of an appeal to neg-raising. I will focus here on Winans's discussion because she develops more reasons for and against classifying *will* as a neg-raiser. Unlike Todd, Winans favors a quantificational modal theory, but this difference is immaterial to whether the neg-raising strategy works.

Here I must make a small concession. Some of the evidence that is accounted for by a scopeless analysis can also be captured by a neg-raising analysis. Specifically, the members of the following pairs strike me as equivalent:

(14)   a.   No teacher believes Ed will pass if he goofs off.
       b.   Every teacher believes Ed will fail if he goofs off.

As a philosopher, I am acutely aware that there is a gap between not believing something and believing its negation. An agnostic teacher would be a counterexample to (14-b) but not to (14-a). However, because of implicature or magic, I don't hear this gap when I compare (14-a) and (14-b). If neg-raisers generally behave like this, then the scopelessness hypothesis is not the only hypothesis that predicts the rough equivalence of *no student will pass if he goofs off* and *every student will fail if he goofs off*.

The concession is that the neg-raising hypothesis can capture a small sliver of the data supporting a scopeless analysis. Despite this concession, my argument stands virtually unharmed.

To start, Winans herself recognizes that *will* does not pattern with traditional neg-raisers (Winans, 2016, section 6.2). For one thing, while the neg-raising interpretation of *think* and *believe* is optional, the (alleged) neg-raising interpretation of *will* is not. This is our familiar point: There is no way of attaching a higher negation onto *will*. Using Winans' own examples, (15-a) but not (15-b) can be optionally interpreted as having wide scope negation.

(15)   a.   It's not the case that John thinks Mary is home.
        b.   It's not the case that John will be home.

In a similar spirit, (Winans, 2016, section 6.2.1.2) notes that the excluded middle inference of ordinary neg-raisers does not project out of questions, whereas *will* excluded middle does. Contrast:

(16)   a.   Does John think Mary is home?
        b.   Will Mary be home?

It is evident that (16-a) doesn't license the inference that John has an opinion either way, while (16-b) does license the inference that either Mary will be home or she won't.

In sum, as a preamble to defending the view that *will* is a neg-raiser, Winans highlights the main reasons to think that it's not a neg-raiser at all. Because of an antecedent commitment to a quantificational theory, Winans is forced to retreat to the thesis that *will* is a neg-raiser of a "special" kind. Since I think we are best off leaving the quantificational theory behind, I'm happy to just say that it's not a neg-raiser at all. (I'll get to Winans's positive reasons for classifying it as a neg-raiser.)

Since Winans's own worries are very much in the same spirit as my arguments, I will add one more of my own. It is distinctive of neg-raisers that they do not exclude the middle when we consider prejacents that involve verbs that lexicalize negation. The following paradigm is instructive. Suppose that your friends have a basketball team. They just finished a game and you don't know how the game ended. Stipulate, as seems plausible for the sport of basketball, that losing is equivalent to not winning. Then contrast:

(17)   a.   I believe they won or I believe they lost.
        b.   It's likely that they won or it's likely that they lost.
        c.   They will win or they will lose.

Only (17-c) sounds tautological among these. Todd (2020, section 4) tries to bite this bullet, claiming that, if we entertain a "true" branching metaphysics, (17-c) should be false. I'll let you be the judge of that – I said what I thought about this argument at the end of Section 4.5. Even if that were right, the paradigm in (17) shows that there is a critical difference between *will* and bona fide neg-raisers.

In addition, much like the homogeneity maneuvers described in Section 4.6, the neg-raising hypothesis is completely silent on the credence-based arguments, further reinforcing the point that the neg-raising hypothesis is a patch that covers only a fraction of the relevant theoretical constraints. (Indeed, Todd's positive view implausibly predicts that we ought to assign credence 0 to all *will*-sentences.) Moreover, credence arguments and negation-based arguments are related. Only by enforcing NEGATION SWAP can we guarantee that if the probability of *the coin will land heads* is 0.6, the probability of *the coin will land tails* is 0.4.

Winans advances two arguments for treating *will* as a neg-raiser. I find neither of them as compelling as her own evidence that it's not, but here they are. First, *will* licenses strict negative polarity items (NPIs) in its prejacent. Key to this argument is a supposed contrast between *will* and *have to*, which boils down to this difference.

(18) a. John won't have talked to Mary until just now
      b. *John didn't have to have talked to Mary until just now

I have two concerns about this argument, one data-driven and another methodological. The data concern is that (18-b) doesn't seem *that* much worse than (18-a), especially once you factor how much more convoluted it is to begin with. Second, even granting the judgment, this argument doesn't carry much force absent a theory of the licensing of strict NPI. Without such a theory, it is quite consistent that the selectional behavior of *will* makes it different enough from quantificational modals to explain this behavior.

The second argument involves disanalogies like this betwen *will* and *have to*:

(19) a. John doesn't think Mary has to be swimming
      b. John doesn't think Mary will be swimming

Winans notes that (19-a) has no reading corresponding to the scope configuration *think > have to > not*. By contrast, (19-b) has a reading corresponding to the scope configurations *think* > *will* > *not*. If you already thought that *will* was a quantifier, this would be pretty powerful evidence that it's a neg-raiser. But if you think, as I have argued here, that *will* validates the negation swap principle, then this observation is completely disabled.

CHAPTER 5

Basic Selection Semantics

This chapter presents a semantic framework created through a collaboration between Paolo Santorio and myself (Cariani and Santorio, 2018). This framework aims to resolve the apparent tension between the claim that predictive expressions, such as *will*, are modals and their apparent lack of quantificational force. The guiding idea is to generalize Stalnaker's theory of conditionals. According to Stalnaker, the conditional *if you had asked Laura, she would have helped you* is true just in case Laura helped you in the closest world to the actual world in which you asked her. (In general, (*if* A)(B) is true at w if and only if the closest A-world to w is a B-world.)

In Cariani and Santorio (2018), we generalize and extend this insight in three ways. First, the effect of selection is not contributed by the conditional antecedent, but by modals, such as *will* and *would*. Second, when these modals occur without an antecedent within the same sentence, as in *Janice would be the right person to ask*, they select one out of a background domain of possibilities that is fixed by context, including prior elements of the discourse. If there are conditional antecedents that combine with these auxiliaries, they can be understood as restricting that background domain of possibilities. Third, we ultimately favor a version of selection semantics that divorces the idea of selection out of a set of possibilities from the idea of similarity, which instead prominently features in Stalnaker's theory of conditionals.[1]

Section 5.1 gives an informal presentation of the semantics. Section 5.2 states the semantics more precisely. Section 5.3 reviews the standard characterizations of entailments in formal semantics. Section 5.4 combines the work of the previous sections and runs through the most notable logical verdicts of the theory. This begins our analysis of how the basic selection semantics speaks to the problems that motivated it. Section 5.5 explains

---

[1] The theme of closeness without similarity is well trodden. For some recent works, see Hawthorne (2005), Bacon (2015), and Schulz (2014, 2017).

how the semantics solves the "zero credence" problem that plagued the other modal theories. Section 5.6 tackles how the semantics accounts for the modal subordination verdicts. Section 5.7 addresses, in a preliminary way, what might be said in the present framework about the present-directed uses of *will*.[2] In the same spirit, Section 5.8 provides some preliminary thoughts about how predictive expressions interact with the acquaintance inference.

The account of Cariani and Santorio (2018) that is presented in this chapter is just beginning. The theory as presented in that paper is very much in need of update and expansion, as some of the idealizations and simplifications we worked under must be relaxed. Moreover, as I will argue in the next chapters, the semantics needs to better account for the integration between predictive expressions and other modals. These developments will keep us busy throughout Part III.

5.1   Selection Semantics: A First Look

Evaluating *will* A involves "selecting" a world out of a background set of worlds and then evaluating the prejacent, A, at that world. This selection process is biased in an important way toward the actual world. Whenever possible, the selection process will select the actual world – this is generally possible when *will* A occurs unembedded and is not constrained by elements of prior discourse (e.g., by modal subordination). But we must also keep some non-simple cases on our radar. Sometimes we need to select from a set of worlds that doesn't include the actual world. To be a bit more precise, the process of selection needs two inputs: a *modal domain* **h** and a *perspective* world w. The job of the modal domain is to restrict the range of worlds we select from. The job of the perspective world is to identify the world from whose perspective we are selecting.

In articulating his theory of conditionals, Stalnaker (1968, 1976, 1981, 1984) interprets the selection mechanism in terms of similarity to the perspective world. It is helpful to think of this idea algorithmically. Suppose we have some kind of similarity metric in the background, such that given any pair of worlds we might get a "similarity score." For each world v in **h**, consider its similarity score with respect to the perspective world w. The world that is selected (from w's perspective) is whichever world has

---

[2]   This last task is more difficult than the others because I don't think the selection semantics approach *alone* can deliver a fully satisfactory account of the phenomenon. But we will take some first steps here, and then revisit the matter in Chapter 7.

the highest similarity score with respect to w. If there are ties between worlds, or if there is a infinite sequence of worlds, each of which is more similar to w than the preceding one, we must do some extra work (Stalnaker, 1984, chapter 7).

This interpretation of selection in terms of similarity is not forced, and I reject it for *will*. However, it is essential to retain one of its core features – namely, the "centering" assumption: When the perspective world w belongs to **h**, we must select w itself. Centering is entailed by the Stalnakerian algorithm sketched in the previous paragraph, on the plausible assumption that the degree of similarity of every thing to itself is greater than the degree of similarity of any two distinct things. If we give up on the idea of similarity, centering must be stipulated independently.

Having declared the intention to modify Stalnaker's semantics for conditionals so that it applies to modals such as *will* and *would*, an apparent disanalogy presents itself. In the case of conditionals, there is a natural place to select from: the worlds that verify the antecedent. But where do we select from in the case of *will*? Our answer is that we select out of a modal domain – a set of worlds.[3]

To put more flesh on our semantics, we must give a more substantive account of which worlds are relevant to the interpretation of *will*. In Cariani and Santorio (2018), we made a specific proposal:

MODAL DOMAIN. The modal domain in context c consists of all those worlds that exactly match the events in the world of c in all matters of particular fact up to the time of c.

Consider an utterance of *the coin will land heads* occurring at some time t in world w. The modal domain of *will* consists of exactly those worlds that agree with w up to t on matters of particular fact (though they might diverge afterward). Among the facts that such worlds have to agree with w about are things such as how the coin landed on previous flips, facts about its history and structural constitution prior to the toss, and so on. Among the facts that modal domains are allowed to leave unsettled is how the coin

---

[3] Modal domains are akin to *modal bases* in Kratzer's framework for modality. Modal bases are parameters that restrict the set of worlds that matter to the evaluation of a modal expression. They differ in their type: Modal domains are sets of worlds, whereas modal bases are functions from worlds to sets of worlds. Fixing a particular world, determine a modal domain. In Chapter 6, I will argue that we should have used modal bases all along instead of using modal domains. Here, however, I am presenting the semantics as we laid it out in Cariani and Santorio (2018).

will land at the toss in question. Some worlds in **h** might have the coin landing heads; other might have it landing tails.[4]

With some care in formulation, this characterization of the modal domain can be seen to be neutral between the main metaphysical options about the nature of the future. Recall the distinction between branching and divergence metaphysics from Chapter 2. Branching theorists believe that worlds may overlap (i.e., share parts) and branch, while divergence theorists believe that worlds may at most be duplicates of each other up to a point, and diverge thereafter. The characterization of the modal domain presented here is immediately interpretable for divergence theorists. Any context of linguistic utterance is associated with a unique world – the world in which the utterance happens – and the domain consists just of those worlds that are appropriately related to that world.

Things are a little trickier on the branching metaphysics, but not that much. Branching theorists deny that any context of utterance is associated with a unique world – the world in which the utterance happens. Instead, they typically maintain that a context of utterance might be simultaneously located in multiple worlds. However, even branching theorists accept that all candidate worlds are duplicates of each other (up to the time of utterance). That entails that there is a unique, determinate modal domain that these worlds agree is relevant to the evaluation of a given utterance.

Let's illustrate this point with some examples. Figure 5.1 adds some new coding to one of our earlier branching diagrams. The letters above each terminal node mark whether A is true or false at that node. Suppose we want to evaluate *will* A as uttered at the large diamond-shaped node on the rightmost branch of the tree. Regardless of the metaphysical interpretation we put on the diagram, as long as sharing an initial segment means that two worlds are at least duplicates, the modal domain at that node must consist of the set $\{w_5, w_6, w_7\}$.

Divergence theorists add to this description the claim that any utterance that takes place at the diamond-shaped node must, in fact, be located on exactly one timeline – say, the one that is marked by a solid line. The rectangular nodes on that timeline represent the moments that belong to the actual future of the utterance. One of our central assumptions about selection, the *centering* requirement, is that when selecting out of a modal domain M from the perspective of a world that belongs to it, we must

---

[4] The restriction to matters of particular fact is important. Without it, we cannot rule out the possibility that w might contain at t some tensed facts about the future, such as the fact that the coin will land heads n time units hence (Prior, 1976).

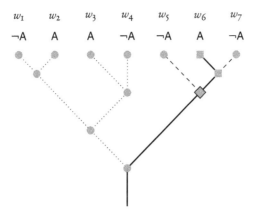

Figure 5.1   Branching diagram with valuation on A

choose that world itself. For example, if selecting from $\{w_5, w_6, w_7\}$ from the perspective of w_6, we must choose w_6 itself. So, to evaluate *will* A as uttered at the diamond-shaped node (from the perspective of w_6), we must check that A is true in w_6 at the appropriate time.[5] If the relevant time is the last time in our model, we must check that A is true at the last time in w_6. Since A is true at the last time in w_6, so is *will* A as evaluated at the diamond-shaped node.

The eagle-eyed reader will have noticed a strange consequence of the picture I have been sketching. We started out aiming to evaluate *will* A at w_6 and we ended up evaluating A … at w_6 itself! All this work to explain the operation of selection seems to have been trivial. This is so when *will* occurs unembedded and without interventions from prior discourse. Fortunately, this is not the general case and we did not define a trivial operator. The operator is nontrivial when we consider embeddings and other ways of affecting the modal domain (e.g., via modal subordination). That difference will be crucial for us to account for the cluster of data that motivate modal analyses.

To see an illustration of this, consider the case of evaluating a conditional (*if* B)(*will* A) (diagrammed in Figure 5.2). Let us adopt the orthodox Kratzerian idea that the job of conditional antecedents such as *if* B is to restrict with **B** the domains of modals in its scope. For now, take this idea at a purely intuitive level (I will have much more to say about it in Chapter 8). To consider how this might play out, add a distribution of truth-values for

[5]   We have not yet said how such times are determined.

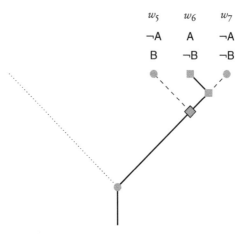

Figure 5.2   Detail of branching diagram with valuation on A and B

B to our diagram. (To avoid clutter, ignore what happens on the left side of the diagram.) To evaluate at the diamond-shaped node, start, as usual, with the modal domain at w_6 – namely, $\{w_5, w_6, w_7\}$. Evaluating the conditional antecedent *if* B narrows down the modal domain to the singleton set $\{w_5\}$ by ruling out the worlds at which B does not hold. Since we must select out of this set, the only world we can select is w_5 itself. When we check whether A holds at the appropriate future node, we find that it does not: (*if* B)(*will* A) is false at w_6.

The upshot is that given a mechanism for restriction, and more generally given any mechanism for modal domain intervention, the outputs of selection operators are nontrivial. The differential treatment of unembedded and embedded occurrences of *will* is as it should be. Our proposal is that *will*'s modal nature only shines through in certain embeddings or when elements of prior discourse affect its interpretation.

5.2   Basic Versions of Selection Semantics

We are ready to formulate the account of Section 5.1 more rigorously. We assume that *will* carries a proprietary argument for a variable *h* whose value is a modal domain. The logical form of *it will rain* might look roughly like this:

[*will* [*h*, it rains]]

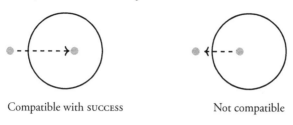

Compatible with SUCCESS   Not compatible

Figure 5.3   Success

The variable *h* is interpreted in the usual way by the assignment function *g*. I will try to distinguish typographically between the variable *h* (the
linguistic item in the logical form) and its semantic value *g*(*h*) (the modal
domain). To keep the notation simple, I write **H** instead of *g*(*h*).[6] For
example, I will write *will*$_h$(**A**) to indicate that the sentence is to be evaluated
against a domain consisting of the worlds in **H**.

Next up, we define selection functions and include them in our models.

Definition 5.1 (selection function)   A selection function ***sel*** over a set of
worlds Ω is a function from $\mathcal{P}(\Omega) \times \Omega \mapsto \Omega$ subject to two constraints.

SUCCESS. For all $\mathbf{A} \in \mathcal{P}(\Omega)$ and all $w \in \Omega$, if $\mathbf{A} \neq \varnothing$, ***sel***$(\mathbf{A}, w) \in \mathbf{A}$.

CENTERING.   For all $\mathbf{A} \in \mathcal{P}(\Omega)$ and all $w \in \Omega$, if $w \in \mathbf{A}$, ***sel***$(\mathbf{A}, w) = w$.

(Properly Stalnakerian selection functions involve two more constraints, to
be discussed in more detail in Section 8.2.)

Figures 5.3 and 5.4 illustrate the different requirements imposed by these
two constraints. The circle represents the worlds we select from; the dashed
arrow represents the selection function; the origin of the arrow is the world
whose perspective we select from; and the target of the arrow is the selected
world.

Definition 5.2 (skeletal selection models)   A *skeletal selection model* is
a triple $\langle \mathcal{W}, v, \textit{\textbf{sel}} \rangle$ with $\mathcal{W}$, a non-empty set of worlds; *v*, a valuation
function mapping sentence radicals to truth-values relative to a world; and
sel, a selection function over $\mathcal{W}$.

---

[6] The reason why '**H**' is capitalized is to stay consistent with the notational choice of using capital
letters to refer to sets of worlds, which **H** is.

Compatible with CENTERING   Not compatible

Figure 5.4   Centering

What makes these models skeletal is the fact that, unlike the linear models of Chapter 1 and the branching models of Chapter 2, they lack a temporal dimension (we will stay skeletal until Chapter 7).

In Cariani and Santorio (2018), we proposed this basic semantic entry for *will*:

SKELETAL SELECTION SEMANTICS.

$$\llbracket will_h\, A \rrbracket^w = 1 \text{ iff } \llbracket A \rrbracket^{sel(\mathbf{H},w)} = 1$$

Informally, replace the input world w with the world that is selected out of the modal domain **H** from the perspective of w; then evaluate the prejacent at this shifted point of evaluation.

Naturally, the skeletal analysis is only a preliminary sketch. An important part of the semantic function of *will* is to help us talk about the future – and nothing in the skeletal selection semantics reflects this role. For this reason, we also hinted at an extension of the semantics that integrates a temporal component. First, add selection functions to the models of Chapter 2.

Definition 5.3 (temporal selection models)   A *temporal selection model* is a quintuple

$$\langle \mathcal{S}, <, \sim, v, \textbf{\textit{sel}} \rangle$$

with $\mathcal{S}$, a non-empty set of moments; $<$, a branching order over the points in $\mathcal{S}$; $\sim$, a cross-world simultaneity relation; v, a valuation function mapping sentence radicals to truth-values relative to a world; and $\textbf{\textit{sel}}$, a selection function (over the set of worlds generated by $\mathcal{S}$ and $<$).

Remember that even though worlds and times are not primitive components of such models, they can be reconstructed out of their primitive ingredients.

Combining the skeletal selection semantics with the idea of linear shift along a temporal dimension introduced in Chapter 1 yields a hybrid between selection semantics and Ockhamism:

HYBRID SELECTION SEMANTICS.

$$\llbracket \mathit{will}_h \, \mathsf{A} \rrbracket^{w,t} = 1 \text{ iff } \exists u > t, \llbracket \mathsf{A} \rrbracket^{sel(\mathrm{H},w),u} = 1$$

This theory predicts that *it will rain* is true at world w and time t iff it rains at the world that is selected from w's perspective at some time after t.

In Chapter 7, I will reject this hybrid analysis, on the grounds that it actually fails to deliver scopelessness. At that point, I will replace it with something that can account for both the future orientation of *will* and the scopelessness facts. For now, however, it stands as proof-of-concept that the idea behind selection semantics is compatible with the important observation that *will* is future-oriented.

5.3 Notions of Validity: A Primer

Part of the task ahead of us is to check that certain schemas we expect to be valid do, in fact, come out valid. For example, we want to establish the validity of WILL EXCLUDED MIDDLE. Establishing this requires a definition of what it is for a schema to be valid.

There are many ways of defining entailment in formal semantics. My basic strategy will be to check those target inferences against one of the strictest notions.

POINT CONSEQUENCE.
$\mathsf{A}_1, \ldots, \mathsf{A}_x \models_p \mathsf{B}$ iff for every model $\mathcal{M}$ and for every point of evaluation π based on $\mathcal{M}$, if $\llbracket \mathsf{A}_1 \rrbracket^{\mathcal{M},\pi} = 1, \ldots, \llbracket \mathsf{A}_x \rrbracket^{\mathcal{M},\pi} = 1, \llbracket \mathsf{B} \rrbracket^{\mathcal{M},\pi} = 1$.

POINT LOGICAL TRUTH.
A single sentence A is a logical truth iff $\models_p \mathsf{A}$.

POINT EQUIVALENCE.
A and B are logically equivalent iff $\mathsf{A} \models_p \mathsf{B}$ and $\mathsf{B} \models_p \mathsf{A}$.

Establishing that an argument is a point consequence immediately establishes that it is valid according to the other, more permissive notions to be introduced later.

Note that this way of characterizing entailment is both schematic and modular. The SKELETAL SELECTION SEMANTICS and the HYBRID SELECTION SEMANTICS disagree about what counts as a model as well as about what

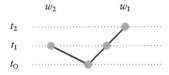

Figure 5.5   Worlds with different lifespans

counts as a point of evaluation. However, the preceding analysis of entailment combines modularly with both semantics, and indeed for any other
semantics.

As Kaplan (1989b, pp. 522–523) famously argued, for the analysis of
languages involving context-sensitive expressions, it is helpful to define a
less strict concept of entailment – one that is mediated by the notion of
a context of utterance. To illustrate the need for this concept, consider a
system with points of evaluation of the form $\langle w, t \rangle$. However, imagine that
different possible worlds have different lifespans. As in Figure 5.5, imagine
that w_1 lasts for three ticks of the clock, t_0, t_1, and t_2, while w_2 lasts for only
two ticks, t_0 and t_1.

Then any point whose world coordinate is w_2 and whose time coordinate
is t_2 will be improper. Even though $\langle w_2, t_2 \rangle$ does not denote an actual point
in our model, nothing in our characterization of points of evaluation rules
it out. Kaplan calls such points *improper* in the sense that no context could
be located at them. Intuitively, we want the valid arguments to be just those
arguments that preserve truth at *proper points of evaluation*.

With the concept of a proper point of evaluation in hand, we can
rewrite the earlier definitions by restricting them to only proper points of
evaluation. The result is a notion of entailment (and associated concepts
of single-sentence validity and equivalence) that is sometimes called "diag-
onal." Since all proper points are points, everything that is point valid is
diagonally valid. However, in the general case, not every point is proper, so
not everything that is diagonally valid is point valid.

There are a few other options for defining logical consequence. In
Chapter 6, following insights by Veltman (1996) and Yalcin (2007), we will
find it useful to introduce "informational consequence." The crucial thing
to remember at that point is that because these notions are more permissive
than point consequence, all the results about validity established here persist
in that setting, although some invalid inferences become valid.

5.4   Logical Features of Selection Semantics

The skeletal selection semantics threads through the desiderata we have accumulated thus far. The first such result to notice is that it validates WILL EXCLUDED MIDDLE. There is no world w such that $[\![will_h \text{ A} \vee will_h \text{ not A}]\!]^w = 0$. The reason is that any world that s might select, no matter the input, must be either a world in which A is true or one in which it is false. In the first case, $[\![will \text{ A}]\!]^w = 1$, and hence the schema is true, given that we are assuming a Boolean account of disjunction. In the second case, $[\![will \text{ not A}]\!]^w = 1$ is true.

We extend this reasoning to establish the validity of several related patterns.

NEGATION SWAP. *will not* A is equivalent to *not will* A.

As we saw in Chapter 4, given the classical law of excluded middle – the principle that A $\vee$ *not* A is a logical truth – NEGATION SWAP entails WEM. The converse entailment does not go through in general: NEGATION SWAP can fail even if WEM is valid. However, NEGATION SWAP does hold in the skeletal selection semantics, for the same reason that WEM is valid.

If we add the assumption that conditionals restrict modal domains, we can derive a limited version of *conditional* excluded middle.

LIMITED CEM. $(if \text{A})(will \text{ B}) \vee (if \text{A})(will \text{ not B})$ is a logical truth.

This version is limited because it covers only conditionals with *will* in their consequents. We will have much more to say about conditionals and the principle of conditional excluded middle in Chapter 8.

The situation with respect to these inferences is a bit different when we consider the hybrid selection semantics. Because of the existential quantification over times, NEGATION SWAP fails. *will not* A might be true even if *not will* A is false – that is, even if *will* A is true. If today is Monday, and I am going to have tacos on Tuesday and pasta on Wednesday (and if both Tuesday and Wednesday are part of the relevant interval), the semantics predicts the truth of *I will have tacos* as well as the truth of *I will not have tacos*. The failure of NEGATION SWAP does not witness a failure of WEM: It is not that both disjuncts of WEM are false, but rather that both are true (albeit because of different times). In more abstract terms, the failure of NEGATION SWAP is due to the fact that in the hybrid system this principle fails:[7]

---

[7] It does not seem as if this problem can be avoided by moving to a more permissive notion of validity.

WILL NON-CONTRADICTION (WNC). *not (will* A & *will not* A) is a logical truth.

Incidentally, the framework of MacFarlane (2014) avoids this problem only by declining to give a semantic value to *will*. In MacFarlane's basic object language, the only predictive expression is *tomorrow*, to which he assigns a Ockhamist semantics. Relative to w and t, *tomorrow* A is true iff A is true in w but 24 hours hence. The idea that there is shift to a specific future instant is admittedly simplistic semantics even for *tomorrow*, and it plainly won't generalize to *will*.

5.5   Solving the Zero Credence Problem

Recall the zero credence problem: How might a modal theory assign intermediate credence (i.e., credence strictly between 0 and 1) to future contingent claims? We saw that quantificational theories face inescapable obstacles in making sense of this. The problem is more easily addressed within the context of selection semantics. I illustrate the critical points with the skeletal selection semantics, but they extend smoothly to the hybrid variant as well.

Credences, I will suppose, attach to contents. I also suppose that the content $\|A\|$ of A in context c is the set of worlds in which A is true when the remaining parameters are set to their context-initialized values. Borrowing a bit of Stalnakerian terminology (Stalnaker, 1978), we define:

Definition 5.4 (Horizontal content) $\|A\| = \{w \mid [\![A]\!]^w = 1\}$

A credence function is attached to the elements of a σ-algebra generated by a set of worlds W. (A σ-algebra over a set W is a set of subsets of W that includes $\emptyset$ and is closed under complementation and countable unions.)

In the skeletal selection semantics, there is a limited correspondence between the content of *will* A and the set of presently possible worlds at which A is true. The correspondence is limited because, although these two sets are not *generally* identical, they contain exactly the same worlds once we restrict them to the historical possibilities.[8]

LIMITED TRANSPARENCY.   For all A, $\|will_h A\| \cap \mathbf{H} = \|A\| \cap \mathbf{H}$.

---

[8]   For a proof of LIMITED TRANSPARENCY, suppose that $w \in \|will_h A\| \cap \mathbf{H}$. Then $w \in \{v \mid [\![will_h A]\!]^v\} = 1$ and $w \in \mathbf{H}$. Because $w \in \mathbf{H}$, $sel(\mathbf{H}, w) = w$, and so $1 = [\![will_h A]\!]^w = [\![A]\!]^{sel(\mathbf{H},w)} = [\![A]\!]^w$.

Informally, this says the historically possible worlds in which *the coin will land heads* is true are exactly those historically possible worlds in which the coin lands heads.

This result gives us the beginnings of an answer to the zero credence problem. Rational agents may assign $\|will_h\ heads\|$ an intermediate degree of credence. Agents might even be *required* to assign this proposition some specific credence, such as one half. This would depend on whether our view of epistemic rationality includes a chance-credence principle such as the Principal Principle, and of course it would depend on the agent's beliefs about chances.

This is the first step of a solution to the zero credence problem. However, a complete account of future credence ought to be significantly more general than this supposition. Such an account is at best preliminary in two respects. For one thing, the limitation of transparency to the set of historically possible worlds turns out to be problematic in ways I will explore in Chapter 6. For another, it is not enough to ensure that bare *will* claims have the probabilities we expect them to have. We would want a story about credence for the whole language, including for the contents of those sentence in which *will* appears embedded.

Fortunately, there is a layer of generalization of LIMITED TRANSPARENCY that is readily accessible. It turns out that the LIMITED TRANSPARENCY result generalizes to embeddings of bare *will* claims under Boolean operators.

BOOLEAN LIMITED TRANSPARENCY.

(i) $\|will_h\ not\ A\| \cap H = \overline{\|A\|} \cap H$

(ii) $\|will_h\ A\ and\ B\| \cap H = (\|A\| \cap \|B\|) \cap H$

(iii) $\|will_h\ A\ or\ B\| \cap H = (\|A\| \cup \|B\|) \cap H$

As a special case of BOOLEAN LIMITED TRANSPARENCY, we can also deduce that any rational agent who is certain in **h** is required to have credence 1 in any one instance of WEM.

It is critical here that Boolean transparency covers only the Boolean fragment of the language. The transparency result fails as soon as we add conditionals to the picture.

5.6 Modal Subordination

A wealth of competing accounts of modal subordination exist. It would be immodest for us to suppose that intervening on the semantics of predictive expressions could immediately clarify the nature of modal subordination.

Nevertheless, to show that we made progress, we need a general sense of *how* it might help. Somehow, we must steer an intermediate course between having enough of a vision about modal subordination that we can understand how the modal future hypothesis helps us make sense of the data from Chapter 3 and not picking up too many commitments about what a comprehensive account of modal subordination might look like.

With that need for balance in mind, we outline an account of modal subordination. The value of the modal domain variable that attaches to *will* (as well as any analogous variables that might attach to other modals) is initially assigned a value by the context of utterance. This value can be affected in two ways. Most immediately, compositional interactions with other elements of the same sentence might shift the modal domain away from its initial, context-provided value. The canonical example is conditional antecedents, which are generally viewed as contributing a restriction to the modal domain. In addition, discourse-level interactions might shift the modal domain away from its initial value. This is precisely what I claim happens in those cases in which *will* is subordinated.

Let us reconsider the examples from Chapter 3.

(1)   a.   If Edna forgets to fill the birdfeeder, the birds will get hungry. She <u>will</u> feel very bad.
       b.   If Katie travels to Berkeley, she will shop at Amoeba Records. She <u>will</u> buy a boxed set and a dozen used LPs.
       c.   One day I might visit Morocco; I <u>will</u> go to the desert and to the mountains.

In outline, the phenomenon we are attempting to model has the following structure. The first sentence of each discourse stores a proposition to which later modals can latch on as a restriction. Importantly, this proposition is not the semantic value of the given sentence: In cases like (1-a) and (1-b), it is the conditional antecedent, as opposed to the whole conditional. To be more specific, in (1-a) the discourse stores the proposition that Edna forgets to fill the birdfeeder and in (1-b) the proposition that Katie travels to Berkeley. By contrast, what is stored in (1-c) is the prejacent of the modal claim in the first sentence – that is, the proposition that I visit Morocco. In each of these cases, the *will* that occurs in the second sentence can be restricted by the stored proposition, resulting in restricted interpretations that are roughly equivalent to the following:

(2)   a.   If Edna forgets to fill the birdfeeder, she will feel very bad.

  b. If Katie travels to Berkeley, she will buy a boxed set and a dozen
used LPs.

  c. If I visit Morocco, I will go to the desert and to the mountains.

 As noted at the beginning of the discussion, this is not a fleshed-out
account of modal subordination. Many complex problems arise in spelling
out such an account. For example, there is disagreement about the exact
distribution of which modals allow for subordination as well as about
potential conflicts between different types of subordinating material. Even
so, this sketch touches on essential components that are shared by many
fully fleshed accounts of modal subordination.

5.7 Present-Directed Uses of *Will*

In Cariani and Santorio (2018), we were noncommittal about how to
account for the epistemic uses of *will*. Here is an example of this kind of
use:

(3) The laundry will be done by now.

At that time, we simply remarked that treating *will* as a modal opens
up the possibility of such a unified account. That's true, but it is not a
full explanation. Do the so-called epistemic uses of predictive expressions
share a lexical entry with the future-directed *will*? If not, is this a case of
polysemy? Ambiguity? If yes, do the data support a uniform treatment?

 If *will* were polysemous, we would expect it to share a meaning with
epistemic *must*. This would make good sense of the fact that (3) seems to
mean something very similar to:

(4) The laundry must be done by now.

The similarities between (3) and (4) even extend to the fact that both license
a kind of evidential inference. A simple – probably too simple – way to
think about this inference is as being to the effect that the speaker does not
have direct evidence that the laundry is done. Call the putative meaning
of *will* the "present-directed *will*." Given that epistemic *must* is generally
believed to express universal quantification over some information state, we
might expect present-directed *will* to behave in the same way.

 The alternative view is that present-directed *will* might itself be a
selection modal. If this is right, the present-directed use of *will* differs from
the future-directed use in two ways: The domain is not set by some objective

criteria and the reference time for the prejacent is not in the future. Such a view is consistent with my proposal to understand the shift in modal domain as an instance of context sensitivity. This is famously how Kratzer (1977, 1981, 1991b, 2012) retrieves the variety of modal flavors. Nothing prevents us from extending these ideas to selectional modals.

The claim that epistemic *will* is a selectional modal carries with it certain implications and predictions. We must check that these predictions are borne out by the data. The most obvious such prediction is that present-directed *will* should give rise to the same scopelessness effects as does future-directed *will*. If that is correct, we should expect similar phenomena to the ones that supported our rejection of quantificational theories (Chapter 4). Thankfully, reality cooperates: (5) has the force of a tautology.

(5)   Either the laundry will be done by now or it won't be.

This judgment contrasts with the parallel judgment:

(6)   Either the laundry must be done by now or it must not be.

Another relevant class of judgments involves comparing propositional attitude claims for attitude verbs that lexicalize negation, as we did in the context of justifying WEM. So, for instance, (7-a) sounds equivalent to (7-b), while (7-c) does not sound equivalent to (7-d);

(7)   a.   I doubt that the laundry will be done by now.
        b.   I believe that the laundry will not be done by now.
        c.   I doubt that the laundry must be done by now.
        d.   I believe that the laundry must not be done by now.

It seems possible to interpret (7-c) as expressing that the laundry's not being done is compatible with the relevant information. Some speakers resist these judgments because they find (7-b) and (7-d) problematic. But even for these speakers, it is possible to generate a similar phenomenon by using negative quantifiers. Contrast these two cases:

(8)   a.   We're arriving early. No musicians will be seated yet (# but, as it happens, the cellists are seated).
        b.   We're arriving early. No musicians have to be seated yet (but, as it happens, the cellists are seated).

This sort of argument strongly suggests that the central difference between present-directed *will* and future-directed *will* is not that the former is, and the latter is not, a quantificational modal. If so, there is no general need to tell a story according to which the difference between present-directed and future-directed uses of *will* is a form of polysemy or ambiguity. I have suggested informally in this section that there might be a difference in modal base to mimic *must* – but even that is not obligatory. In Chapter 7, I will develop the account of future-directed *will* a bit more without relying on that hypothesis.

5.8   Revisiting the Acquaintance Inference

Recall that the acquaintance inference paradigm (Section 3.5) consists of inferences to the effect that certain predicates of personal taste require certain associated experiences.

(9)   a.   That soup tastes disgusting ↪ I have tasted that soup.
       b.   That soup tasted disgusting ↪ I have tasted that soup.

The crucial phenomenon is that modals and future-directed *will* suppress it:

(10)   a.   That soup must taste disgusting ↛ I have tasted that soup.
        b.   That soup will taste disgusting ↛ I have tasted that soup.

One might expect at this point that we will provide some kind of explanation, based on our preferred theory, of why acquaintance inferences are suppressed.

This would be a mistake: As these data already reveal, there is nothing specific about selection semantics that requires it to be involved in an account of the suppression of acquaintance inferences. These inferences are suppressed by quantificational modals, such as *must*, just as much as they are suppressed by selectional modals, such as *will*.

The explanatory target, then, must be why *modals* in general suppress it. I try my hand at this task in Chapter 13. But I also want to insist that to some degree these are separable projects. The way that acquaintance inferences figure into the argument for selection semantics is unusual and a bit different from the other theoretical constraints. In the cases of the other constraints, we argued that these were not collectively satisfied by quantificational and non-modal analyses, but were satisfied by selection semantics. In the case of the acquaintance inference, our argument is rather different: We are using suppression of the acquaintance inference as a *diagnostic* for modality – not as a theoretical constraint. More specifically, we argue that, in light of the fact that there are several other diagnostics for modality that group *will* and *would* together and with other modals, the fact that there is one more respect in which this category is unified provides us with additional evidence that we ought to sort *will* as a modal.

PART III

Developing Selection Semantics

Between Will *and* Might

Future talk is not an isolated compartment of our linguistic practice. It behooves us to see how our theory of future discourse connects with a more general theory of modal discourse. Of particular interest are entailments (e.g., do *will* claims entail *might* claims?) and embeddings (e.g., are there interesting effects of embedding predictive expression under epistemic modals?).

The bad news is that both versions of selection semantics from Chapter 5, the skeletal and the hybrid, run into some trouble when they are integrated with the rest of the modal system. They make some odd entailment predictions and they mismanage interactions with other modals and propositional attitude verbs. The source of these troubles is a bug in the formulation of semantics for *will*. The good news is that the bug is fixable. Even better, it is fixable with some off-the-shelf technology. However, the fix requires reconsidering some important details in the theory, as well as developing some new theoretical themes.

This is the first of three technical chapters in which I assume that the fundamental vision of the selectionist approach is correct, but attempt to settle on a specific implementation of the view. All three chapters are, by design, much drier fare than the rest of the book.

6.1   The Bug

The skeletal and hybrid theories assign the wrong modal profile to *will* sentences. This can be shown by focusing on interactions between *will* and possibility operators. Let $\Diamond$ be a vanilla possibility operator, taking as arguments a modal base and a proposition. Let $\mathbf{f}$ be a modal base in Kratzer's sense (a function from worlds to sets of worlds). To identify the bug, it will

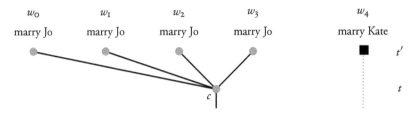

Figure 6.1   Oedipus's merely possible non-incest

be useful to think of ◇ as tracking possibility relative to some information state that is pinned down by the modal base at w.

(1) $\llbracket ◇_f \text{A} \rrbracket^w = 1$ iff $\exists v \in \mathbf{f}(w), \llbracket \text{A} \rrbracket^v = 1$

The first symptom of the bug is that composing this possibility operator with the analysis of *will* from the Chapter 5 yields some obviously wrong predictions.

Before unpacking these predictions, let me stress that the argument itself doesn't require (1) to be the correct analysis of epistemic possibility. You can follow along by filling in your own judgments and theories about epistemic modal claims. The relevant problems will arise anyway.

With that said, let's move to the argument. Suppose that all of the historical possibilities – all the worlds that duplicate the actual world up to now – agree that Oedipus will unknowingly marry his mother Jocasta ("Jo" for friends). At the point at which we join this story, this is an inevitable historical fact: It lies in the future, but it is a settled matter. However, suppose also that, due to its fallibility, the epistemic state picked out by $\mathbf{f}$ at w is compatible with some possibilities that are not historical possibilities. In these merely epistemic possibilities, Oedipus marries a woman named Kate who bears a vague resemblance to Jocasta, but no interesting relation to her.

Figure 6.1 depicts a situation like this: Worlds w_0, w_1, w_2, and w_3 comprise the historical possibilities in context c. Saying that w_0 is the actual world and that $\mathbf{f}(w_0)$ is the relevant epistemic state from the perspective of world w_0 lets in a merely epistemic possibility w_4 in which Oedipus avoids incest.

Now consider the status of the sentence *It is possible that Oedipus will avoid incest* from the perspective of context c located in w_0. Intuitively, assuming that the modal is epistemic, this sentence should be true. Accordingly, we expect the semantics to predict:

(2) $[\![\Diamond_f(\textit{will}_h(\text{avoid incest}))]\!]^{w_0} = 1$

Unfortunately, the basic selection semantics does not deliver this. In particular, reflecting on the model, we expect w_4 to witness the truth of the prejacent of $\Diamond_f$ in (2) relative to the context c. That is, we expect:

(3) $[\![\textit{will}_h(\text{avoid incest})]\!]^{w_4} = 1$

This expectation is frustrated. Even if we are evaluating from the point of view of w_4, the selected world must come from the modal domain **H**. However, **H** is the set of historical possibilities in the original utterance context. In the example, $\mathbf{H} = \{w_0, w_1, w_2, w_3\}$. Because of the success constraint on selection, this requires $\textit{sel}(\mathbf{H}, w_4)$ to be within **H** – that is, to be a world where Oedipus marries Jo, which is incompatible with the constraint in (3).

   The bug is not limited to epistemic possibility claims, but can also be illustrated with attitude reports. Let $\textsc{bel}_s$ be a belief operator, endowed with a quantificational semantics: s (an agent we'll later reference as "Sara") believes that Oedipus commits incest iff Oedipus commits incest in all of s's belief worlds. More formally, let $d(\cdot)$ be a function that outputs s's doxastic state in w. (Sara's doxastic state in w identified with the set of worlds that are compatible with what Sara believes in w. For a more fine-grained model, we might want add a further relativization to times.) Ignoring times, a simple entry for this sort of belief operator is:

(4) $[\![\textsc{bel}_s\ \mathbf{A}]\!]^w = 1$ iff $\forall v \in d(w), [\![\mathbf{A}]\!]^v = 1$

Consider evaluating *Sara believes Oedipus will commit incest* on the assumption that Figure 6.1 represents Sara's doxastic state. In this doxastic variant of the problem, think of w_4 as a mere doxastic possibility for Sara (i.e., a doxastic possibility that isn't historical). Because of this, Sara's doxastic state doesn't settle that Oedipus will commit incest. It should then be false that Sara believes that it will rain. The problem is that Sara's belief state diverges from what is historically settled in the context itself, and it is the latter that fixes the modal domain.

   To make this more precise, we want the semantics to generate this prediction:

(5) $[\![\textsc{bel}_s(\textit{will}_h(\text{Oedipus commits incest}))]\!]^{w_0} = 0$

This should be false because Sara's doxastic possibilities include a world, w_4, in which Oedipus avoids incest and marries Kate. In other words, we would expect:

(6) $[\![will_h(\text{Oedipus commits incest})]\!]^{w_4} = 0$

Just as in the previous case, this expectation is frustrated. The selected world at w_4 must come from $\mathbf{H}$ – that is, it must come from $\{w_0, w_1, w_2, w_3\}$. This requirement, together with the success constraint, requires $\boldsymbol{sel}(\mathbf{H}, w_4)$ to be an incest world, since the historical possibilities in the utterance context were stipulated to all be worlds where Oedipus commits incest.

6.2   The Bug Amplified: Future *Might* Contradictions

The bug has ripple effects in other parts of the dialectic. Kissine (2008, 2014) argues against quantificational theories of *will*. His central objection is that they cannot explain the perceived inconsistency of sentences such as:

(7)   a.   *Oedipus will marry Jo but it is possible that he won't.
       b.   *Oedipus won't marry Jo but it is possible that he will.

Call sentences like these *future might contradictions* (FMCs for short). As my terminology suggests, FMCs have something in common with "epistemic" contradictions (Yalcin, 2007). Epistemic contradictions are sentences like (8), in which *might* is given an epistemic interpretation.

(8)   * It's raining but it might not be.

An important observation made by Yalcin is that epistemic contradictions, in addition to sounding defective when unembedded, sound significantly degraded in embeddings under propositional attitudes:

(9)   Sara supposes that it's raining but it might not be.

Here, it seems as if Sara is viewed as entertaining an inconsistent supposition. Similarly, the injunction *Suppose it's raining but it might not be* sounds like an injunction to entertain an inconsistent supposition.

   Like epistemic contradictions, (7-a) and (7-b) are conjunctions of an epistemic possibility claim and a contrasting claim about the state of the world. Indeed, some sentences in the style of (7-a) and (7-b) even more closely resemble epistemic contradictions. For example:

(10)   a.   *Oedipus will marry Jo but he might not.
        b.   *Oedipus won't marry Jo but he might.

The difference between (10-a) and (10-b), on the one hand, and (7-a) and (7-b), on the other hand, is that (10-a) and (10-b) do not involve embeddings of *will* under *might*.[1]

In light of the discussion in Section 6.1, (7-a) and (7-b) are problematic for the bug-affected semantics. This is easy to see since these sentences involve embeddings of *will* under *might* and Section 6.1 establishes that the skeletal and hybrid semantics mishandle these embeddings. More surprisingly, the bug rears its ugly head even in the case of (10-a) and (10-b), despite the anatomical differences between them and (7-a) and (7-b) – specifically, despite the fact that these do not involve an embedding of *will* under *might*.

To see why, let us analyze (10-a) and (10-b) more carefully. To start, notice that they are classically consistent (in the terminology of Chapter 5, they are point-consistent). The formal model associated with the story of Oedipus's merely possible non-incest illustrates this for the case of (10-a). Consider, again, a context c occurring in world w_0; it is true in c that Oedipus will commit incest, but plausibly it is also true in an epistemic sense that he might not, since it's compatible with the epistemic possibilities. A similar model could be set up for (10-b), suggesting that the defectiveness of (10-a) and (10-b) is not accounted for in terms of classical inconsistency. This is unsurprising and independent of whether *will* is given a purely temporal or a modal interpretation.

The next thought might be that the defectiveness of (10-a) and (10-b) is related to the defectiveness of epistemic contradictions. According to Yalcin, epistemic contradictions like (8) are infelicitous because they are *informationally inconsistent*. In Yalcin's system, information states (modeled as sets of worlds) play two roles: One role is to provide a domain of quantification for epistemic modals such as *might*, and the other is to figure in the characterization of a distinctive notion of entailment and consistency that is adopted from Veltman's (1996) system. While classical entailment implements the idea that valid arguments preserve truth, Yalcin's

---

[1]   These cases Some people have reacted to this point by worrying that unless they contain an implicit *will*, won't be inconsistent because the *might*claim is not about future eventualities, whereas the *will* claim is. This is plainly false. Sentences such as *Oedipus might marry Jo* are by default future oriented – i.e., the possibilities that they describe must occur in the future. This should be intuitively evident, but to see how it works in detail without positing an implicit *will*, see Chapter 7 and more generally works like Condoravdi (2002).

"informational entailment" implements the idea that valid arguments preserve acceptance by an information state.

ACCEPTANCE. Information state s accepts **A** iff for every world w in s, $[\![A]\!]^{s,w} = 1$.

To illustrate, our twist on the Oedipus story sets up an information state in which it is accepted that Oedipus will marry someone – either Jocasta or Kate. However, it is not accepted that he will marry Jocasta and it is not accepted that he will marry Kate.

This notion of acceptance underpins the definition of informational entailment.

INFORMATIONAL ENTAILMENT. $A_1, \ldots, A_x \models_i C$ iff there is no state i that accepts all of $A_1, \ldots, A_x$ but does not accept **C**.

A sentence **A** is informationally inconsistent iff there is no state s such that s accepts **A**.

According to Yalcin, epistemic contradictions are infelicitous because they are informationally inconsistent – that is, because no information state can accept them. Indeed, any information state that accepts that it might not be raining must contain a world in which it's not raining – but then the information state cannot accept that it is raining. The strength of this explanation is proportional to the degree to which one recognizes informational inconsistency as an important explanatory tool. Indeed, much of Yalcin's argument focuses on establishing the explanatory importance of this notion of inconsistency.[2]

I will not attempt to probe whether informational consequence has the appropriate level of explanatory significance. I am open to a variety of accounts of the defectiveness of epistemic contradictions. The question I would like to consider is this: Would a Yalcin-style explanation extend to FMCs like (10-a) and (10-b), even if just as a proof of concept?

There are two obstacles in going for this extension. First, we cannot assume at the outset that the *might* in FMCs is epistemic. I will have more to say about this issue once we fix the bug. (An alternative view is that these operators are historical, as suggested by Klecha, 2016.) Second, even granting that the occurrence of *might* in (10-a) is epistemic, the bug

---

[2]   Here I am not focusing on the complex dialectic concerning whether Yalcin has the correct account of epistemic contradictions. For alternatives to Yalcin's account, as well as relevant discussions of the dialectic, see Dorr and Hawthorne (2013), Mandelkern (2019), Mandelkern (2019a, 2019c), Stojnić (in press), and Ninan (2018).

blocks the Yalcin-style explanation because (10-a) does not turn out to be informationally inconsistent.

Here is why: It follows from ACCEPTANCE that an information state accepts a conjunction if it accepts each of its conjuncts. Hence, (10-a) will be consistent if there is an information state that accepts both (11-a) and (11-b).

(10-a)   * Oedipus will marry Jo but he might not.

(11)   a.   Oedipus will marry Jo.
          b.   Oedipus might not marry Jo.

We do not have to look very hard to find an information state that does accept both (11-a) and (11-b). Consider again the information state from the Oedipus scenario (Figure 6.1), consisting of the set $\{w_0, w_1, w_2, w_3, w_4\}$. This state accepts (11-a) because every world in it verifies that (at the salient time) Oedipus will marry Jo. This is evident, and plausible, for worlds w_0, w_1, w_2, and w_3. In light of our discussion of the bug, it is also true, but *implausible*, that w_4 also verifies (11-a) as uttered at any of $\{w_0, \ldots, w_3\}$. As before, the selection function must select from the perspective of w_4 but out of the historical domain at the base world – that is, out of $\{w_0, w_1, w_2, w_3\}$. But the only worlds that can be selected out of this domain are incest worlds. Every world in the information state makes (11-a) true, so it is accepted.

The state also plausibly accepts (11-b). (11-b) is true at $\mathbf{f}(w)$ iff there is a world in $\mathbf{f}(w)$ at which Oedipus avoids incest. Indeed, under our assumptions about $\mathbf{f}$, there is such a world in $\mathbf{f}(w)$ in which he does avoid incest – namely, w_4 itself.

Putting the pieces of this argument together, it becomes clear that due to the bug, the basic selection semantics cannot predict the informational inconsistency of FMCs. Insofar as we are committed to implementing a Yalcin-style explanation, we need a semantic package for which the analogue of this fact fails. But even if we are not committed to implementing a Yalcin-style explanation, the particular way in which the explanation fails suggests that something is wrong with the semantics.

6.3   Kissine's Argument

In a pair of papers, Kissine (2008, 2014) develops an objection against quantificational modal theories of *will* that reply on the interpretation of some FMCs. Kissine views these objections as targeting modal theories of *will*, so addressing them is an important part of completing the modal theorist's agenda. Kissine focuses on FMCs that involve embedding of *will* under *might*, such as:

(12)   *will* A & *might not will* A

(13)   Oedipus will marry Jo and it might be that it's not the case that he will marry Jo.

Such conjunctions sound infelicitous, and perhaps even inconsistent, as do all FMCS.

    However, Kissine notes that simple universal modal theories, such as Peircean semantics, make them (classically) consistent, even assuming that *might* and *will* have the same modal base **f**. After all, the truth-conditions of the two conjuncts of (12) are, respectively:

(14)   a.   Every world v in $\mathbf{f}(w)$ is a A-world.
       b.   There is a world v in $\mathbf{f}(w)$ such that there is a world z in $\mathbf{f}(v)$ in which A is false.

It is a simple exercise in modal logic to note that these truth-conditions are compatible: If the world z that is mentioned in (14-b) does not belong to $\mathbf{f}(w)$, (14-a) won't constrain it.

    Kissine concedes that his opponent might make the two conjuncts of (12) incompatible by stipulating the transitivity of the relation that undergirds **f**. Putting the constraint directly in terms of **f**, it amounts to:

TRANSITIVITY. If $v \in \mathbf{f}(w)$ and $z \in \mathbf{f}(v)$, then $z \in \mathbf{f}(w)$.

Under this constraint, we can indeed predict the inconsistency of (12). Transitivity requires that the world z in (14-b) belong to $\mathbf{f}(w)$, which by (14-a) must mean it's an A-world.

    But then, Kissine notes, the quantificational theory needs a separate patch for sentences of the following form:

(15)   *not will* A & *might will* A

(16)   It's not the case that Oedipus will marry Jo, but it might be that he will.

The conjuncts of (15) unpack to:

(17)   a.   Some world v in $\mathbf{f}(w)$ is not an A-world.
       b.   Some world v in $\mathbf{f}(w)$ is such that every world z in $\mathbf{f}(v)$ is an A-world.

The problem now is that (15) is also incorrectly predicted to be consistent. Moreover, this prediction is not affected by stipulating transitivity. All that transitivity entails is that the A-world that is in $\mathbf{f}(v)$ according to (17-b), must also be in $\mathbf{f}(w)$. But that's not enough, since the model might well be a fork model.[3] A further condition is required to rule this out:

EUCLIDEANNESS. If $v \in \mathbf{f}(w)$ and $z \in \mathbf{f}(w)$, then $z \in \mathbf{f}(v)$.

Under EUCLIDEANNESS, we can reason that $\mathbf{f}(w)$ must contain a ¬A-world w_1 from (17-a) and a world w_2 such that $\mathbf{f}(w_2)$ only includes A-worlds (by (17-b)). By EUCLIDEANNESS, w_1 must belong to $\mathbf{f}(w_2)$ – but that contradicts the fact that everything in $\mathbf{f}(w_2)$ is a A-world.

The problem that pops up after making these additions is that, once the system is enhanced with transitivity and euclideanness, *might will* A turns out to be equivalent to *will* A. Validating simple logical principles governing the interactions of *will* and *might* implies an unpalatable collapse result.

To sum up Kissine's argument, under a classical quantificational background, we either fail to predict the badness of some FMCs or we have to collapse *will* A and *might will* A. The background includes two critical assumptions: that the basic semantics for *will* is universal and that entailment is preservation of truth at a point. The selection semantics I have been developing does not live within the space of quantificational theories. For this reason, Kissine's argument does not directly apply to it. It remains to be seen whether that is enough to avoid the objection. After fixing the bug, I will show one way to address Kissine's objections. Following the insights from Yalcin's account of epistemic contradictions, I will insist that the inconsistency of FMCs can be diagnosed as related to informational inconsistency (though the property I will appeal to will not always be informational inconsistency).

6.4 The Epistemic Patch

One approach to the bug could be to give *will* an epistemic domain – perhaps the same informational domain that Yalcin's semantics assigns to *might*. This move amounts to making *will* partly an epistemic modal,

---

[3] Though this point is immediate for those who are familiar with modal logic, it might not be so otherwise. The point is that we might have a system of worlds $\{w_0, w_1, w_2\}$ such that $\mathbf{f}(w_0) = \{w_1, w_2\}$, $\mathbf{f}(w_1) = \{w_1\}$, and $\mathbf{f}(w_2) = \{w_2\}$. Suppose now that A is true at w_1 but false at w_2. Under the present semantic assumption, this model verifies (15).

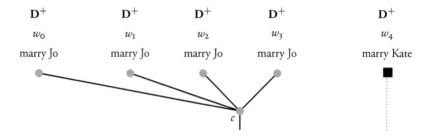

Figure 6.2   Enriching the Oedipus model with a fixed domain

though it would still not be entirely epistemic, because we continue to assume that its meaning involves a selection function.

Following are the bare bones of such a semantics. Note that this relies on what Yalcin calls a "domain" semantics for *might*, and not on the relational semantics in (1):

i. for radical A, $[\![A]\!]^{s,w} = 1$ iff $w(A) = 1$
ii. $[\![\textit{will } A/\textsc{woll } A]\!]^{s,w} = 1$ iff $[\![A]\!]^{s,\textit{sel}(s,w)} = 1$
iii. $[\![\textit{might } A]\!]^{s,w} = 1$ iff $\exists v \in s, [\![A]\!]^{s,v} = 1$
iv. $[\![A \And B]\!]^{s,w} = 1$ iff $[\![A]\!]^{s,w} = 1$ and $[\![B]\!]^{s,w} = 1$

This system delivers much of what we wanted. Under this revised semantics, it is no longer true that the basic scenario from Figure 6.1 accepts *Oedipus will marry Jo* and *Oedipus will commit incest*, because the informational epistemic domain for *will* includes the world in which Oedipus marries Kate (w_4). Figure 6.2 depicts this revised structure. More specifically, regardless of which world is actual, the domain for *will* $\mathbf{D}^+$ is the entire set $\{w_0, w_1, w_2, w_3, w_4\}$. Because w_4 is included in the domain of selection, the selection function must return w_4 itself when provided s and w_4 as inputs. Happily, that means that *Oedipus will marry Jo* is false at w_4. Once this fact is reflected in the agent's epistemic state, our initial problem concerning the embedding of *will* under *might* can also be addressed. If there is a world in $\mathbf{D}^+$ in which Oedipus avoids incest (such as w_4 in our example model), then that world will also be a witness for *it is possible that Oedipus will avoid incest* or *it is possible that Oedipus will not marry Jocasta*).

Another happy result is that FMCs turn out to be informationally inconsistent. This is immediate for FMCs such as:

(10-a) Oedipus will marry Jo but he might not.

To accept (10-a), a state must accept both of its conjuncts. Any state s that accepts that Oedipus might not marry Jo must contain a world in which they do not marry. But then s cannot accept that they will marry, since it would have to be true at every world in s.

We can try developing answers to the other bug-related problems. I won't elaborate on this strategy any further here, because I believe that some serious and more general problems arise with the epistemic approach.

First, this approach faces variants of the bug if the language allows embeddings of *will* in contexts such that *will* can reach outside of an initially provided information state. For example, the language might have operators that express concepts of historical or objective possibility that are broader than epistemic possibility. It is doubtful that all these chunks of modal discourse would involve an epistemic component.

Second, it is difficult to hold on to the idea that *will* and *would* have related meanings if we essentially tie the meaning of *will* to information states. After all, it does not seem plausible that the meaning of *would* as it occurs in, for example, subjunctive conditionals is tied to information states in this way. Moreover, mixing up our first and second points, *would* typically occurs in counterfactual consequents. Such environments typically allow the semantics to reach beyond the informationally relevant possibilities.

Third, and most seriously, this approach runs into trouble in presence of operators for historical necessity. Here I will use *it is settled that* as my lead example. It is natural to suppose that such operators quantify over the historical possibilities in the context of utterance. In effect, we are supposing that the Peircean semantics is correct for *settled* even if it is not correct for *will*.

SEMANTICS FOR SETTLEDNESS. $[\![\textit{it is settled that } \mathsf{A}]\!]^w = 1$ iff $\forall v \in \mathbf{H}, \mathbf{A}(v)$

The problem is that this analysis of settledness runs into its own version of the bug. In the Oedipus scenario, it predicts the falsehood in our sample model:

(18)   It is possible that it is not settled that Oedipus will commit incest.

The problem again is that even at w_4 it isn't settled that Oedipus will commit incest, since the domain $\mathbf{H}$ is set by context.

Similarly, the fixed-domain semantics for settledness predicts that *Sara believes that it is settled that Oedipus will commit incest* is true iff it is settled that Oedipus will commit incest.[4] Finally, it predicts that analogues of FMCs like (19) should sound consistent when they don't actually sound consistent.

(19)   It is settled that Oedipus will commit incest but he might not.

To summarize the point, if we solve the bug for *will* by giving it an epistemic domain, we also have to find a way to solve the analogue problem for *it is settled that*. That second problem cannot evidently be solved by giving *it is settled that* an epistemic domain.

6.5   The Relational Patch

There is a better fix involving a simple, standard move. Instead of requiring the domain of *will* to be fixed once and for all by context, let it be generated by something like a Kratzerian modal base. That is, let it be generated by a function **h** that inputs a world and outputs a modal domain.[5] With this approach, we adopt the following analysis:

RELATIONAL SKELETAL SEMANTICS. $[\![\textit{will}_h \text{ A}]\!]^w = 1$ iff $[\![\text{A}]\!]^{sel(\mathbf{h}(w),w)} = 1$

This intervention on the lexical entry for *will* demands matching interventions in other parts of the theory. We must replace the old metasemantic principle governing the initialization of the domain with a new principle governing the initialization of the modal base. In discussing the baseline semantics, I said that the domain **H** is initialized as the set of historical possibilities in a given context. In algorithm form:

(i)   Find the world w that is fixed by context c.
(ii) Find the set **H** of w's duplicates up to the time of c.
(iii) Set the domain of *will* to that set.

---

4   There may be a way of working around this problem if we assign a substantial theoretical role to *local contexts*. Perhaps the epistemic modal and the attitude operator can shift the domain for settled away from its original value and toward some "local" value (e.g., the worlds that the holder of the attitude takes to be historical possibilities). The *locus classicus* for the notion of local context is offered by Schlenker (2009), but I specifically expect some moves in the style of Mandelkern (2019) or in the rather different style of Boylan and Schultheis (in press) to be potentially effective here. I won't pursue how such a strategy might work in detail and what kinds of trade-offs might be involved.

5   Obligatory footnote here: Technically, modal bases are functions from worlds to sets of propositions that determine modal domains. The concept of "modal base" I use here is a simplification of Kratzer – a simplification that ignores the mechanics and the explanatory benefits of a system of premises.

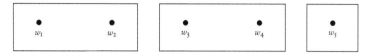

Figure 6.3   Partition representation of $\mathbf{h}_c$

In the relational system, the domain is determined by a modal base function $\mathbf{h}(\cdot)$. I propose the following algorithm for $\mathbf{h}(\cdot)$:

(i) For each world w, consider the set of w's duplicates up to the time of the context.
(ii) Define the function $\mathbf{h}(\cdot)$ such that, on input w, it returns precisely the set of duplicates of w up to the time of c.
(iii) Set $\mathbf{h}$ as the initial modal base in context c.

If we assume, as seems plausible, that duplication up to a time is an equivalence relation, then $\mathbf{h}(\cdot)$ is a function that maps each world to a cell in the appropriate duplication partition (Figure 6.3).

The move to modal bases also forces us to reconsider the centering property. In the original framework, centering was the claim that whenever w belongs to $\mathbf{H}$, $sel(\mathbf{H}, w) = w$. Since the domain parameter has been relativized, we can simplify things. First note how centering applies to sets of the form $\mathbf{h}(w)$:

CENTERING ON MODAL BASES (PRELIMINARY) If $w \in \mathbf{h}(w)$, then
$\quad sel(\mathbf{h}(w), w) = w$.

Because we think of $\mathbf{h}(w)$ as denoting the historical possibilities in w, and w is always a historical possibility with respect to itself, w is guaranteed to be in $\mathbf{h}(w)$. Thus, the antecedent of the centering condition is trivially satisfied. When selecting directly from a historical modal base, this simplifies to:

CENTERING ON MODAL BASES. $sel(\mathbf{h}(w), w) = w$

Note that this simplification is only available when we apply the centering property of selection functions to sets that are specified in this way.

In particular, the centering constraint need not be operative when we consider modal bases that have been updated with some information. Consider updating modal base $\mathbf{h}$ with the information in proposition $\mathbf{A}$. This update is defined by intersection:

$$\mathbf{h}(w) + \mathbf{A} = \lambda w.(\mathbf{h}(w) \cap \mathbf{A})$$

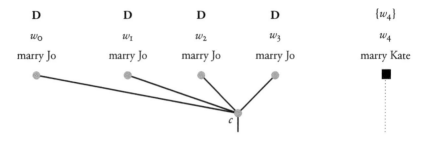

Figure 6.4   Enriching the Oedipus model with variable domains

There is no guarantee that w belongs to $\mathbf{h}(w) + \mathbf{A}$ – and, in fact, it won't whenever w is not in $\mathbf{A}$. Thus, there is no guarantee that w be selected out of this set.

Let us move to checking that the revised analysis delivers the key predictions involved in the bug. Recall that we wished to predict (2), repeated here with its original numbering, in the Oedipus scenario:

(2) $[\![\Diamond_f(will_h(\text{avoid incest}))]\!](w_0) = 1$

Figure 6.4 revises that diagram with information about how the modal base might be set up in this scenario. Let $\mathbf{D} = \{w_0, w_1, w_2, w_3\}$. What is critically important is that the domain for *will* is free to vary across worlds. It is this variability that allows us to capture our desiderata. For example, in the context diagrammed in Figure 6.4, it is not accepted that Oedipus will marry Jo. Recall that we wanted to predict this by having:

$$[\![will_h(\text{avoid incest})]\!](w_4) = 1$$

Indeed, our modified semantics achieves this, because w_4 is the only selectable world out of $\mathbf{f}(w_4)$.

The revised analysis allows us to state a much more general transparency result than what we could achieve in the original setup.

GENERALIZED TRANSPARENCY. For all A, $\|will_h \, \mathsf{A}\| = \|\mathsf{A}\|$.

GENERALIZED BOOLEAN TRANSPARENCY.
  (i) $\|will_h \, not \, \mathsf{A}\| = \overline{\|\mathsf{A}\|}$
  (ii) $\|will_h \, \mathsf{A} \, and \, \mathsf{B}\| = (\|\mathsf{A}\| \cap \|\mathsf{B}\|)$
  (iii) $\|will_h \, \mathsf{A} \, or \, \mathsf{B}\| = (\|\mathsf{A}\| \cup \|\mathsf{B}\|)$

Fact 6.1 *The relational semantics satisfies the generalized transparency principles.*

This fact shows that the relational patch behaves exactly as intended. (This and all subsequent facts are proven in the appendix to this chapter.)

It follows immediately from generalized transparency that questions about FMCs generally reduce to questions about the correct modeling of ordinary epistemic contradictions. In particular, it means, that Kissine is right in claiming that *possibly it will be sunny* and *it won't be sunny* are classically consistent. However, since our claim is that FMCs are no worse than epistemic contradictions, we need to check whether the resources that are typically brought to bear to account for epistemic contradictions successfully deliver an account of the inconsistency of FMCs.

It is easy to show, given the transparency result and the earlier characterization of informational entailment, that if the possibility operator in FMCs is interpreted epistemically – and specifically as quantifying over the same information state that is relevant to the definition of consequence – then FMCs turn out to be informationally inconsistent.

To see the point with greater precision, consider this semantic package:

i. for radical A, $[\![A]\!]^{s,w} = 1$ iff $w(A) = 1$
ii. $[\![\textit{will}_h \; A]\!]^{s,w} = 1$ iff $[\![A]\!]^{s,\textit{sel}(h(w),w)} = 1$
iii. $[\![\textit{might} \; A]\!]^{s,w} = 1$ iff $\exists v \in s, [\![A]\!]^{s,v} = 1$
iv. $[\![A \; \& \; B]\!]^{s,w} = 1$ iff $[\![A]\!]^{s,w} = 1$ and $[\![B]\!]^{s,w} = 1$
v. $[\![\textit{not} \; A]\!]^{s,w} = 1$ iff $[\![A]\!]^{s,w} = 0$
vi. $[\![\textit{settled}_h \; A]\!]^{s,w} = 1$ iff $\forall v \in h(w), [\![A]\!]^{s,w} = 1$

So that we can identify this system by name in the appendix to this chapter, let's agree to call it the *domain analysis*.

A notable fact about the domain analysis is that it is an unusual mix of modals that read a contextually provided modal base as well as an epistemic *might* that quantifies over the same information state that is quantified in the definition of acceptance. It turns out that this foundation is enough for our present purposes.

Fact 6.2 *The domain analysis predicts the informational inconsistency of* FMCs *and their analogues involving the* settled *operator.*

6.6   On Coordinated Informational Entailment

Things get trickier if the *might* that occurs in FMCs is not an epistemic modal in Yalcin's sense. Such a case might demand both conceptual and formal modifications to the framework. In this section, I consider how one might appeal to a more permissive notion of consequence, without modifying the semantics.

Suppose that the future-directed *might* in *Oedipus might marry Jo* or *it might rain* is understood as a historical modal, endowed with a relational semantics:

(20) $[\![might_h \, \mathsf{A}]\!]^w = 1$ iff $\exists v \in \mathbf{h}(w)$, $[\![\mathsf{A}]\!]^v = 1$

I used $\mathbf{h}$ for the modal base here both to reflect the assumption that it is historical and to indicate that it is the same as the modal base for *will*. Now suppose that historical FMCs are those conjunctions such as *it will rain and it might not* in which both modals are co-indexed and attached to the same, historical modal base.

It is easy to see that a simple appeal to informational consequence won't help predict the defectiveness of historical FMCs. Unless the language contains lexical items that are responsive to an information state parameter, informational consequence and point consequence collapse on each other.[6]

It follows from this collapse, and from the fact that FMCs are point-consistent, that historical FMCs are informationally consistent.

There might be a cheap way out of this problem if we had reason to think that historical FMCs should be consistent. If that were the case, our work would be done, since this is what the semantics predicts. Unfortunately, such sentences are defective, although perhaps not in the exact same way in which epistemic contradictions are defective. For one thing, if historical FMCs were not defective, two distinct readings of FMCs should be detectable: a defective one associated with epistemic possibility and a nondefective one associated with historical possibility. In fact, there is no trace of that consistent reading. For another things, if there are objective chances or similar objective modalities, modal language should allow us to talk about them directly. Perhaps we have operators such as *there is some objective chance that* and perhaps these operators can latch onto such objective modalities. However, just as FMC's are defective, so are sentences like this one:

(21)   It will rain, but there is some objective chance that it won't.

---

[6] It is already established that every point-valid argument is informationally valid. If no lexical items depend on an information state parameter in the index, the converse is also true: Every informationally valid argument is point-valid. To see this, suppose that an argument was point-invalid; then there should be a world v that makes the premises true but the conclusion false. Now, consider the information state $\{v\}$: v must accept the premises but fail to accept the conclusion. Hence, the argument is informationally invalid.

There is no cheap way out. We must find some way of predicting the unacceptability of historical FMCs.

Without unnecessarily complicating the discussion with a parallel discussion of objective chances, I will develop some ideas in the pragmatics of modal discourse to explain the relationship between *will* and a historical, objective *might* operator.

One important point of difference between (21) and ordinary epistemic contradictions is that the defectiveness of (21) is not embedded in quite the same way. Yalcin observed that the infelicity of embedded epistemic contradictions does not carry over to historical FMCs. Embedding (21) under *suppose* does not sound degraded in the same way.

(22)   Suppose that it will rain but there is some objective chance that it won't.

This suggests that although historical FMCs are defective, the account of their inconsistency should not follow the *exact* same playbook as the account of the inconsistency of epistemic contradictions.

My account of the defectiveness of historical FMCs leverages a pragmatic expansion of the concept of informational validity.[7] The key idea is that even if the lexical entries do not constrain information states, coordination relations must exist between the context of utterance and the information states that are accessed by the semantics. These coordination relations shrink the class of eligible models.

Classical entailment involves quantification over contexts, whereas informational entailment involves quantification over information states. My idea for an expansion of informational entailment involves both kinds of quantifications – the first instance over contexts, and in the second case over information states that are "eligible" with respect to those contexts. Besides the specific application I have in mind, I suspect that this sort of strategy may have applications whenever contextual parameters interact with background information states.

The task is to specify which information states are eligible in the relevant sense. With that aim in mind, define:[8]

---

[7] Though I regard the concept I am about to define as pragmatic, it is defined with the same level of precision as ordinary concepts of logical consequence, much as Stalnaker (1976) gives a precise characterization of the concept of reasonable inference. By calling it an *expansion* of informational validity, I mean to say that every argument that is informationally valid is classified as acceptable according to this relation.

[8] Though I generally omit context notation, it is useful to make it explicit here. Thus, contexts will reappear in the notation for the remainder of this discussion.

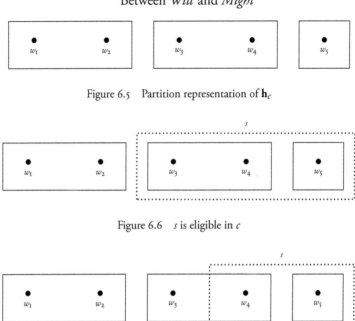

Figure 6.5   Partition representation of $\mathbf{h}_c$

Figure 6.6 s is eligible in c

Figure 6.7 s is not eligible in c

HISTORICALLY ELIGIBLE STATES. Information state s is *historically eligible* in context c if and only for every world $w \in s$, $\mathbf{h}_c(w) \subseteq s$.

Informally, for each context c, we zero in on those information states s such that the relevant historical modal base function in c never maps from inside to outside of s. Because historical modal bases represent equivalence relations (specifically, duplication up to a time), they induce partitions. Under these assumptions, the eligible information states (in c) can be equivalently characterized as those states that do not cut through the cells of the historical partition determined by $\mathcal{M}$ at the time of c.

The distinction between the eligible and ineligible information state is easy to grasp diagrammatically. Suppose we have five worlds. To check whether s is eligible in c, consider the historical modal base in c, $\mathbf{h}_c$ depicted in Figure 6.5. Figure 6.6 illustrates an example of an eligible state, while Figure 6.7 illustrates an example of an ineligible state.

To reflect the fact that our semantics includes index coordinates that are explicitly initialized by context, the concept of acceptance needs to be revised. For example, if our system has intervals and assignment functions as index coordinates, we might want to define this relativized concept of acceptance as follows. Let π_c stand in for any parameters in the index of evaluation that depend on c.

CONTEXTUAL ACCEPTANCE. Information state s *accepts* A (in context c) iff for all $v \in s$, $[\![A]\!]^{v,\pi_c} = 1$.

The centerpiece of the account is the definition of the appropriate generalization of informational entailment:

COORDINATED INFORMATIONAL ENTAILMENT.
An argument with premises $A_1, \ldots, A_x$ and conclusion C is a *coordinated informational entailment* (written $A_1, \ldots, A_x \vdash_{c\text{-}info} C$) iff for any context c, no information state s that is *historically eligible* in c accepts each of the A_i's (in c) but fails to accept C (in c).

Our account of the unacceptability of historical FMCs centers on two important facts about coordinated informational entailment.

Fact 6.3 *Anything that is valid in the classical sense (i.e., in the sense of point consequence) is informationally valid.*

This is a standard fact about informational consequence that also holds for its coordinated variant.[9]

From the point of view of our target in this section, the key observation is:

Fact 6.4 *Historical FMCs are classified as inconsistent by coordinated informational consequence.*

Informally, there is no context c and no information state s that is eligible in c such that s accepts a historical FMC. The upshot is that depending on which interpretation we impose on the *might* that occurs in FMCs, there is a package that can help account for their inconsistency in broadly informational terms.

6.7 Epistemic Relationalism?

Signing up for the relational patch allows us to hold on to the historical analysis of *will* while addressing the bug and accounting for the

---

[9] In a sufficiently expressive language, the relation between classical, informational, and coordinated informational entailment is strict inclusion. Epistemic contradictions are inconsistent in the informational sense and in the coordinated informational sense; FMCs are only inconsistent in the coordinated informational sense.

inconsistency of epistemic and historical FMCs. The dialectic offers up one last wrinkle for us to consider. Why not *combine* the relational insight and the epistemic insight? The resulting view is a relational skeletal semantics that replaces the historical metasemantics with a epistemic metasemantics:

HISTORICAL METASEMANTICS.

> For each input world w, the modal base h outputs the set of worlds that are duplicates of w up to the time of c.

EPISTEMIC METASEMANTICS.

> For each input world w, the modal base h outputs the set of worlds that are indistinguishable from w by some relevant epistemic state at the time of the context c.

To compare these metasemantic modules, let us make two simplifying assumptions. First, assume both the historical and the epistemic modal base determine equivalence relations, and hence both partition the set of all worlds. Second, assume that the partition that is determined by the epistemic modal base is strictly coarser than the partition determined by the historical modal base. This second assumption amounts to the philosophical insight that an epistemic state anchored to a time t cannot discriminate between states of the world that are exact duplicates of each other. While this assumption is dangerously close to a form of skepticism about the future, we will entertain it here for the sake of argument.

Under these assumptions, there is very little to choose between the epistemic version and the historical version of the relational semantics. Both satisfy generalized transparency results like the ones noted in Section 6.6, so the theories are essentially predictively equivalent within the space of unembedded *will* claims and Boolean combinations thereof.

This is not to say that there is absolutely nothing to choose between them. For one thing, the historical approach is much closer to completely spelled out as it stands. The epistemic metasemantics owes an account of what it means to be the relevant epistemic state in different contexts. The problem is not that no such account is forthcoming, but rather that different commitments will generate a semantic with different profiles.

On the other side of the ledger, Simon Goldstein and John Hawthorne (personal communication) offer an argument on behalf of the epistemic approach. Suppose that conditionals are interpreted as restrictors of modal bases (more on what this means in Chapter 8). Consider the following conditional:

(23)   If Ann took the test yesterday, it will be graded tomorrow.

Suppose we evaluate (23) in a world w in which Ann took the exam two days ago. For this reason, all the worlds in $\mathbf{h}(w)$ agree that Ann took the exam two days ago. When we add to $\mathbf{h}(w)$ the supposition that Ann took the exam yesterday, we end up with an empty domain, so that (23) evaluates as vacuously true. No such problem arises if the modal base is epistemic, as long as we assume that it isn't known in the relevant sense when Ann took the exam.

I will address this objection as I move to discuss conditionals in selection semantics in Chapter 8 (and more specifically, in Section 8.6). Assuming that the argument can be disarmed, the upshot is that within a relational selectionist framework, there is little to choose between the historical version of the semantics and the epistemic one. I will stick with the historical formulation largely for continuity with the preceding semantic tradition, to highlight the connection between settledness talk and future talk, and to keep *would* anchored to a historical meaning.

Appendix: Proofs

Fact 6.1 Generalized transparency.

Claim: For all A, $\|will_h \, \mathsf{A}\| = \|\mathsf{A}\|$.

Proof. We just observe:

$$\|will_h \, \mathsf{A}\| = \{w \mid [\![\mathsf{A}]\!]^{sel(\mathbf{h}(w),w)} = 1\} = \{w \mid [\![\mathsf{A}]\!]^{w} = 1\} = \|\mathsf{A}\|$$

The middle equality, which is the only significant one, is justified by the fact that the historical modal base is realistic in the sense that it guarantees for every w, $w \in \mathbf{h}(w)$. The Boolean extension of generalized transparency follows by standard induction on the complexity.

□

Fact 6.2 The domain analysis predicts the informational inconsistency of FMCs

Claim: For all A, the domain analysis predicts *will$_h$* A & *might not* A $\vDash_{info} \perp$.

Proof. Suppose by way of *reductio* that s accepts *will$_h$* A & *might not* A. Then s accepts *will$_h$* A and also accepts *might not* A. This means:

(i) For all $w \in s$, $\llbracket A \rrbracket^{s,sel(h(w),w)} = 1$.
(ii) For all $w \in s$, $\exists v \in s$, $\llbracket not\ A \rrbracket^{s,v} = 1$.

By centering (i), simplifies to:

(iii) For all $w \in s$, $\llbracket A \rrbracket^{s,w} = 1$.

This directly contradicts (ii). Furthermore, it is easy to see that this reasoning extends to statements of the form *settled$_h$* A & *might not* A. $\square$

Fact 6.3 Coordinated informational consequence extends point consequence.

Claim: If $A_1, \ldots, A_x \vDash_p C$, then $A_1, \ldots, A_x \vDash_{c-info} C$

Proof. Suppose $A_1, \ldots, A_x \vDash_p C$. Let c be a context. Suppose s is an eligible information state at c that accepts all of the premises. That is, for all $v \in s$ and $y \leq x$, $\llbracket A_y \rrbracket^{v,\pi_c} = 1$. Assume z is an arbitrary world in s. We must show $\llbracket C \rrbracket^{z,\pi_c} = 1$. Because $z \in s$, all the premises are true at the index z, π_c. But then, since C is a point consequence of the premises, it must be true at this index as well. $\square$

Fact 6.4 H istorical FMCs are coordinated informational contradictions.

Claim: *will$_h$* B, *might$_h$*$(\neg B) \vDash_{c-info} \perp$

Proof. For the purposes of this proof, I assume that a context is (or determines) a triple $\langle M, w, t \rangle$ consisting of a background model, world, and time. Fix any context $c = \langle M, w, t \rangle$. Suppose both premises are accepted (relative to c) by an information state s that is eligible relative to c. Fix a world $z \in s$.

Because *might$_h$*$(\neg B)$ is accepted in s, we must have $\llbracket might_h(\neg B) \rrbracket^z = 1$. This unpacks to:

$$\exists v \in h(z), \llbracket \neg B \rrbracket^v = 1$$

Fix this particular v with the property that it is a $\neg B$-world. Because $z \in s$ and $v \in h(z)$, since s is historically eligible with respect to the context that generates h, $v \in s$. Informally, since z and v are duplicates up to the time fixed by c, either both are in s or neither is. Because *will$_h$* B is accepted in s and $v \in s$, $[\![\textit{will}_h \text{ B}]\!]^v = 1$. Hence:

(a) $[\![\text{B}]\!]^{\textit{sel}(\mathbf{h}(v),v)} = 1$

Since $\mathbf{h}$ is historical, $v \in \mathbf{h}(v)$. By centering, $\textit{sel}(\mathbf{h}(v), v) = v$, so (a) simplifies to:

(b) $[\![\text{B}]\!]^v = 1$

But this contradicts the prior claim to the effect that v was a $\neg$B-world.

$\square$

CHAPTER 7

Future Orientation

Strikingly, we have made it far in the analysis of predictive expressions without saying much about the rather obvious fact that predictive expressions are devices of future reference. The symmetric paradigm for the analysis of tense was founded upon the idea that there are three tenses: future, present, and past. I reject this, but I do not deny the obvious fact that sentences involving *will* are usually about the future.

Something stronger seems true: In many languages, sentences involving predictive expressions such as *will* are the primary vehicles of future discourse. In languages such as English, they sharply contrast with sentences without predictive expressions. Consider, for instance, the effect the frame adverbial *tomorrow*:

(1) a. I will eat pasta tomorrow.
     b. * I eat pasta tomorrow.

Unlike (1-a), (1-b) is only acceptable on a "scheduled" reading (e.g., if there is a schedule according to which pasta is on the menu for me tomorrow). To some extent, this behavior of (1-b) is a quirk of English. In other languages, such as Italian, present tense is compatible with a future reference time even without such a scheduled reading.

(2) Domani   piove.
     Tomorrow it rains.

One might be excused here for having the thought that predicted rain is similar enough to scheduled rain. Perhaps forecasts are attempts at a report about the divine schedule. The problem is that this strategy would leave us without an explanation for why *it rains tomorrow* is bad in English, unless what counts as a schedule varies from language to language.

But I digress. The fact that other devices of future reference exist is immaterial to the dialectic I want to address. What matters is that predictive expressions allow us to speak about the future (in those languages that have them) and are usually among the primary devices for such discourse. It's not that *will* has some magical semantic powers that no other English expression has. (Indeed, I will shortly argue that the way in which *will*-sentences get to be about the future is not at all special.) Instead, the point is that there is an element of the semantic contribution of *will* that we have not captured and that needs to be captured. This much is also true, *mutatis mutandis*, of languages such as German and Italian, which are much more liberal in allowing bare present tense to convey information about the future.[1]

So this is where we are: An adequate account of the semantic contribution of predictive expressions must capture their potential for future-directed displacement. The semantic proposals I have considered thus far within the selection semantics framework punt on this task. It is time to tackle this unfinished bit of the agenda.

7.1 Revisiting the Formalism

For reasons of convenience, this chapter diverges from the setup I have used until now and relies instead on the non-syncategorematic formalism that is canonical in compositional semantics. Accordingly, instead of writing clauses like:

(3) $[\![\mathit{will}_h\ \mathbf{A}]\!]^w = 1$ iff $[\![\mathbf{A}]\!]^{sel(\mathbf{h}(w),w)} = 1$

I write:

(4) $[\![\mathit{will}_h]\!] = \lambda\mathbf{A}\lambda w.\mathbf{A}(sel(\mathbf{h}(w),w)) = 1$

The informal gloss on (4) is that *will* combined with its syntactic argument *h* denotes a function that inputs a proposition **A** and a world *w* and outputs 1 if and only if **A** is true at the world that is selected out of **h**(*w*) from the perspective of *w*.[2]

We continue to leave relativity to a model implicit. Note that the standard way (and likely the only correct way) of making the model

---

[1] This is also not to say that the use of (what is ordinarily classified as) future morphology is sufficient for future reference. It is well documented that Italian has an even richer present-directed future than English. For some recent developments in this burgeoning subfield, see Giannakidou and Mari (2013), Frana and Menéndez-Benito (2019), and Ippolito and Farkas (2019).

[2] For those unfamiliar with it, 'λ' is an operator that binds a variable in its input string and generates a term that denotes a function. For example, '$\lambda x.x + 1$' denotes the successor function. As a further notational convention, when the scope of a string of lambda expressions is a first-order formula,

explicit would be to understand (4) as providing the semantic value of its input expression relative to a model. This contrasts with an alternative interpretation, according to which we should read (4) as characterizing a function from models, propositions, and worlds to truth-value.

One last bit from the legal department. Though I have described this as a change of notation, there are respectable points of view from which this is a more substantial change of *framework*. I shall not engage with these debates here.

7.2   Hybrid Approaches

Cariani and Santorio (2018) float an analysis of *will* that makes it *both* a selectional modal and a quantifier over times. To develop this idea, assume that sentences denote functions from world/time pairs to truth-value. Let **p** range over such functions. Next, extend the selection semantics insight so as to predict the (typical but not universal) future orientation of *will*-sentences.

HYBRID ANALYSIS.

$$[\![will_h]\!] = \lambda \mathbf{p} \lambda w \lambda t . \exists t' > t, \mathbf{p}(\textit{sel}(\mathbf{h}(w), w), t')$$

According to this analysis, *will* makes two primary contributions. First it selects a world *via* the selection function, and then it quantifies over future times. When centering is active and selection is idle, this operator collapses on the standard linear tense. In this sense, it is a hybrid of selectional and linear tense operators.

The hybrid analysis fails because it undermines a key element of the motivation for selection semantics. Specifically, it predicts nontrivial scope interactions between *will* and negation, because the existential quantifier in the denotation of *will* combines differently with negations scoping over or under it. As a consequence, *will(not(rain))* says that there is a future time at which it does not rain, and *not(will(rain))* says that at every future time it

---

we think of the lambda expression as stating the characteristic function of the relevant property, possibly relevant to some parameters. To illustrate:

$$\lambda x. x \text{ is an integer and } \exists y(2y = x)$$

pins down the characteristic function of the even integers. In contrast, the open string

$$\lambda x. x \text{ is an integer and } (2y = x)$$

only pins down a function relative to some way of fixing a value for the parameter *y*.

does not rain. Only the latter structure seems to correspond to a proper meaning for the English sentence *it will not rain.* (I do not know of a single other language in which the former scope configuration is available.)

Someone who had not paid attention to my argument so far, or simply didn't care for it, might posit that the negation in *I will not eat tomorrow* is supposed to scope outside of *will,* and go on to adopt a semantics in which *will* involves existential quantification over times. Under these stipulations and assumptions, bare forecasts such as *I will eat tomorrow* get assigned existential truth-conditions, while *I will not eat tomorrow* gets assigned universal truth-conditions. It should come as no surprise (in light of the discussion in Section 4.7) that this account won't work. Neither forcing negation to take a wide scope nor introducing existential quantification over times is an admissible move in this argument. We can force negation to scope in special ways by using lexical items that force their scope. For example, according to the present proposal, *I will not pass* is not equivalent to *I will fail.* Similarly, if *I stay dry* and *I get wet* are contraries, the sentences *I will not stay dry* and *I will get wet* are not equivalent. We have as much reason to insist on scopelessness now that times are in the picture as we did in Part II, where we focused only on the modal aspect of *will*'s behavior.

7.3 Temporal Selection

Selection functions helped account for scopelessness at the world level, but they might also help at the level of times. A relevant hypothesis is that *will* initiates both selection of a single world and selection of a single time. Let ▶ be a function that maps a time t to a time t' that occurs no earlier than t:

SINGLE-TIME SELECTION SEMANTICS.

$$[\![will_h]\!] = \lambda\mathbf{p}\lambda w\lambda t.\mathbf{p}(\textit{sel}(\mathbf{h}(w), w), \blacktriangleright(t))$$

Partial inspiration for this approach comes from referential theories of tense in the style of Partee (1973). An even more direct inspiration is the semantic proposal in MacFarlane (2014, chapter 9). MacFarlane's (broadly) Ockhamist semantics for *tomorrow* involves shifting a temporal coordinate of evaluation by exactly 24 hours.

MACFARLANE'S "TOMORROW."

$$[\![tomorrow]\!] = \lambda\mathbf{p}\lambda w\lambda t.\mathbf{p}(w, t + 24 \text{ hours})$$

Like my single-time selectionist analysis, MacFarlane's account of *tomorrow* is scopeless with respect to negation.

Both these theories achieve this result at the cost of presupposing a sharp temporal shift that does not seem to match elementary intuitions about temporal shift in natural language. Consider first MacFarlane's account: If at 3 PM of Monday I say, *I will eat dinner tomorrow*, then I say something true if and only if I eat dinner exactly 24 hours hence. But obviously this cannot be accepted, except as some kind of toy idealization: My Monday afternoon utterance is plainly true if I eat dinner at 7 PM on Tuesday. And this prediction gets worse. Consider the negation of *I will eat dinner tomorrow*:

(5)   I will not eat dinner tomorrow

Evidently, the truth of (5) requires that I do not eat dinner at any point tomorrow. However, the account predicts that (5) is true if asserted on Monday at 7 PM, and I go on to eat Tuesday's dinner at 8.

Similar points apply to the single-time selection semantics. Although this semantics uses a temporal selection function, it is still wedded to the idea that for each *will*-sentence, there is an exact time at which its prejacent is true. It does not seem plausible to expect speakers who make a prediction about what will happen tomorrow to have to answer to any one specific time. As a result, the view seems to incur a significant metasemantic cost, only to account for the scopeless behavior of *will* with respect to negation.

Instead of trying to develop the temporal selection approach into a more plausible view, I choose to adopt a different starting point and use it to construct an alternative view. I expect the greater naturalness of my proposal will be apparent once it is fully developed. In the final section of the chapter, I will also stress a potential empirical advantage of my approach over temporal selection approaches.

7.4   The Future Orientation of Modals

This alternative involves abandoning the idea that temporal sentences are evaluated relative to times and moving instead to a framework in which they are evaluated relative to intervals. In the semantics literature, many arguments are advanced in support of this move (Bennett and Partee, 1972; Ogihara, 2007). Since these arguments appeal to controversial, and in my view dubious, assumptions about the metaphysical structure of events, I won't rely on them to justify my recourse to intervals. I will still land on an interval-based semantics by following an influential paper by Condoravdi (2002). Condoravdi proposes that the future orientation of *will* is due to the fact that *modals* can extend intervals of evaluation into the future.

The technical task I will pursue is to integrate selection semantics with a modified version of Condoravdi's system for the future orientation of modals. Condoravdi observes that we can obtain future shift with modals without overt traces of future tense. Think of examples such as these:

(6) a.   She might win.
     b.   He must enroll.

In these examples, her win and his enrollment must occur at times that are in the future with respect to the time of utterance. This is suggested both by direct intuition and by the patterns of adverbial modification that the sentences in (6) license. An example of the latter sort of argument relies on the contrast between the felicity of *she might win tomorrow* and the infelicity of *she might win yesterday*.

Condoravdi argues persuasively that this persistent ability of modals to shift the evaluation of their prejacent toward the future is not a coincidence. Nor is it correctly modeled by supposing that there are direct interactions between these modals and tense, such as those that are postulated by the hybrid selection semantics.

Like me, Condoravdi works under the hypothesis that *will* is a modal. She claims that *will* gets its future orientation in the same way that *might* does: by allowing evaluation of the prejacent at non-past points (except in those cases in which we have independent restrictions on the interval of evaluation). However, Condoravdi (2002, p. 13) appeals to the quantificational analysis of *will* I rejected earlier. As an alternative, I propose that *will* performs world selection and interval extension. This intervention showcases the fruitful effects of integrating selection semantics with Condoravdi's system.

7.5   Theoretical Background

Before presenting the system in detail, it is worth taking some time to illustrate some of the main ideas that lie in its theoretical background. Assume that clauses have a fundamental architecture governing the standard arrangement of tense and aspect (Beck and von Stechow, 2015). In particular, assume this structure:

[TENSE [PERFECT [ASPECT (*radical*)]]

Sentence radicals are tenseless descriptions of events or states. Accordingly, they are further classified at a very coarse level as *eventive* or *stative*.

Aspect concerns distinctions among different kinds of temporal structure that the eventuality described by the sentence radical might be viewed as having. For instance, the trio of sentences in (7) differ in how they represent the eventuality of my reading the book in question.

(7)   a.   I read that book.
      b.   I used to read that book.
      c.   I was reading that book.

Perfective aspect, as in (7-a), represents an event as a single, complete whole. Perfective aspects contrasts with a plurality of *imperfective* aspects – different ways of viewing the temporal structure of an event. An example of imperfective aspect is *habitual* aspect, which indicates that an event occurred frequently over a period of time. Another example is *progressive* aspect, illustrated by (7-c), which involves viewing an event as it is unfolding.

Due to the complexities of giving semantic analyses for imperfective aspects, I focus exclusively on perfective aspect. This again follows Condoravdi's treatment, since her formal system doesn't even entertain aspect as a separate element in the semantic analysis. This idealization allows us to simplify the clause architecture to:

[TENSE [PERFECT (*radical*)]]

In Condoravdi's system, the standard contribution of the perfective aspect is bundled into the evaluation of sentence radicals.

Tense fixes the temporal perspective of the clause. Simple tenses are present and past. In addition to simple tenses, the perfect is an optional device to create composite tenses. For example, the perfect allows reference to times that precede the times picked out by past tense – as in *I arrived and she had already finished her homework.*

In Condoravdi's system, modals are required to scope below the TENSE level, but they can float above or below the PERFECT level. In particular, all three of the following are possible clause configurations with a modal MOD:

(i) PRES(MOD(·))

(ii) PRES(PERF(MOD(·)))

(iii) PRES(MOD(PERF(·)))

These scope configurations help illustrate an important part of Condoravdi's picture – the distinction between the *perspective* and the *orientation* of a modal. The *perspective* is the time that anchors the modal parameters of the modal. For example, if it's a deontic modal, the perspective is the time at which the relevant obligations are supposed to hold. The *orientation* of the modal is the time, or time interval, at which the prejacent is being evaluated. These can be seen as distinct in the contrast between the following examples:

(8) a. They look happy coming off the team bus. *They must have won the match.*

b. Everyone was excited. At that point, *they should have won the match.*

The difference between these is that (8-a) states a present epistemic necessity about a past fact. In Condoravdi's terminology, it has present perspective but past orientation. By contrast, (8-b) states a past necessity with a non-epistemic flavor (perhaps circumstantial, or deontic): The modal has past perspective and it is future-oriented with respect to that past point.

According to Condoravdi's analysis, this difference emerges from the scope of the perfect with respect to the modal. When perfect scopes over the modal, we get the past perspective; when it scopes under the modal, we get the present-perspective and past-oriented reading.

7.6 Selection Semantics, Condoravdi Style

Language

Moving on to the formalism, we consider a language involving sentence radicals (which we first discussed in Chapter 1), as well as the following pronounced expressions: *not, and,* and *will.* We continue to decompose *will* and *would* in terms of tense, and the modal morpheme WOLL. In particular, we decompose *will* as PRES+WOLL. (We will refrain from having past tense as well – but if we had it, we'd also decompose *would* as PAST+WOLL.) The system allows composite tenses *via* a perfect operator PERF. Finally, in Section 7.7, we will consider an expansion of the language with other modal operators such as *might*.

Models

I interpret this language against $W \times T$ structures (Thomason, 1984), extended to include events and states. Specifically, define a model $\mathcal{M}$ as a 7-tuple $\langle W, T, \mathcal{E}, \approx_t, <, \tau, v \rangle$, where:

- W, T, and $\mathcal{E}$ are respectively non-empty sets of worlds, times, and eventualities (events or states).
- $\approx_t$ is a relation between worlds indexed to a time ($T \mapsto W \times W$). Intuitively, $w \approx_t v$ iff w and v are duplicates up to time t.
- $<$ is an irreflexive, transitive, and linear relation on times ($T \times T$). Interpret this as the temporal precedence relation. I occasionally abuse notation and use $<$ to relate *intervals* (i.e., convex sets of times), so that $\mathcal{I}_1 < \mathcal{I}_2$ iff every point in $\mathcal{I}_1$ precedes every point in $\mathcal{I}_2$.
- τ is a function from event/world pairs to intervals ($\mathcal{E} \times W \mapsto \mathcal{P}(T)$). Intuitively, $\tau(e, w)$ is the temporal trace of e in w – that is, the set of instants that the eventuality e stretches over.
- v is a valuation function that inputs a sentence radical A, an event e, and a world w. It outputs 1 if e is an eventuality in w and A is a type of event that describes e, and 0 otherwise.

For a guiding example of what it means for a radical to describe a type of event, think about the relationship between *they win* and events of winning by the referenced group.[3]

It is convenient to state the semantics with the help of the following abbreviations:

- If $\mathcal{I}$ is any interval, EXT($\mathcal{I}$) is the extension of $\mathcal{I}$ toward the future.

  EXT$(\mathcal{I}) = \mathcal{I} \cup \{x \in T \mid \text{for all } t \in \mathcal{I}, x > t\}$

- *now*: the present moment, given a context (not an interval).
- *sel*: a selection function, satisfying:

  <u>success:</u> for $w \in W$, $\mathbf{A} \subseteq W$ with $\mathbf{A} \neq \emptyset$, *sel*$(\mathbf{A}, w) \in \mathbf{A}$
  <u>centering:</u> for $w \in W$, $\mathbf{A} \subseteq W$ with $w \in \mathbf{A}$, *sel*$(\mathbf{A}, w) = w$

[3] Condoravdi does not use valuation functions in her semantics. However, my use of them doesn't reflect any commitments that are not already commitments of Condoravdi's system. When A is eventive or stative, she writes A$(e)(w)$ to mean that e is an event of the type described by A and occurs in world w. This is obviously equivalent to writing $v(\mathbf{A}, e, w) = 1$.

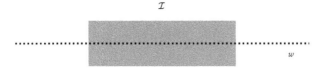

Figure 7.1   Interval

- f: a modal base (provided as an argument to WOLL).
- ○: the overlap relation between intervals – that is, the relation that holds between those intervals that have non-empty intersection.

Semantics

Onward to the semantic theory – starting with the evaluation of radicals.

> If **B** is an eventive sentence radical, $[\![\mathbf{B}]\!] = \lambda w \lambda \mathcal{I}.\exists e(v(\mathbf{B}, e, w) = \text{1}$ & $\tau(e, w) \subseteq \mathcal{I})$.
>
> If **C** is a stative sentence radical, $[\![\mathbf{C}]\!] = \lambda w \lambda \mathcal{I}.\exists e(v(\mathbf{C}, e, w) = \text{1}$ & $\tau(e, w) \circ \mathcal{I})$.

An eventive radical, such as *I go home*, is true at w and $\mathcal{I}$ iff the temporal trace of my going home in w is wholly included in $\mathcal{I}$. A stative radical, such as *I be home*, is true at w and $\mathcal{I}$ iff the temporal trace of my staying home overlaps $\mathcal{I}$.[4]

As is often the case, it's useful, to diagram the difference that supports this distinction. Start by identifying an interval $\mathcal{I}$ in a world w (Figure 7.1). Suppose, to get a concrete intuition, that this interval is the hour that just passed. Consider the stative radical *I be home*. This radical has a trace – roughly the set of instants at which I am home. It is enough for *I be home* to be true at w and $\mathcal{I}$ that the trace merely overlap $\mathcal{I}$ (Figure 7.2). This seems to be a close enough match for our intuitions.

Let's consider some examples all dressed up in tense to identify these intuitions. Suppose that on Monday I went to bed at 11 PM. I woke up on Tuesday at 7 AM and was out for the rest of the day past midnight. I would be speaking truly if I said *I was home on Tuesday*. There might be pragmatic reasons not to assert it (maybe I wasn't home for some salient portion of the day), but I haven't spoken falsely.

---

[4]   A side note for those who want to truly go deep in comparing the present system with Condoravdi's. Her system also entertains "temporal properties." I have slightly modified the setup to make them unnecessary in presenting the semantic clauses.

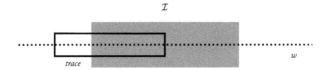

Figure 7.2   Trace and interval overlap

Things are different with eventive radicals and the eventive claims that embed them. Suppose I say, *I played a tennis match on Tuesday*. In fact, my match started on Monday, and it finished on Tuesday. Then there is much stronger pressure to say that I spoke falsely. Truly, I played a tennis match between Monday and Tuesday.[5]

Let's move on from the analysis of radicals. In this system, sentences denote functions from worlds to truth-values. However, much of the semantic computation engine manipulates functions from world/interval pairs to truth-values. Call such functions *interval intensions* and assume that the uppercase bold variables we used for functions from worlds to truth-values can also range over them. In this system, an important job of tense is to input interval intensions and output propositions (i.e., sets of worlds). Indeed, tenses head clauses and part of their semantic role is to saturate temporal interval arguments. In particular, the semantic entry for PRES is:

$$\llbracket \text{PRES} \rrbracket = \lambda \mathbf{A} \lambda w . \mathbf{A}(w, \{now\})$$

This particular analysis makes PRES an indexical: pres*(I be home)* is true at a world w just in case there is a state corresponding to me being home that occurs in w and overlaps the time of context of utterance. Several well-known anaphoric effects involving tense cannot be captured under this indexical analysis (see Partee, 1973, and Grönn and von Stechow, 2016, for recent reviews). The present tense for the two verbs in (9) is clearly not interpreted indexically:

(9)   Every time I hit this switch that light goes on.

Such effects may be captured by an alternative analysis in which the interval of evaluation for PRES is set by a covert variable. I won't chase such

---

[5] I do think that sometimes you can get away with this. It seems okay to say *I returned home on Tuesday*, describing a trip that started Monday night in Los Angeles and ended Tuesday morning in Chicago. Nevertheless, I don't think these marginal cases undermine the generalization to which Condoravdi is appealing.

complications here, but instead stick to the Condoravdi framework (including its adoption of an indexical present). I believe that the complications can be addressed in a modular fashion.

Condoravdi also provides an analysis for perfect in terms of temporal precedence of intervals.

$$[\![\text{PERF}]\!] = \lambda\mathbf{A}\lambda w\lambda\mathcal{I}.\exists\mathcal{I}^* < \mathcal{I}, \mathbf{A}(w,\mathcal{I}^*)$$

Note that unlike tenses, PERF outputs an interval intension. Because of this difference in type, it can scope above and below tense.[6]

We can now integrate the selection semantics for WOLL. In accordance with our design specifications, WOLL makes two contributions: It selects a world out of the historical modal base and it extends the interval of evaluation into the future.

$$[\![\text{WOLL}]\!] = \lambda\mathbf{f}\lambda\mathbf{A}\lambda w\lambda\mathcal{I}.\mathbf{A}(\textbf{\textit{sel}}(\mathbf{f}(w),(w)), \text{EXT}(\mathcal{I}))$$

Neither effect involves quantification and, as we will see shortly, the resulting theory happily predicts that *will* and *not* commute.

The system needs negation to operate at two different types. Clausal negation operates on propositions. However, we must also allow for structures such as PRES(*might*(*not*(*he be sad*))). Such structures require negation to operate at the sub-clausal level and thus to apply to interval intensions:

$$[\![\textit{not}]\!] = \lambda\mathbf{A}\lambda w\lambda\mathcal{I}.\mathbf{A}(w,\mathcal{I}) = 0$$

I will be neutral here on how this behavior is derived – whether by type-shifting, polymorphism, or even ambiguity. As for conjunction, we will only need clause-level conjunction, endowed with standard Boolean semantics.

Here is an illustration of the truth-conditions that this system projects on bare forecasts with eventive prejacents, such as *I will eat*:

(i) $[\![\textit{will}_h(\textit{I eat})]\!] = [\![\text{PRES}(\text{WOLL}(\text{h}, \text{I eat}))]\!] = [\![\text{PRES}]\!]([\![\text{WOLL}(h, \textit{I eat})]\!])$
(ii) $[\![\text{WOLL}(h, \textit{I eat})]\!] =$
  $= \lambda w\lambda\mathcal{I}.\exists e(v(\textit{I eat}, e, \textbf{\textit{sel}}(\mathbf{h}(w), w)) = 1 \quad \& \quad \tau(e, \textbf{\textit{sel}}(\mathbf{h}(w), w)) \subseteq \text{EXT}(\mathcal{I}))$

---

[6] To expand on this point, what I'm saying is that in this system, tenses input an interval intension and output a proposition, whereas perfect inputs an interval intension and outputs an interval intension, just like modals.

Putting (i) and (ii). together and saturating the interval argument with PRES:

(iii) $[\![will_h(I\ eat)]\!] =$

$= \lambda w.\exists e(v(I\ eat, e, \textbf{\textit{sel}}(\textbf{h}(w), w)) = 1 \quad \& \quad \tau(e, \textbf{\textit{sel}}(\textbf{h}(w), w)) \subseteq$
$\text{EXT}(\{now\}))$

Informally, *I will eat* is true at world w iff there is an event consisting of me eating that takes place in $\textbf{\textit{sel}}(\textbf{f}(w), w)$ and whose temporal trace in this world falls entirely within the non-past interval EXT(now).

The truth-conditions for stative prejacents, such as *I will be happy*, are derived in the same way, but differ in the point at which we evaluate the stative radical:

(iv) $[\![will_h(I\ be\ happy)]\!] =$

$= \lambda w.\exists e(v(I\ be\ happy, e, \textbf{\textit{sel}}(\textbf{h}(w), w)) = 1 \quad \& \quad \tau(e, \textbf{\textit{sel}}(\textbf{h}(w), w)) \circ$
$\text{EXT}(\{now\}))$

Informally, *I will be happy* is true at world w iff there is a state consisting of me being happy that takes place in $\textbf{\textit{sel}}(\textbf{h}(w), w)$ and whose temporal trace in this world overlaps with the non-past interval EXT(now).

7.7 Applications

In this section, I identify and prove some general facts that show the semantics satisfies the design constraints that motivated it. First, by inspecting the result of the derivation in Section 7.6, we see that the semantics does have bare forecasts that shift the evaluation of their prejacents toward the future. That was what we intended to inject into our system. What remains to be shown is that this goal was achieved in a way that is consistent with the motivation of selection semantics.

The basic desideratum, inherited from Cariani and Santorio (2018), was to have the system be such that *not* and *will* commute. We have achieved this. Indeed, in general, *will* A and *will not* A have complementary truth-conditions.

Consider the case of eventive prejacents and recall the truth-conditions for *will* A we just derived:

$\lambda w.\exists e(v(A, e, \textbf{\textit{sel}}(\textbf{h}(w), w)) = 1 \quad \& \quad \tau(e, \textbf{\textit{sel}}(\textbf{h}(w), w)) \subseteq \text{EXT}(\{now\}))$

Now contrast this with the truth-conditions for *will not* A (A eventive):

(i) $[\![will_h (not \text{ A})]\!] = [\![\text{PRES}(\text{WOLL}(h, \text{ not A}))]\!] = [\![\text{PRES}]\!] ([\![\text{WOLL}(h, \textit{not } \text{A})]\!])$

(ii) $[\![not]\!] ([\![\text{A}]\!]) = \lambda w . \lambda \mathcal{I} . \neg \exists e (v(\text{A}, e, w) = 1 \ \& \ \tau(e, w) \subseteq \mathcal{I})$

(iii) $[\![\text{WOLL}(h, \textit{not } \text{A})]\!] =$

$= \lambda w . \lambda \mathcal{I} . \neg \exists e (v(\text{A}, e, \textbf{sel}(\textbf{h}(w), w)) = 1 \ \& \ \tau(e, \textbf{sel}(\textbf{h}(w), w)) \subseteq \mathcal{I})$

(iv) $[\![will_h (\text{not A})]\!] =$

$= \lambda w . \neg \exists e (v(\text{A}, e, \textbf{sel}(\textbf{h}(w), w)) = 1 \ \& \ \tau(e, \textbf{sel}(\textbf{h}(w), w)) \subseteq \text{EXT}(\{now\}))$

Incidentally, these derivations highlight a second fact – a distinctive feature of Condoravdi's framework. Bare forecasts quantify existentially over events, whereas sentences of the form *will not* A quantify universally over events. The traditional Ockhamist semantics for *will* gave it existential force by supposing that it quantifies over times. In Condoravdi's framework, it is the quantification over events – and not any kind of quantification over times – that accounts for why bare forecasts have existential force.

Let us move on to a different aspect of the theory. There are some important differences between the present framework and Condoravdi's framework when it comes to analyzing present-directed uses of *will*. Consider again examples such as the following:

(10)   The laundry will be done by now.

Condoravdi assumes that these examples require assigning *will* an epistemic modal base. Part of her account is devoted to explaining why the epistemic reading of the modal in (10) seems obligatory. Her account is as follows:

HISTORICITY. If the modal base of *will* is not epistemic, it is historical (i.e., consists of all the duplicates of the actual world up to the time of the context).

AGREEMENT. All the worlds in the historical modal base at context *c* agree on the status of the purely present directed prejacents.

DIVERSITY. Evaluation for a claim of the form *will* A requires a modal base that is diverse with respect to the proposition A.

Condoravdi reasons that if the modal base for *will* in (10) were historical, then all the worlds in it would agree about present-directed prejacents. However, this would violate DIVERSITY.

I reject both HISTORICITY and DIVERSITY. My reasons for rejecting historicity are not very interesting. I just think that there is no reason to narrow our focus to a dichotomy of historical and epistemic modal bases, since we already acknowledge other kinds of modal bases (e.g., circumstantial and other objective modal bases that are not historical). Why couldn't present-directed *will* have one of these nonhistorical, non-epistemic modal bases?

My reasons for rejecting DIVERSITY are, I hope, much more interesting. I reject it because the key argument supporting it is strictly incompatible with the theory I have been building up this point. Condoravdi reasons that if we attributed to present-directed *will* a historical modal base, then *will* A would collapse onto A. Because she thinks collapse is a bad idea, we shouldn't attribute to *will* a historical modal base. According to the account I have developed, this kind of limited collapse is precisely the prediction we want to endorse for future-directed *will*. The generalized transparency property Chapter 6 just is the kind of limited collapse result Condoravdi wants to avoid.

I can now say a bit more about present-directed *will* than I said in Section 5.7. The ground floor of my account of present-directed *will* is that *the laundry will be done by now* is true at world w just in case *the laundry is done* is true in w during the interval {*now*}. Incomplete as this is, it is already enough to explain a few significant facts. Consider, for instance, the acknowledged fact that present-directed uses of *will* can only involve *stative* prejacents. Contrast these two sentences:

(10)   The laundry will be done by now.

(11)   * They will win the match (by) now.

The generalization in this neighborhood is that present-directed *will* is not available with stative prejacents.

The story I have sketched so far can capture this, provided we are granted a stipulation about events. To start, suppose that the semantic function of *by now* is to restrict the interval of evaluation to the interval {*now*}.

$$\llbracket \textit{by now} \rrbracket = \lambda A \lambda w \lambda \mathcal{I}.\mathbf{A}(w, \mathcal{I} \cap \{\textit{now}\})$$

For the purposes of applying operations in the right order, we need *by now* to scope over *will*; otherwise, *will* will reextend the interval that is narrowed down by *by now*. It is possible to avoid this stipulation if we are happy to complicate the semantics, but I won't pursue this here.

Given this, and the rest of our analysis, (10) says that there is a state in *w* involving the laundry being done whose temporal trace *overlaps* with the singleton present interval in *w*. By contrast, (11) says that there is an event of match-winning that is wholly included in the interval {*now*}. I submit that the prejacent of sentences such as (11) must have an instantaneous temporal trace for it to be fully included in {*now*} – and it cannot be. If the prejacent of a *will*-sentence describes an event that cannot be instantaneous, sentences that state it fits into a singleton interval will generally sound defective, and indeed they do.

Several people have noted in conversation that there is a felicitous way of hearing (11). Suppose we are in the last three seconds of a basketball game. Our team is down two points, but our best player has the ball. In those three seconds, the player pulls up for a three-point shot. At the same time, I say:

(12)   They will win the match ... NOW!

That last word coincides with the three-point shot going in, and our team pulling ahead just as time expires. The fact that this eventive present-directed sentence is available is, if anything, further evidence in favor of the story that I have told. As a possible interpretation of what is happening here, we might state that it is only because the win is conceived as a punctual event that it can fit the tight constraints of present-directed *will*.[7]

The ability to account for the contrast between stative and eventive pre-jacents when it comes to being available for present-directed *will* showcases another respect in which the interval-based analysis is superior to the single-time reference analysis of Section 7.3.

---

[7]   It is also possible to think of this example as involving a mid-sentence context shift, in which case it neither supports nor undermines my view.

CHAPTER 8

Neo-Stalnakerian Conditionals

The roots of the selection semantics for *will* lie in Stalnaker's selection semantics for the conditional (Stalnaker, 1968, 1976). A major difference between the present theory and Stalnaker's model concerns which items the selectional behavior is associated with. In Stalnaker's system, it is associated with the conditional. According to the present view, it is contributed by selectional modals such as *will* and *would*.

This distinction opens up some exciting and novel theoretical possibilities. Consider, for instance, unembedded *will*-conditionals such as *if Mick sings, Keith will play*. Suppose that these have roughly the truth-conditions that would be predicted by Stalnaker semantics: The unique relevant world in which Mick sings is one in which Keith plays (at a non-past time). The observation that opens up the line of inquiry of this chapter is that it is possible to reconstruct those truth-conditions on the basis of rather different technology. Specifically, I explore a theory of *will*-conditionals according to which *if* merely restricts modal bases, while *will* and *would* contribute world selection to the truth-conditions of the conditional. This recarving of the structure of Stalnaker's conditional yields a unique and under-explored semantic profile and a different set of predictions about the acceptability of inferences.

Once we identify this approach to *will*-conditionals, we also begin to see the contours of a bolder hypothesis about conditionals generally. We might think of bare conditionals, such as *if Mick sang, Keith played*, as themselves involving covert selectional modals. I will develop this bolder idea as well. Ahead of that development, it is important to stress that the semantics for future-directed discourse I have constructed in the previous chapters does not stand or fall with this additional development.

This chapter is structured as follows. Section 8.1 introduces some key distinctions and concepts. Section 8.2 introduces Stalnaker's semantics for conditionals. Section 8.3 develops an account of *will*-conditionals within my preferred version of the selection semantics framework and illustrates how it results in a recarving of the Stalnakerian truth conditions for the conditional. Section 8.4 illustrates how my recarving of the Stalnakerian truth-conditions yields new logical predictions for the conditional. Section 8.5 explores how these ideas about selectional conditionals might be molded into a view about conditionals in general. Sections 8.6–8.8 discuss some objections to the approach.

8.1 Preliminaries

Start by distinguishing six different kinds of conditional sentences. The bases for these distinctions are the different configurations of modal and temporal operators they exhibit. I illustrate them with specific English examples:

WILL. If Mick sings, Keith will play.
PRES-PRES. If Mick sings, Keith plays.
PAST-PAST. If Mick sang, Keith played.
PAST-WOULD. If Mick sang, Keith would have played.
HAD-WOULD. If Mick had come, Keith would have played.
WERE-WOULD. If Mick were to come, Keith would play.

These categories are in no way meant to be exhaustive.[1] Furthermore, the individual examples are not necessarily representative of the entire category: There are interesting differences within each class due to the type of eventuality picked out by the antecedent.[2]

My main focus will be the first three kinds of form – that is, *will*-conditionals and bare conditionals. My theory does make baseline predictions about *would*-conditionals as well, but it is not possible for me to say everything I would like to way about such conditionals without radically altering the course of this book. All I will do here is nod approvingly toward Khoo's (2015) account of the differences in meaning between these conditionals and anticipate that what I would like to do is replicate the core predictions of that framework in my preferred setup.

---

[1] For instance, for each of these classes, there are parallel sentences involving overt necessity or possibility modals – e.g., *if Mick sings, Keith might play* and *if Mick sings, Keith must play*.
[2] For example, *will*-conditionals with stative antecedents behave somewhat differently from ones with eventive ones (Kaufmann, 2005). Consider, for instance, how *if Mick is happy, Keith will play* differs from *if Mick sings, Keith will play*. The former, but not the latter, can be interpreted so that its antecedent constrains the present time. That is, *if Mick is happy, Keith will play* can be read as saying that if Mick is happy *now*, Keith will play *later*. By contrast, *if Mick sings, Keith will play* cannot be read this way: The supposed event of Mick's singing must be in the future.

8.2   Stalnaker's Semantics for Conditionals

The basic idea of Stalnaker's semantics is that a conditional *if A, then B* is true at world w if and only if B is true at the most similar A-world to w. To represent the relevant concept of similarity, Stalnaker recruits selection functions. Letting '>' denote the Stalnaker conditional, we have:

STALNAKER CONDITIONALS.

$$[\![A > B]\!]^w = 1 \text{ iff } sel(A, w) \in B$$

Recall that the selection function *sel* is provided by the model which is omitted from my notation, but is always implicitly present.

Because Stalnaker's selection functions represent similarity relations, they are more constrained than the selection functions I recruited in the semantics for *will*. In addition to the familiar principles of success and centering, Stalnakerian selection functions must satisfy some other structural assumptions. The most important of them is the conditional substitution principle, also known as CSO:

CONDITIONAL SUBSTITUTION.

if $sel(A, w) \in B$ and $sel(B, w) \in A$, then $sel(A, w) = sel(B, w)$

In conjunction with centering, conditional substitution ensures that the selection function can be modeled as choosing the highest available world from a well-order (parametrized to a world) and also that every world is maximally similar to itself.

Stalnaker's other notorious assumption is invoked to handle conditionals with impossible antecedents, Stalnaker enriches the stock of worlds in his models, with the "absurd world" λ – a world in which everything is true. Stalnaker then stipulates the principle that the absurd world is selected when, and only when, the propositional input to the selection function is the empty set.

ABSURDITY. $sel(\emptyset, w) = \lambda$

The effect of this is that $(if A)(B)$ is true at every w and for every B whenever A is impossible. The absurdity principle will play a very minimal role in my discussion: It will be necessary to assume it in the background in some of the formal results, but it doesn't play any specific role in deriving truth-conditions for any of the specific sentences we'll consider.

To maximize comparability with my preferred framework, I will find it convenient to formulate the Stalnaker conditional so that it also references a modal base.[3]

STALNAKER CONDITIONALS (WITH MODAL BASES).

$$[\![A >_f C]\!]^w = 1 \text{ iff } \textbf{\textit{sel}}\,(\mathbf{f}(w) \cap \mathbf{A}, w) \in \mathbf{C}$$

Stalnaker's conditional famously, though not uncontroversially, validates:

CONDITIONAL EXCLUDED MIDDLE. $\vdash (A >_f C) \vee (A >_f \textit{not } C)$

This is an elementary by-product of the fact that the selection function outputs a single world. As noted in Chapter 5, validating CEM is empirically desirable for a variety of reasons – specifically, ones involving the apparent scopelessness of conditional constructions with respect to negation and possibly reasons involving the probabilities of conditionals.[4]

Just as central as CEM is a classic set of invalidities predicted by the Stalnaker conditional. Among the design specifications for the Stalnaker conditional is the fact that it invalidates antecedent strengthening.

ANTECEDENT STRENGTHENING. $A >_f C \nvdash (A \;\&\; B) >_f C$

Some of the other invalidities are much more controversial. A notable example is the principle of import/export.

IMPORT/EXPORT. $A >_f (B >_f C)$ is equivalent to $(A \;\&\; B) >_f C$.

If this principle were valid, right-nested conditionals such as

(1)   if Mick sings, then if Keith comes, the band will be reunited,

should be equivalent to

(2)   if Mick and Keith come, the whole band will be reunited,

As is well known, import/export fails in both directions in Stalnaker's semantics. Figure 8.1 is a diagram of a model that shows why. Think of

---

[3] Adding a modal base does not, obviously, result in a completely equivalent theory. But the differences won't be significant to my main observations.

[4] In light of triviality results, I want to be extremely careful about using the probabilities of conditionals as a criterion of theory choice. Every theory I know that systematizes the probabilities of conditionals has some degree of non-classicality. Nonetheless, as Santorio (2017) emphasizes, under very basic assumptions the project of systematizing the probabilities of very simple conditionals in ordinary contexts suggests strongly that CEM should be valid.

Figure 8.1   Visualization of a countermodel to import/export in Stalnaker's semantics

points in the diagram as individual worlds, and think of spatial distance in the diagram as representing closeness of worlds. To evaluate $A >_f (B >_f C)$ at w, we must evaluate $B >_f C$ at v – the closest A-world to w. But to evaluate $B >_f C$ at v, we must evaluate C at the closest B-world to v, namely z. Since C is true at z in this model, $A >_f (B >_f C)$ is true at w. By contrast, to evaluate $(A \ \& \ B) >_f C$ at w, we must evaluate at the closest world to w in which $A \ \& \ B$ is true. In the sample model, this is y; since C is false there, $(A \ \& \ B) >_f C$ is false at w.

This appears to be a problem. It would be desirable to account for the generalized acceptability of instances of import/export at least for indicatives (see Mandelkern, in press, for some arguments). For semantic theories that invalidate import/export, this means developing some other story – e.g., a pragmatic one – that makes sense of the fact that it feels acceptable, when it does.

A powerful and well-known challenge to import/export comes from a famous result by Allan Gibbard. Gibbard (1981) proves that import/export plus little else collapses the conditional onto the material conditional (also see Khoo, 2013, for an insightful reconstruction of Gibbard's result). Let '$\rightarrow$' range over arbitrary conditional connectives. The two assumptions that generate this collapse result are:

MATERIAL ENTAILMENT. $A \rightarrow B \vdash A \supset B$

LOGICALITY. Either $A \nvdash B$ or $\vdash A \rightarrow B$

Fact 8.1 MATERIAL ENTAILMENT, LOGICALITY *and* IMPORT/EXPORT *entail* collapse – i.e., that $A \rightarrow B$ and $A \supset B$ are equivalent.

The standard proof is replicated in the appendix to this chapter.

It is possible to interpret Gibbard's proof as implicitly supporting Stalnaker's theoretical choice to invalidate import/export. After all, both of the other assumptions appear to be eminently plausible at first. The former is very closely related to *modus ponens*, and the latter captures the plausible insight that if a single-premise argument is valid, the corresponding conditional must be a logical truth. Given that, Stalnaker's system might be designed after the best out of a bunch of bad choices. If logical space is

Figure 8.2   Visualization of a countermodel to semi-closure

arranged in such a way that *all* choices are undesirable (i.e., all choices involve sacrificing something important), then the intuitive plausibility of denying import/export carries less weight, and invalidating it is less burdensome.

A second well-trodden problem for Stalnaker's semantics is that it projects the wrong truth-conditions on conditionals that embed other modals like:

(3)   If Mick sings, then Keith might come.

Imagine here combining Stalnaker's conditional with a vanilla, Kratzer-style analysis of *might*. The predicted truth-conditions for claims like (3) are:

$$[\![A >_f might_f B]\!]^w = \exists v \in \mathbf{f}(sel(\mathbf{f}(w) \cap \mathbf{A}, w)), v \in \mathbf{B}$$

This combined analysis invalidates some eminently plausible inference patterns, such as:

SEMI-CLOSURE. $might_f$ A, $(if A)(might_f$ B) $\vdash might_f$ (A & B).

Figure 8.2 depicts a counterexample.

To see how this might work as a counterexample, suppose that the base world is w and that $\mathbf{f}(w) = \mathbf{f}(v) = \{w, v, z\}$. The first premise says that A is possible within $\mathbf{f}(w)$. This is true because of world v. The second premise says that once we select an A-world from w's perspective, there will be a B-world v accessible from that selected world. Here, $sel(\mathbf{A}, w) = v$. Because $\mathbf{f}(v) = \{w, v, z\}$ and z is a B-world, the second premise is true. The problem is that the conclusion of the argument is not true at w, or indeed at any other point in the model.

A related and more frequently voiced concern (Lewis, 1973, p. 80) is that we might want to validate *might/would* and *might/will* duality principles. Yet, Stalnaker's theory invalidates both of the following:

MIGHTY INCOMPATIBILITIES.
A $>_f$ *will* B, A $>_f$ *might not* B $\vdash \bot$
A $>_f$ *would* B, A $>_f$ *might not* B $\vdash \bot$

This point is widely accepted in the lore, even if strictly speaking Stalnaker does not give separate semantic analyses for *will* and *would*. Presumably, the implicit assumption is that he intends to treat the former as just tense and the latter as part of a single idiomatic *if … would …* construction. In any case, it's easy to see why the mighty incompatibilities pose a problem for Stalnaker. Assuming the rules of *reductio* and disjunctive syllogism, CEM collapses *might*-conditionals onto their *will/would* counterparts. Here is a sketch of this classical proof for the special case of *will*-conditionals:

1. Suppose $A >_f$ *might* B.
2. By *reductio* and the mighty incompatibilities, *not* ($A >_f$ *will not* B).
3. By CEM, ($A >_f$ *will not* B) *or not* ($A >_f$ *will not* B).
4. By disjunctive syllogism (applied to 2 and 3), $A >_f$ *will* B.

The unpalatable consequence is that, under our present assumptions, *might*-conditionals entail their *will* counterparts. The converse direction (that *will*-conditionals entail their *might* counterparts) is independently plausible. Hence, collapse of *might*-conditionals and *will*-conditionals ensues.

In Stalnaker's framework, this argument fails at the first step, as the mighty incompatibilities are invalid. Those who go down this route owe an account of their intuitive justification. To accomplish this, Stalnaker (1981) heroically disavows the obvious logical forms of the mighty incompatibilities. He suggests that *if … might …* conditionals be construed so that *might* takes wide scope over an ordinary conditional. Stalnaker gives this wide-scoped *might* an epistemic interpretation. So, (3) would be roughly paraphrasable as *it might be that (if Mick sings, Keith comes)*. It's fair to say that not many scholars have been persuaded by this move, and that it is not an established response among contemporary philosophers of language.[5]

In the sections to follow, I build up to a semantics for conditional sentences that retains the Stalnakerian truth-conditions for unembedded conditionals, accounts for the motivation for conditional excluded middle and import/export, and allows for the beginnings of a response to the objection from the MIGHTY INCOMPATIBILITIES.

---

[5] For arguments against it, see Bennett (2003, section 73) and Williams (2010, footnote 30). Especially pertinent to the focus of this book, Stalnaker's reinterpretation maneuvers lose sight of the connection between the mighty incompatibilities and FMCs, and more generally of the connection between the mighty incompatibilities and epistemic contradictions. See the discussion in Santorio (2017).

8.3   *Will*-Conditionals in Selection Semantics

Let us start small. The formal fact at the center of this chapter is that within a selectionist framework for *will*, it is possible to reconstruct Stalnakerian truth-conditions for *will*-conditionals by a different route. This route generates a different set of predictions about the validity of inference patterns. (I want to say a different *logic for the conditional*, but the syntactic differences don't make a proper logical comparison straightforward.) This section takes up these points in turn.

Following the discussion in Cariani and Santorio (2018), start with Kratzer's theory for *if*. According to Kratzer, conditionals work as restrictors of modal domains, which in turn are fixed by modal bases. In the formal development given earlier, I chose to treat modal bases as (values of) variables. This means that if *if*-clauses are to restrict modal bases, they must be able to shift the assignment function (whose job it is to interpret variables).

Here I consider two ways of implementing this sort of shift. The first is simpler but inflexible – and descriptively inadequate in some cases. The second is more flexible but also more complex. After presenting them, I will generally use the first approach to illustrate how the semantics works in various examples. That will always be done in the spirit of simplification, since the second approach is clearly the preferable one.

The simpler approach starts by sorting the variables into two kinds: ordinary variables for individuals and variables for modal bases. Conditionals are then interpreted via a rule that shifts the assignment for modal base variables without affecting ordinary individual variables. If $\mathbf{f}(w)$ is the old modal base, we want to shift the assignment to a new modal base consisting of the intersection of $\mathbf{f}(w)$ with the proposition expressed by the antecedent. Toward that goal, let us define an auxiliary concept.

Definition 8.1   The *update* of modal base $\mathbf{f}$ with proposition $\mathbf{A}$ (notation $\mathbf{f}+\mathbf{A}$) is the pointwise intersection of $\mathbf{f}$'s outputs with $\mathbf{A}$ – i.e., $\lambda w.\mathbf{f}(w) \cap \mathbf{A}$.

In our system modal bases are values of variables, so we must also define an update operation over assignments.

Definition 8.2   The update of assignment g with $\mathbf{A}$ ($g+\mathbf{A}$) is the pointwise update of all of the modal base variables in g with $\mathbf{A}$.

The proposal is that conditional antecedents update the assignment function in this localized way and leave the other coordinates of the assignment function untouched.

CONDITIONALS (SIMPLE BUT INFLEXIBLE).

$$\llbracket (\textit{if}\,\mathbf{A})(\text{TENSE}(\text{MODAL}_f\;\mathbf{B}))\rrbracket^{w,\mathcal{I},g} = \llbracket \text{TENSE}(\text{MODAL}_f\;\mathbf{B})\rrbracket^{w,\mathcal{I},g+\mathbf{A}}$$

Since my notation omits assignment function, I will generally write expressions like the right side of this equality as $\llbracket \text{TENSE}(\text{MODAL}_{f+\mathbf{A}}\;\mathbf{B})\rrbracket^{w,\mathcal{I}}$. Strictly speaking, however, this notation is abusive.

What makes this approach inflexible is the fact that it forces us to update all modal bases at once. It is sometimes desirable to have the expressive capacity to restrict some, but not all, of the modal bases. A more complex and flexible approach limits the shift to some selected modal base variables.[6] More specifically, assume that:

(i) Modal base variables come with indices (e.g. f_1, f_2, f_3 and so on).
(ii) *If*-clauses similarly have indices.
(iii) Conditional antecedents affect "selectively" only the modal bases they are co-indexed with.

For example, the LF of *if Mick sings, Keith will play* might be as in (4):[7]

(4)   [If$_4$ Mick sings] *will*$_{f_4}$ [Keith play].

Definition 8.3 The *fine update* of assignment function g with proposition **A** and index n ($g + \langle \mathbf{A}, n \rangle$) is the update of the modal base variable with index n.

CONDITIONALS (FLEXIBLE BUT MORE COMPLEX).

$$\llbracket (\textit{if}_n\,\mathbf{A})(\text{TENSE}(\text{MODAL}_{f_n}\;\mathbf{B}))\rrbracket^{w,\mathcal{I},g} = \llbracket \text{TENSE}(\text{MODAL}_{f_n}\mathbf{B})\rrbracket^{w,\mathcal{I},g+\langle\mathbf{A},n\rangle}$$
where $g + \langle \mathbf{A}, n \rangle$ is the assignment that is exactly like g except that it reassigns the nth modal base variable, setting its value to $f_n + \mathbf{A}$.

This flexible approach is preferable if we have to model sentences with stacked modals, where we might want *if* to restrict only some of the relevant modal base variables. In the following discussion, I default to illustrating things with the simpler approach, falling back on the more complex approach only when needed.

---

[6] This account is, in essence, what we proposed in Cariani and Santorio (2018), following von Fintel (1994).
[7] Though I find it convenient to write the variable index right next to *if*, it is meant to apply to the entire *if*-clause.

To see this theory at work, let us give Mick and Keith one more go on the main stage:

(5)   If Mick sings, Keith will$_f$ play.

Consider updating modal base **f**, with the following proposition:

$$\mathbf{L} = [\![\text{Mick sings}]\!].$$

Then we predict:

$$[\![(5)]\!]^w = [\![\textit{will}_{f+\mathbf{L}}(\text{Keith play})]\!]^w$$

To further unpack these truth-conditions, summon Chapter 7's semantics for *will*. Let $\Theta(e)$ abbreviate the claim that event e is wholly included in interval EXT($\{now\}$).

(i) $[\![\text{Keith will}_f \text{ play}]\!]^w =$
   $\exists e(v(\textit{keith play}, e, \textbf{sel}(\mathbf{f}(w), w)) = 1 \ \& \ \Theta(e))$
(ii) $[\![\text{If Mick sings, Keith will}_f \text{ play}]\!]^w =$
   $\exists e(v(\textit{keith play}, e, \textbf{sel}(\mathbf{f}(w) \cap [\![\text{Mick sing}]\!], w)) = 1 \ \& \ \Theta(e))$

Informally, the truth conditions of (5) can be restated as follows:

> $[\![(5)]\!]^w = 1$ iff there is an event e described by the radical *Keith play* (plausibly this means that there is a playing event e whose agent is Keith) such that:
>
> • e occurs in world v, where v is the world that is selected when **sel** is given as input the set of the historical alternatives (to w) where Mick sings and
> • the temporal trace of e in w is wholly included in the future extension of the input interval $\mathcal{I}$.

Of course, because of the effect of selection on an updated modal base, this playing event need not occur in the actual world.

This analysis of WILL-conditionals is in broad agreement with Stalnaker's theory about their truth-conditions: (*if* A)(B) is true at w if B is true at the A-world v that is selected from w's perspective. To see the similarities (as well as the differences) between the factorized theory and Stalnaker's model, it's convenient to inspect the truth-conditions of, for example, (5) side by side.

According to the simplest version of Stalnaker's semantics, these truth-conditions are:

$$\lambda w.\textbf{sel}(\llbracket \text{Mick sing} \rrbracket, w) \in \llbracket \text{keith play} \rrbracket$$

Once we throw in a modal base, we have:

$$\lambda w.\textbf{sel}(\textbf{f}(w) \cap \llbracket \text{Mick sing} \rrbracket, w) \in \llbracket \text{keith play} \rrbracket$$

According to the factorized analysis:

$$\lambda w.\exists e(\nu(\textit{keith play}, e, \textbf{sel}(\textbf{f}(w) \cap \llbracket \text{Mick sing} \rrbracket, w)) = 1 \ \& \ \Theta(e))$$

The differences between these truth-conditions are relatively minor. The selection functions are subject to slightly different constraints (but that's a choice where one might go either way). I've added several bells and whistles onto the factorized analysis, they're close enough that I am comfortable thinking of my analysis as a version of Stalnaker's semantics.[8]

8.4   Logical Patterns in the Factorized Analysis

Although the factorized analysis predicts the same truth-conditions for WILL-conditionals as Stalnaker's analysis, it makes different predictions when it comes to accounting for inference patterns. Like Stalnaker's analysis, the factorized analysis predicts a form of conditional excluded middle restricted to *will*-conditionals:

CEM-W $\vdash$ $(if\,\textsf{A})(will_f\,\textsf{B}) \vee (if\,\textsf{A})(will_f\,not\,\textsf{B})$

Interestingly, the semantics also validates an analogue of import/export, appropriately restricted to *will*-conditionals.

IE-W $(if\,\textsf{A})(if\,\textsf{B})(will_f\,\textsf{C}) \dashv\vdash (if\,\textsf{A}\ \&\ \textsf{B})(will_f\,\textsf{C})$

Some syntactic work is necessary at this point to account for the mechanics of the structure $(if\,\textsf{A})(if\,\textsf{B})(will_f\,\textsf{C})$. I won't carry out this work explicitly, but one basic idea is that two *if*-clauses might occur as separate adjuncts of the modal, so that they sequentially restrict its modal base (Kratzer, 2012, p. 105).[9]

---

[8] If we wanted to bring them in even closer alignment, we could spot Stalnaker a purely temporal analysis of *will*. Proving a proper equivalence in detail would be a bit of a detour here. In Cariani (2019), I work through how a simpler version of selection semantics (in particular, one that is stripped of the work we did in Chapter 7) can exactly match Stalnaker's truth-conditions for *will*-conditionals.

[9] Let me say a bit more. There are two different ways of presenting a restrictor theory (Kratzer has suggested both at different times).

This reconstruction dodges the reason why import/export fails in Stal-naker's system. There are two conditionals in $(if A)(if B)(will_f C)$, but only one in $(if A \ \& \ B)(will_f C)$. As a result, in a proper Stalnakerian system, the former structure involves two selection steps – the first time moving to the closest A-world and the second time moving to the closest B-world to that – while the latter involves only one such step. The factorized analysis does not have this feature because it relies on the restrictor analysis. After all, restricting a modal base $\mathbf{f}$ with $\mathbf{A}$, and then restricting $\mathbf{f} + \mathbf{A}$ with $\mathbf{B}$, takes us to $\mathbf{f} + \mathbf{A} + \mathbf{B}$. That is the exact same modal base we obtain by restricting $\mathbf{f}$ with $\mathbf{A} \cap \mathbf{B}$. Because selection functions are associated with the modals, rather than with the conditionals, we select only once in each case.

It is not news that the restrictor analysis validates import/export, and it is even older news that the analysis validates a limited version of it. What is surprising, though, is that a restrictor analysis (with the accompanying validity of import/export) is consistent with a semantic theory that gives *will*-conditionals broadly Stalnakerian truth-conditions. In consequence, it is possible to have Stalnaker's truth-conditions for unembedded *will*-conditionals while also directly accounting for the intuitions that are usually marshalled in support of import/export.

The restrictor approach also gives an attractive way around Gibbard's collapse result (Khoo, 2013). The principle of material entailment must fail

According to the first way, $(if A)$ denotes a function from propositions to truth-value. Under this interpretation, $(if A)(if B)(will_f C)$, now plausibly to be rewritten as $(if A)((if B)(will_f C))$, is well formed. However, there is no guarantee that *if* will attach to a modal. From the compositional point of view, an *if*-clause should be completely free to attach to any proposition whatsoever. There may be pragmatic reasons to rule out LFs such as $(if A)(B)$ when B is non-modal, since in many cases such LFs will just be equivalent to B. But I haven't often seen restrictor theorists go this way.

According to the second way, modals have two arguments, a restrictor and a scope. That is, *if*-clauses are restricted in their distribution to restrictor arguments of modals. This means, for instance, $(if A)(B)$ can be reconstructed as:

$$\text{MODAL}_f (if A)(B)$$

This expression should not be read as a modal scoping over a conditional, but rather as a modal with its two arguments being saturated by the antecedent and the consequent of a conditional, respectively. Working under this approach, some syntactic magic is necessary to allow $(if A)(if B)(will_f C)$ to be well defined. After all, the direct translation into this formalism would look like this:

$$\text{MODAL}_f (if A \ if B)(C)$$

I am quite confident that this can be implemented somehow or other. What is necessary is some device that takes a (possibly empty) list of *if*-clauses and turns them into a single proposition – the intersection of the contents of all the *if*-clauses or, if the list is empty, the tautological proposition. We have solved harder problems than this one, but I'm sure it takes some work.

in some relatively isolated cases. For example, it must fail in some of the critical instances employed in Gibbard's proof, such as the following:

(6) $(if\,\neg A)((if\,A)(B))$

Here, the outer conditional's antecedent contradicts the antecedent of the inner conditional. In our system, this imposes an inconsistent restriction, making the conditional logically true. If the principle of material entailment held, then (6) should entail $\neg\neg A \vee (if\,A)(B)$, which by a bit of classical reasoning simplifies to:

(7) $A \vee (if\,A)(B)$

But it is implausible to claim that (6) entails (7): (6) involves contradictory suppositions and is plausibly regarded as a logical truth on account of that. By contrast, (7) is in no way guaranteed to be a logical truth: There are false conditionals with false antecedents.

The restrictor analysis also helps us handle *if-might* conditionals in entirely standard ways. Because no *will* is involved, the conditional simply restricts the modal base of *might*.

$$[\![(if\,A)(might_f\,B)]\!]^w = \exists v \in \mathbf{f}(w) \cap A, v \in \mathbf{B}$$

This unproblematically validates semi-closure.

Fact 8.2 SEMI-CLOSURE *is valid; i.e.,* $might_f\,A, (if\,A)(might_f\,B) \models might_f\,(A\,\&\,B)$.

As usual, a proof is in the appendix.

Given this analysis, things get a little trickier for the mighty incompatibilities. After all, the current semantics assigns consistent truth-conditions to:

$$(if\,A)(might_f B)\quad \&\quad (if\,A)(will_f\,not\,B)$$

At this point, we can follow the same strategy we used to explain the badness of "future *might* contradictions" (FMCs) in Chapter 6. In making this move, we follow the playbook established by Santorio (2017) without actually going for Santorio's preferred formalism. Santorio's main point is that these contradictions can be accounted for in terms of something much like informational consequence. However, while Santorio advocates a more sophisticated framework he calls "path semantics," the informational account of the mighty incompatibilities is already available in the relatively simpler framework I have developed up to this point.

Fact 8.3 *The combination of the restrictor analysis for* if *together with the selection semantics of Chapter 7 classifies*

$$\text{(if } A)(\text{will}_f \ B) \ \ \& \ \ \text{(if } A)(\text{might}_f \ \text{not } B)$$

as a coordinated informational inconsistency.

In Chapter 7, we also noted that if we treat *might* as quantifying over an information state, we can treat FMCs as epistemic contradictions. A technical problem arises in extending this reasoning to the mighty incompatibilities. Suppose we introduce this *might* (you will be able to distinguish it from the one that is used in Fact 8.3 because it doesn't carry a modal base argument). We are interested in predicting the informational inconsistency of:

$$(\textit{if } A)(\textit{will}_f \ B) \ \ \& \ \ (\textit{if } A)(\textit{might}_f \ \textit{not } B)$$

The technical problem is that in the account of *if* we have sketched so far, (*if* A) restricts a modal base, and not the information state that *might* is sensitive to. I won't sketch here the kind of semantics that is needed if we treat *might* as quantifying over an information state. But in essence, we have two options. The first possibility is to generalize the domain analysis from Section 6.4. The cost of this would be to give up the relational account I advocated in Section 6.5. The second option would be to have conditionals play a double restricting role – as restrictors of modal bases and as restrictors of information states. I leave the development of such complications to separate work.

8.5 The Generalized Factorization Analysis

Let us take stock of where we are. I have argued that the selectionist account of *will* can match the Stalnakerian truth-conditions for unembedded *will*-conditionals. Moreover, it can do so while allowing a different, and broader, set of logical predictions. As a consequence, some structural problems for Stalnaker's semantics can be approached differently.

However, Stalnaker's semantics was meant to be a fully general account of conditionals – the whole, diverse family of them. Can the present framework replicate that level of generality? A key first step would be to extend the framework to cover bare conditional statements. On the surface, these conditionals do not involve overt modals of any kind. Faced with this task, we might summon a classical component of Kratzer's development of the restrictor analysis (Kratzer, 1991a, 2012). Her idea is to account for bare conditionals by postulating a covert (i.e., unpronounced) modal. This modal is typically assumed to default to an epistemic necessity modal. For example, (8) should be viewed as having a covert necessity operator, roughly as in (9):

(8)   If Mick is English, Keith is English.

(9)   If Mick is English, MUST$_f$ (Keith is English).

The antecedent of (9) restricts the modal base of the covert MUST, so that the sentence ends up having a restricted necessity interpretation. Under this reshaped logical structure, even superficially bare conditionals involve modality after all.

   At this point a natural, though slightly subversive, move suggests itself. We might tweak Kratzer's account to allow the covert necessity operator to be a selection-based modal. Kratzer (2021) does some of the subverting herself, by suggesting that selection modals can *sometimes* be the relevant covert modals. The even more subversive thesis is that they *always* are (this move is also explored and eventually rejected by Mandelkern, 2018).

   For illustration's sake, I assume that this covert modal is *will*. The logical form of (8) might look a little like this:

(10)   (if PRES(Mick be English))(PRES(WOLL$_f$(PRES(Keith be English))))

Abbreviate the proposition expressed by "Mick is English" as follows:

$$\mathbf{E} = \lambda w. \exists e(v(\text{Mick be English}, e, w) = 1 \ \& \ \tau(e, w) \circ \{now\})$$

The truth-conditions of (10) are:

$$\lambda w. \exists e(v(\text{Keith be English}, e, sel(\mathbf{f}(w) \cap \mathbf{E}, w)) = 1 \ \&$$
$$\& \ \tau(e, sel(\mathbf{f}(w) \cap \mathbf{E}, w)) \circ \{now\})$$

More generally, we can state truth-conditions for a (superficially) bare conditional if A, B. To do so, abbreviate the temporal constraint associated with eventuality e as $\theta(e)$. (Recall that this constraint will look different depending on whether e is an event or a state.) Next, calculate the truth-conditions of (if A)($will$ B):

(11) $\lambda w. \exists e(v(\text{B}, e, sel(\mathbf{f}(w) \cap [\![\text{A}]\!], w)) = 1 \ \& \ \Theta(e))$

   Once again, these are Stalnakerian truth-conditions with some extra bells and whistles. The conditional is true iff the selected A-world contains an eventuality corresponding to B that is appropriately related to the time interval of evaluation. If we mentally strip down the temporal part of the proposal, we recognize Stalnaker's truth-conditions for bare conditionals. Call this the *generalized factorization analysis* (GFA).

Under the GFA, we can extend the lessons of Section 8.3 to superficially bare conditionals. That is, the GFA accounts for the plausibility of those surface forms that appear to instantiate the conditional excluded middle, such as the following:

(12)   Either Mick sang if Keith played or Mick didn't sing if Keith played.

More precisely and more generally, the following holds (notational shortcut alert: I omit present tense scoping over WOLL to keep things more legible):

CEM-C. $\vdash$ (*if* A)(WOLL$_f$ B) $\lor$ (*if* A)(WOLL$_f$ *not* B)

As before, in addition to CEM-C, the semantics classically (and thus informationally) validates a pattern that accounts for instances of import/export involving bare conditionals:

I/E-c. (*if* A)(*if* B)(WOLL$_f$ C) $\dashv\vdash$ (*if* A & B)(WOLL$_f$ C)

Interestingly, the system makes available a second logical form for I/E, though it is invalid:

I/E-c2. (*if* A)(WOLL$_f$(*if* B)(WOLL$_f$ C)) $\not\dashv\not\vdash$ (*if* A & B)(WOLL$_f$ C)

I generally omit the routine checks involved in establishing these facts.

There are some interesting things to highlight about I/E-c2. First, it incorporates the fascinating suggestion that there might be a way of defining a binary conditional connective with Stalnakerian truth-conditions *and* logic inside a restrictor theory. To do so, just say that A $\rightarrow$ B = (*if* A)(WOLL$_f$ B). This would make it consistent to say that the selection function is encoded by WOLL while also saying that in any given clause there is a one-to-one correspondence between selection functions and occurrences of *if*. Second, it raises questions about how responsible the theory ought to be for the predictions of these additional structures. Does the validity of I/E-c properly account for the felt intuitive validity of import/export, given that there is a *very nearby* LF that is invalid? I will say a bit more about this issue toward the end of the chapter.

A generalization of the approach presented in Section 8.4 will also deliver the informational validity of an analogue of the mighty incompatibilities:

WM-c. (*if* A)(WOLL$_f$ B), (*if* A)(*might$_f$ not* B) $\vdash_{c\text{-}info}$ $\bot$

WM-c*. $(if A)(\text{WOLL}_f B), (if A)(\textit{might not } B) \vdash_{info} \bot$

Summing up, the GFA is the core of the account of conditionals that emerges if we start with selection modals and work our way out to a general approach to conditional meaning. Its ability to capture intuitions about logical validity is somewhat different from what's available in Stalnaker's framework. Much more substantive work would have to go into defending the GFA as a fully general account of conditionals – it might even have to be the subject of a whole different book. In what is left of this chapter, I take the very first steps by responding to three criticisms of the approach.

8.6   Counterhistorical Restriction

The GFA posits a covert WOLL in the logical structure of bare conditionals. Which modal base should it have? If this covert operator is to parallel overt *will*, we should expect it (in light of our present assumptions) to have a historical modal base. As Simon Goldstein and John Hawthorne (personal communication) note, this hypothesis falters in regard to "counterhistorical" antecedents – those antecedents that are incompatible with the settled history up to the time of the context. Suppose that in w, Ann takes a test on Tuesday. On Wednesday, I say:

(13)   If Ann took her test on Monday, it was graded on Tuesday.

If the restriction of WOLL is historical, $\mathbf{f}(w)$ is the set of worlds that duplicate w up to the time of my utterance. That means that, in every world in $\mathbf{f}(w)$, Ann took the test on Tuesday, so the restriction with the antecedent of (13) is vacuous.[10]

A natural alternative – and a solution to this problem – is to assign that covert WOLL an epistemic modal base. It is convenient, but philosophically quite substantial, to assume that at any given time, the epistemic modal base is a coarsening of the historical one. Let $\mathbf{h}_t$ be the historical modal base at t and let $\mathbf{e}_t$ be the epistemic modal base at t.

$$\forall w, v, \forall t : \text{if } v \in \mathbf{h}_t(w), v \in \mathbf{e}_t(w)$$

---

[10]   Though I haven't specified how the selection function is to operate on the empty set, this is certainly problematic: All counterhistorical conditionals would depend only on what goes on at a single world.

The informal meaning of this constraint is that worlds can only be distinguished by the epistemic modal base (at t) if there is some qualitative difference between them (at t).

The assumption that the covert WOLL has an epistemic modal base correctly handles (13). The spirit of the objection is not yet defeated, however: *Will*-conditionals still rely on historical modal bases. Given that, the problem seems to reappear for counterhistorical *will*-conditionals such as the following:

(14)   If Ann took her test on Monday, it will be graded on Thursday.

I propose that examples like (14) motivate importing an idea that proponents of restrictor approaches have been independently advocating. Sometimes, a covert modal is posited even in the presence of an overt modal (Frank, 1997; Kaufmann and Kaufmann, 2015). As before, the GFA differs from this tradition in positing covert selection modals all the way down. The result is that the logical form of (14) is something like this:

(15)   (if_1 *test monday*)(WOLL$_{f1}$ *will$_{f2}$ grade thursday*)

Suppose that $f1$, which is co-indexed with the *if*-clause, is assigned to the epistemic modal base **e**, while $f2$ is assigned to the historical modal base **h** (at the relevant times). This allows for nonvacuous counterhistorical restriction, because it is **e**, and not **h**, that gets the restriction:

(16) $[\![(15)]\!]^w = [\![grade\ thursday]\!]^{sel(\mathbf{h}(sel(\mathbf{e}(w)\cap \text{test monday},w)),\text{EXT}(now))}$

In support of this move, I note that it is independently needed not only in cases that routinely motivate double modalization, but also in cases that are extremely close to the present dialectic. Suppose that the language contains *some* historical modals like the cumbersome but intelligible *it is historically necessary that*. Then, consider the following conditional:

(17)   If Ann took her test on Monday, it is historically necessary that it will be graded on Tuesday.

For the reasons explored earlier, we cannot treat (17) as involving a counterhistorical restriction on the historical necessity modal. The only sensible strategy within a restrictor analysis is to posit a covert modal for the *if*-clause to restrict.

8.7   On the Proliferation of Covert Modals

Mandelkern Mandelkern (2018) sketches and rejects an account of conditionals like the one from Section 8.3. His first concern is that the heavy reliance on covert modals is suspect for reasons having to do with learnability of conditional constructions across languages (see also Schulz, 2010).

> How do we learn to insert covert modals in all the needed places? And how do we learn which modal to put in? We can imagine a wide array of options that would seem to be open to children concerning what kind of modal we put in (existential? universal? epistemic, deontic, metaphysical?) as well as when to insert them (always? sometimes? never?). How do children (both within and across languages) converge on the correct combination? (Mandelkern, 2018, p. 312)

It is hard to address this challenge without a major digression, and this is not the place for that. Nevertheless, I believe the challenge is not as pressing as Mandelkern suggests. For one thing, figuring out the force and flavor of covert modals is not significantly harder than figuring out the force and flavor of overt ones. Setting this point aside, it is not clear exactly what children are supposed to not be able to do. According to most standard models for acquisition, children can entertain and test syntactic and semantic hypotheses of the relevant complexity: Slotting covert elements into the relevant LFs and fixing the relevant parameter values involves searching and testing a relatively small hypothesis space.

There are also less direct reasons for caution. If there is a problem with covert modals here, then there are problems in all the other places where semanticists have found it plausible to resort to covert modalities. Furthermore, if there is a problem with covert *modals*, then there likely is a problem with covert *elements* more generally. Semantics without covert elements would be a respectable research program, but it comes with a large unfinished agenda. In light of these considerations, I submit that we are allowed to proceed on the assumption that a theory with covert modal elements is not unlearnable.

8.8   Collapse and the Identity Principle

Mandelkern's second concern concerns the logic of the conditional. Accounts that validate import/export fail to deliver the validity of an impressively intuitively compelling schema – the identity schema *if* A, *then* A. Mandelkern (in press) supports this point in two different ways.

First, a restrictor simply cannot validate some instances of the identity schema. Here is an example, illustrated first with a conditional connective →, and then under the GFA. (I added some boxes that help track identical subformulas to assist with legibility.)

(18) a. $(\neg(A \to B) \ \& \ B) \to (\neg(A \to B) \ \& \ B)$
  b. $(if\,(\boxed{\neg(if\,A)(\text{WOLL}_f \ B) \ \& \ B})(\text{WOLL}_f\,(\boxed{\neg(if\,A)(\text{WOLL}_f \ B) \ \& \ B}))$

It's easy to see why this fails on the restrictor account. Evaluating (18-b) requires restricting the modal base of the second WOLL with the proposition corresponding to

$$\neg(if\,A)(\text{WOLL}_f \ B) \ \& \ B$$

In particular, this means restricting to B-worlds alone. But if we do restrict to B-worlds, $(if\,A)(\text{WOLL}_f \ B)$ must be true, so $\neg(if\,A)(\text{WOLL}_f \ B)$ must be false, which then means the entire consequent must be false.

Mandelkern's other challenge to import/export is that it and the Identity principle are involved in a striking collapse result. Let '→' be a variable ranging over conditional connectives. Identity, together with a weak monotonicity constraint (and against a background that licenses substitution of logical equivalents), yields the principle of logicality we encountered when discussing Gibbard's proof:

WEAK MONOTONICITY. $A \to (B \ \& \ C) \vdash A \to B$

LOGICALITY. Either $A \nvdash B$ or $\vdash A \to B$

(Under $A \vdash B$, A is equivalent to $(B \ \& \ A)$, so $A \to A$ entails $A \to B \ \&$ A, which by weak monotonicity yields $A \to B$.) But logicality immediately entails these two schemas:

(19) a. $\vdash (\boxed{\neg(A \to B)} \ \& \ B) \to \boxed{\neg(A \to B)}$
  b. $\vdash ((\neg(A \to B) \ \& \ \boxed{B}) \ \& \ A) \to \boxed{B}$

Both are consequences of logicality because one conjunct in the antecedent is identical to the consequent.

However, applying import/export reasoning to (19-b) yields:

(20) $\vdash (\neg(A \to B) \ \& \ B) \to (A \to B)$

If so, $(\neg(A \to B) \ \& \ B)$ – the common antecedent of (19-a) and (20) – is logically false, by a principle Mandelkern (2019a) dubs *Ad Falsum*, according to which $A \to B$ and $A \to \neg B$ entails $\neg A$.

AD FALSUM. $A \to B$ & $A \to \neg B \vdash \neg A$

Collapse follows at this point by further maneuvers identified in the appendix to this chapter.

Fact 8.4 *Against the background of classical logic for the nonconditional fragment,* IDENTITY, IMPORT/EXPORT, *and weak monotonicity yield collapse of the conditional onto the material conditional.*

Mandelkern rejects the import/export step and develops an impressive theory that accounts for why import/export, though invalid, seems to not fail in the indicative domain.

My first reaction to these arguments, on behalf of the import/export principle, is to reach for a bullet-biting response. Restrict Identity to its non-junk instances,[11] or even more plainly to its instances that do not embed conditionals. The strategy would grant that Identity is a simple-looking principle in conditional semantics, but resist the idea that the intuitive support for it extends to cases in which A is instantiated by complex, conditional-embedding, and possibly even contradictory, sentences such as $((\neg(A \to B)$ & $B)$ & $A)$.

Even if this were the right approach, the dialectic would not end here. Biting this bullet requires a reply to Mandelkern's case for Identity in section 4.2 of Mandelkern (in press). In particular, one would have to address his contention that instances of (18), such as the example in (21), have the distinctive ring of tautology.

(21)   If the match lit, but it's not the case that it lit if it was wet, then it's not the case that it lit if it was wet.

I agree with Mandelkern on the judgment about (21). My hope, however, is that the sort of restrictor theory I have developed has some tools that might support a reply to this argument. In particular, an attentive strategy of indexing for the modal base variable can yield a construal for (21) that is guaranteed to be true.

(22) $(if_2(\neg(if_1 wet)(\text{WOLL}_{f_1} lit) \ \& \ lit))(\text{WOLL}_{f_2}(\neg(if_1 wet)(\text{WOLL}_{f_1} lit)))$

---

[11]   This is part of a more general line of responses to collapse results that is briefly entertained in Cariani and Goldstein (in press). By non-junk instances, I mean the smallest natural class of instances that are directly supported by intuitive data.

The lingering problem would then be to explain why we do not, in fact, detect the co-indexed reading of (21).

In an attempt to address this problem, it is natural to land on a more concessive reply to Mandelkern's objection. We could add the stipulation that stacked occurrences of WOLL just cannot be co-indexed. Then the logical form in (22) wouldn't just be one of two relevant possibilities, but rather would be much closer to what linguistic law mandates as the form for (21).

This addition to the system restores the validity of the Identity principle and forces us to consider Mandelkern's collapse result. Under this stipulation, the analogue of Mandelkern's collapse proof fails in one of two different ways, depending on how we construct the relevant nested conditional. Recall that we identified two different versions of import/export:

I/E-c. $(if\,A)(if\,B)(\text{WOLL}_f\;C)\;\dashv\vdash\;(if\,A\;\&\;B)(\text{WOLL}_f\;C)$

I/E-c2. $(if\,A)(\text{WOLL}_f\,(if\,B)(\text{WOLL}_f\;C))\;\not\dashv\not\vdash\;(if\,A\;\&\;B)(\text{WOLL}_f\;C)$

Under the $(if\,A)(\text{WOLL}_f\,(if\,B)(\text{WOLL}_f\;C))$ form, it evidently fails at the import/export step. Under the $(if\,A)(if\,B)(\text{WOLL}_f\;C)$ form, it is blocked because *Ad Falsum* fails.

This principle is used to derive

(23) $\vdash\;\neg(\neg(A \rightarrow B)\;\&\;B)$

from

(19-a) $\vdash\;(\neg(A \rightarrow B)\;\&\;B) \rightarrow \neg(A \rightarrow B)$

(20) $\vdash\;(\neg(A \rightarrow B)\;\&\;B) \rightarrow (A \rightarrow B)$

But this reasoning step does not work in the system I sketched here. This is easier to see if we first convert (19-a) and (20) into the LFs they would have in the system:

(24)   a. $\vdash\;(if\,[\neg(if\,A)(\text{WOLL}_f\;B)\;\&\;B])(\text{WOLL}_f\neg(if\,A)(\text{WOLL}_f B))$
        b. $\vdash\;(if\,[\neg(if\,A)(\text{WOLL}_f\;B)\;\&\;B])(if\,A)(\text{WOLL}_f\;B)$

What is apparent when we represent things this way is that, technically speaking, this is not even an instance of *Ad Falsum*.

The last thing I want to note concerns what to do with the form I/E-c2. In Cariani (2019), I prove that it is possible to implement Mandelkern's strategy for accounting for it as a Strawson entailment in my system, by switching the presuppositions he associates with the conditional from *if* to WOLL. If that strategy is successful, it might yield an interesting by-product. Perhaps I/E-c2 it can help explain why we don't detect much of a difference between I/E-c and I/E-c2. Once the presuppositions of WOLL are factored in, both principles turn out to be Strawson-valid.

Appendix: Proofs

Fact 8.1 Gibbard's proof.

Claim: MATERIAL ENTAILMENT, LOGICALITY and IMPORT/EXPORT entail COLLAPSE.

IMPORT/EXPORT. $A >_f (B >_f C)$ is equivalent to $(A \ \& \ B) >_f C$
MATERIAL ENTAILMENT. $A \rightarrow B \vdash A \supset B$
LOGICALITY. Either $A \nvdash B$ or $\vdash A \rightarrow B$
COLLAPSE. $A \supset B \dashv\vdash A \rightarrow B$

Proof. We are given one direction of the equivalence for free, in the form of the material entailment principle. This is normally regarded as the "intuitively plausible" direction because of its relation to *modus ponens*. For the converse direction, suppose $A \supset B$. This is definitionally equivalent to $\neg A \lor B$. Reason by cases: Suppose first that $\neg A$ is true; then by logicality and $\neg A \land A \vdash B$, we have $\vdash (\neg A \land A) \rightarrow B$. By import/export, $\vdash \neg A \rightarrow (A \rightarrow B)$. By the supposed truth of $\neg A$ and MATERIAL ENTAILMENT, $A \rightarrow B$. In the second case, suppose that B is true; then by LOGICALITY and $(B \land A) \vdash B$, it follows that $\vdash (B \land A) \rightarrow B$. By import/export, $B \rightarrow (A \rightarrow B)$, but because we supposed B we can derive $A \rightarrow B$. This concludes the collapse proof.   □

Fact 8.2 SEMI-CLOSURE is valid.

SEMI-CLOSURE. $might_f A, (if A)(might_f B) \vdash might_f (A \ \& \ B)$.

Proof. Suppose the model is such that $might_f A$ is true at w. Then there is a world $v \in \mathbf{f}(w)$ such that A is true at v; because $(if A)(might_f B)$ is also true at w, and because by the first premise it is not vacuously true, there is a world $v \in \mathbf{f}(w) \cap \mathbf{A}$ such that $v \in \mathbf{B}$. But then the conclusion must be true at v.   □

Fact 8.3 The mighty incompatibilities are coordinated informational inconsistencies.

Claim: $(if\,A)(will_f\,B)$ & $(if\,A)(might_f\,not\,B) \models_{c-info} \bot$

Proof. The truth-conditions for the two conjuncts are, respectively:

(i) $\exists e(v(B, e, \mathbf{sel}(\mathbf{f}(w) \cap \mathbf{A}, w)) = 1$ & $\Theta(e))$

(ii) $\exists v \in \mathbf{f}(w) \cap \mathbf{A}, \neg\exists e(v(B, e, v) = 1$ & $\Theta(e))$

Suppose s is a state that accepts both (i) and (ii) and that is eligible for $\mathbf{f}$. Consider an arbitrary w in s. By (ii), there must be a $z \in \mathbf{f}(w) \cap \mathbf{A}$ with the negative property in (ii) – so in particular, this world doesn't contain a B even within the relevant time frame. Because s is eligible, $z \in \mathbf{f}(w)$, and $w \in s$, we must have $z \in s$. That means, in particular, that (i) should be true at z. Moreover, since $z \in \mathbf{f}(w) \cap \mathbf{A}$, by centering, $sel(\mathbf{f}(z) \cap \mathbf{A}, z) = v$. But now z is required to have incompatible properties – in particular, it's required by (i) to contain an event that makes B true and by (ii) to lack such an event. ☐

Fact 8.4 Mandelkern's proof.

Claim: Against the background of classical logic for the nonconditional fragment, IDENTITY, IMPORT/EXPORT, AD FALSUM, and WEAK MONOTONICITY yield collapse of the conditional onto the material conditional.

IMPORT/EXPORT. $A >_f (B >_f C)$ is equivalent to $(A$ & $B) >_f C$
IDENTITY. $\vdash A \rightarrow A$
WEAK MONOTONICITY. $A \rightarrow (B$ & $C) \vdash A \rightarrow B$
AD FALSUM. $A \rightarrow B, A \rightarrow \neg B \vdash \neg A$

Proof. In the main text, following a proof from Mandelkern (2019a), we used identity, monotonicity, and *Ad Falsum* to derive $\vdash \neg(\neg(A \rightarrow B)$ & $B)$. By classical reasoning, $\vdash (A \rightarrow B) \vee \neg B$, or equivalently $B \vdash A \rightarrow B$. Substitute $\neg B$ for B, so as to get:

(i) $\quad \neg B \vdash A \rightarrow \neg B$

This, together with $A \rightarrow B \vdash A \rightarrow B$, yields $(A \rightarrow B)$ & $\neg B \vdash (A \rightarrow B)$ & $(A \rightarrow \neg B)$. So, by the monotonicity of classical entailment:

(ii) $\quad (A$ & $(A \rightarrow B))$ & $\neg B \vdash (A \rightarrow B)$ & $(A \rightarrow \neg B)$

By *Ad Falsum*, (A & (A → B)) & ¬B ⊢ ¬A, which by classical reasoning yields the principle of material entailment we introduced when introducing Gibbard's proof. From this point on, since we established logicality and we also have import/export, Gibbard's argument takes us the rest of the way to collapse.   □

Assertion, Prediction, and the Future

I am about to turn this record over to its side B. Side A focused on semantics, finishing off with an extended discussion of complicated technical matters. I indulged in the temptation because the complicated puzzles involving the integration of predictive expressions with the modal system cannot go unremarked. Side B turns to less-technical concerns about future-directed discourse, assertion, and all that.

The guiding question of Part IV is whether there is a sense in which the future is open. Part V will turn to some epistemic and cognitive questions about future-directed thought.

My aim in Part IV is not to address metaphysical questions without doing metaphysics, but rather to work out what consequences different metaphysical views concerning the nature of the future would have for a theory of linguistic communication. As an example of this kind of question, consider whether the intuition that the future is open should be viewed as having an effect on the truth-conditions of statements about the future.

The semantic framework of Parts II and III did not require much of a stand on these questions. This strikes me as an element of good design, but the semantics and the pragmatics of future discourse do impact the metaphysical dialectic concerning the open future. Conversely, fundamental metaphysical commitments can impact the overall theory of future-directed discourse. In Part IV, I seek to elaborate some of these connections.

The core negative argument starts in Chapter 10. Here I remix an old problem for the branching metaphysics. Following in the footsteps of Lewis (1986a), Besson and Hattiangadi (2014), and others, I claim that thinking about assertion poses a difficult challenge for some standard accounts of the intuition that the future is open. More specifically, I argue that widely accepted claims about the rules of assertion conflict with the idea, common among branching theorists, that the openness of the future should be interpreted in terms of the claim that future contingents are neither true nor false. In Chapter 11, I develop a positive account of how one might retrieve a sense in which the future is open without claiming that future contingents are neither true nor false. While the account is more or less independent of the formal semantics I have developed in Parts II and III, the two proposals dovetail nicely.[1]

This dialectic is moot, however, if there are no assertions about the future. Moreover, some theorists have maintained that we do not truly make assertions about the future. Instead, we make mere *predictions*, which are speech acts that are less committal than assertions. We saw this attitude in a quote from Huddleston and Pullum (2002). Let me repeat that quote one more time:

> There is a close intrinsic connection between futurity and modality: our knowledge of the future is inevitably much more limited than our knowledge about the past and the present, and what we say about the future will typically be perceived as having the character of prediction rather than an unqualified factual assertion.

It is puzzling that Huddleston and Pullum slide from a semantic claim (that there is a connection between futurity and modality) to an epistemic one (that our knowledge of the future is limited) to a speech-act theoretic one (that "what we say about the future" is a prediction, as opposed to an unqualified factual assertion). My aim is to disentangle the different components of this slide and to reach an individually coherent understanding of the semantics, the epistemology, and the pragmatics of future discourse.

But back to the main dialectic, if we don't make assertions about the future – if there is a special-purpose speech act that is reserved for future discourse – there is no point in thinking about how assertions of future-directed claims constrain the interface between semantics and metaphysics. For this reason, that ground needs to be cleared right away with a defense of the thesis that we do make assertions about the future. This is the job of Chapter 9, where I develop a theory of the speech act of prediction.[2] This theory makes it clear that accepting that prediction is a distinctive speech act is not incompatible with, and in fact *invites*, the thesis that we make assertions about the future.

---

[1] I emphasize that this account does not signal acceptance of the idea that the future is open in some objectively significant sense. I view Part IV as an exploration of a non-negligible portion of my philosophical credence function – the portion I allocate to open future theses.

[2] This chapter is published with minor differences as a self-standing piece, Cariani (2020), in the journal *Ergo*.

CHAPTER 9

On Predicting

Predicting is widely believed to be a matter of making assertions (or speech acts that are assertion-like) about the future. Both pieces of that understanding are questionable. Predicting is not essentially asserting, though it sometimes is; and the contents of acts of prediction are not essentially about the future, though they often are. In this chapter, I propose a theory of predicting that captures its relation to asserting as well as the sense in which it appears to essentially involve the future. Although predicting is not essentially asserting, I will claim that many speech acts about the future count as *both* predictions and assertions.

My discussion is structured around two puzzles. The *subject-matter* puzzle challenges the thesis that the contents of predictions must be about the future. The *speech act puzzle* concerns the relationship between predicting and asserting. I lead with them to establish the goalposts for the inquiry. With the puzzles on the table, I identify the views of some fellow travelers who agree that predictions are not essentially about the future: I consider first the view that predicting requires future discovery, and then a proposal by Benton and Turri (2014; henceforth *B&T*) to the effect that predictions are characterized by a constitutive norm (analogous to, but weaker than, the knowledge norm for assertion). I argue that each of these views captures something important about predicting and formulate an account that synthesizes their virtues. It is distinctive of my proposal, and an important part of my argument, that the speech act of prediction is multiply realized: Some predictions are also assertions, while others are not.

Parts of this chapter are drawn from my article by the same title ("On Predicting") to be published in *Ergo*. Per the journal policy, I retained the copyright to this material. But in any case, it is reprinted here with the informal approval of the *Ergo* editors, and I thank them for that.

The arguments to come require us to have minimally reliable heuristics for determining what counts as an act of prediction. I propose two, very rough, sufficient conditions:

PERFORMATIVE PREDICTION. An act is a prediction if it is a speech act whose vehicle is a sentence of the form *I predict that* ….

The idea behind this terminology is to analogize predictions to promises, apologies, and other speech acts that are canonically executed by performing another speech act – e.g., by asserting or, as Searle and Vanderveken (1985) prefer, by *declaring* something. The classification of predictions as performatives is supported by standard tests for performativity such as "hereby" insertion (Austin, 1975), as in *I hereby predict that they will lose the match*. And indeed, "predict" is typically treated as a performative verb, e.g., in Searle and Vanderveken (1985).

As a point of terminology, I say that the content of a performative prediction *I predict that* **A** is the proposition that **A** – as opposed to the proposition that the speaker predicts that **A**. Again, an analogy with promises can help illuminate this point. When I promise that I will take the kids to the park, the content of my promise (i.e., what I promise) is that I will take the kids to the park.

Evidently, not all predictions are performative. One can predict that it will snow overnight just by uttering the sentence *it will snow overnight*. For this reason, I distinguish a second kind of predictive speech act:

TRANSPARENT PREDICTION. A prediction that **A** is *transparent* if and only if its vehicle expresses the proposition that **A**.

How to recognize transparent predictions? I propose the *voiceover heuristic*: Individual speech acts are classified as predictions if we can felicitously imagine a voiceover continuation like *that prediction turned out to be right (/wrong)*. Some examples:

(1)   a.   *A*: This plane will land on time.
             Voiceover: That prediction turned out to be wrong.
       b.   *B* (staring out of a window): It's raining.
             Voiceover: * That prediction turned out to be wrong.

There might be predictions that are neither performative nor transparent, but in such cases I set them aside.[1]

---

[1]   It is an established point in speech-act theory that we should be wary of linking speech acts with hard-and-fast principles connecting a sentence's form and the force of its uses (Green, 2017). So there

One last piece of ground-clearing before we begin in earnest. In addition to its speech-act meaning, "prediction" has a meaning in which it picks out theoretical predictions, as in:

(2)   Special relativity predicts that a twin in a high-speed rocket, as viewed by her Earth-bound sister, will have a slower-ticking clock.[2]

There are clear limits on how tight the connection between predicting and theoretical predictions can be. To start, theoretical predictions differ from speech acts in their ontological status. Speech acts are widely understood to be events and endowed with the kind of structure that is distinctive of acts. In particular, *qua* acts are events that have an agent. Thus, they can meaningfully be said to be subject to norms – and in particular, to the sort of norms that Benton and Turri (2014) and I invoke in our respective characterizations. By contrast, theoretical predictions are not events, but propositions. In particular, the predictions of a theory T are some (but not all) of the propositions that T entails. As such, they have whatever ontology propositions have.[3] If, for instance, propositions are abstract objects (e.g., sets of worlds), then theoretical predictions are those very same abstract objects. Then, if a normative theory of the speech act of prediction is correct, there is no unified analysis that can capture both acts of prediction and theoretical predictions. Nonetheless, I will argue in the final section of the chapter that this pessimistic observation leaves us room to theorize about how these concepts are connected.

9.1   Predicting ≠ Forecasting: An Easy Piece

Sappose that a forecast is an assertion-like speech act whose content is entirely about the future. According to the *future content* hypothesis, predictions are forecasts in this sense.

Authors with disparate commitments and diverse backgrounds accept the future content hypothesis. According to Searle (1985), prediction is

---

might well be predictions that are neither performative nor transparent. However, none of the points made in this chapter strictly depends on this distinction being exhaustive, and ignoring this complication streamlines the presentation.

[2]   https://physics.aps.org/synopsis-for/10.1103/PhysRevLett.113.120405

[3]   Of course, each act of prediction is also associated with a proposition – the content of the prediction. (Suppose that the contents of acts of prediction are *S*-predictions.) Unfortunately, the existence of *S*-predictions is not enough to forge a tight connections between theoretical predictions and acts of prediction. Although propositions are involved in both cases, *S*-predictions can, and theoretical predictions cannot, be characterized in terms of norms governing the behavior of an agent.

an assertive (i.e., it signals commitment to truth and has a word-to-world direction of fit) with future subject matter:

> The differences … between a report and a prediction involve the fact that a prediction must be about the future whereas a report can be about the past or present. (Searle, 1985, p. 6)

Sperber and Wilson (1986, p. 245) follow suit:

> [W]hat makes an utterance a prediction is that [the speaker] ostensively communicates an assumption with a certain property, that of being about a future event at least partly beyond her control.

And here is Isaac Levi (2007, p. 1):

> Prediction … can be understood to express full belief in the truth of some claim about the future or a judgment as to how probable some conjecture about the future is to be true.

The problem for the future content hypothesis is that some predictions are not about future events. Indeed, it is possible to make predictions that are entirely about the present or the past (see also Benton and Turri, 2014, section 2). Here are two cases that illustrate two different ways in which predictions may concern past events.

(3)   Steph Curry is about to take a free throw. Elena is watching the game and says, "I predict he'll make it." But the game is actually on tape delay. Curry has already made the free throw.

(4)   Simona takes a test at 9 AM, then leaves for vacation. The test is graded instantly but Simona has not let her friends know the outcome. One of her friends goes on to say, "I predict that she passed."

In the first case, the actual temporal reference seems to have been replaced by a "story-internal" temporal reference, as if the basketball game was a fiction endowed with its own temporal sequence. To illustrate, when reading *Dr. Zhivago*, one might predict that Yuri Zhivago will die – meaning that he will die *by the end of the story*. Yuri's death is not in the future with respect to the predictor's context, but rather is in the future within the timeline of the story. Perhaps prediction can operate on the basis of such a simulated timeline. If that is true, then (3) does not by itself refute a suitably modified future content view.

Things are different with (4). The speech act in (4) meets our sufficient conditions for qualifying as a prediction: It is a flawless performative prediction.[4] Moreover, (4) is a more striking counterexample than (3), since it does not suggest futurity with respect to a surrogate timeline. What seems to have to be in the future in (4) is the time at which the participants will receive conclusive evidence on the question whether Simona passed (I consider an account that builds on this hunch in Section 9.3).

As another example in this vein, imagine a classroom of preschoolers playing a game in which they have to guess, without looking, what object is inside a box. The teacher might ask: *Do you have any predictions about what is in the box?* A student answers: *It's a toy car!* The student made a prediction but nothing about the subject matter of the prediction is in the future.

Our first puzzle then is, how should we conceive of prediction if not in terms of the future content hypothesis? The etymology suggests that predicting involves saying something *ahead of* something else. Of course, that etymology might well not be worth taking seriously. But if it is, we might wonder what that something else is, given that it's not the content of the prediction that relates it to the future.

9.2 Predicting versus Asserting

On to the second puzzle: How are predicting and asserting related? Two conflicting ideas spring to mind.

THE SUBKIND THESIS. Every act of prediction is also an assertion.
THE INCOMPATIBILITY THESIS. No act of prediction is also an assertion.

A paradigmatic implementation of the subkind thesis is the idea that predictions are assertions about future states of affairs. A paradigmatic implementation of the incompatibility thesis is the idea that prediction and assertion are incompatible speech acts that share some traits because they belong to a common genus. An example of this view is the idea, mentioned earlier, that there is a class of "assertives" that includes speech

---

[4] It is easy to imagine a simple variation on the story in (4) in which Simona's friend makes a felicitous transparent prediction.

acts as diverse as asserting and guessing.⁵ Of course, acknowledging that they have commonalities is consistent with the incompatibility thesis.

One's choice among such options is consequential for the theory of assertion. Several theorists (e.g., Williams, 1994; Weiner, 2005) express the intuition that the epistemic standards for prediction are weaker than knowledge. If that supposition is accepted, and if one accepts the subkind thesis, the standard for assertion must sometimes be weaker than knowledge.⁶ Alternatively, a defender of the knowledge account of assertion might feel tempted to reverse this argument and conclude that predictions cannot be assertions.

The subkind thesis cannot be right, as can be shown by focusing on an interesting and under-appreciated datum involving performative predictions. Unlike assertions, performative predictions can felicitously be followed by Moorean professions of ignorance in the predicted proposition.⁷

(5)   I predict that she will win but I don't know that she will.

However, it is a fundamental characteristic of assertions that they cannot be followed by professions of ignorance.

(6)   * She won but I don't know that she did.

Relatedly, performative predictions are permissible even if based on purely statistical evidence. In a fair lottery, one may felicitously utter *I predict that my ticket will not win*. But one may not outright assert *my ticket will not win*.

The upshot is that performative predictions fail to satisfy two important tests that are plausibly requirements of assertion. Such tests are often

<hr>

⁵ I want to take this opportunity to highlight some fresh, currently unpublished work on guessing by Kevin Dorst and Matt Mandelkern and (separately) by Ben Holguin. In future work, I hope to explore more systematic connection between predicting and guessing.

⁶ Some views of assertion suggest that the standard for assertion is context-sensitive and can sometimes be knowledge, and sometimes weaker than knowledge (Levin, 2008; Goldberg, 2015). In the main text, I have in mind a non-context-sensitive knowledge norm.

⁷ An anonymous reviewer for *Ergo* highlighted (though not as an objection to this point) that it is bad to say:

I predict that she will win but I don't know that I predict that she will.

This might be thought of as (mild) evidence that *I predict that* A is an assertion whose content is that I predict the proposition that A. Of course, it is important to keep in mind the gap between this and the further commitment of the subkind thesis – namely, that a speech act whose vehicle is *I predict that* A predicts the proposition that A. It is this further commitment that is up for criticism in the main text.

leveraged in support of the knowledge account of assertion (Williamson, 2000), but accepting the tests as diagnostics for assertion does not require commitment to the knowledge account.[8] Instead, all that is required is that assertions be incompatible with professions of ignorance, however that incompatibility might be explained, and that they be defective if made on the basis of purely statistical evidence. Given that sentences like (5) are felicitous, that they are predictions, and that their felicity does not exploit specific features of context, we must conclude that some predictions are not assertions.

One can undoubtedly resist this argument by insisting that the tests are not requirements of assertion. The ensuing dispute would be partly terminological. Although I am not authorized to issue fines to those who delimit assertion differently than I do here, there is a theoretically valuable class of speech acts for which the tests *are* diagnostic. Referring to the class of speech acts that are pinned down by these tests as "assertions" is, in my view, a legitimate way to use the term. With that said, this argument can be extended by noting related contrasts involving other concepts:

(7)   a.   I predict that she will win but I am not committed to that.
      b.   I predict that she will win but I am not certain.
      c.   I predict that she will win but she might not.

(8)   a.   * She won but I am not committed to that.
      b.   * She won but I am not certain she did.
      c.   * She won but it might be that she did not win.

These asymmetries are pervasive and distinguish performative predictions from ordinary assertions on a broad variety of views about assertion, including commitment views in the style of Brandom (1994) and context update views in the style of Stalnaker (1978).

The failure of the subkind thesis should not be taken as support for the incompatibility thesis. In fact, I think the incompatibility thesis is also false: Acts of transparent prediction have all the hallmarks of assertion. Of course, defenders of the incompatibility thesis would agree that there are important similarities between predictions and assertions, but still insist that they are different – much as two species within the same genus might be different. However, if the incompatibility thesis were true, transparent predictions would have to lack some of the critical features of assertion.

---

[8]   Proponents of the truth rule of assertion often agree with Williamson about such data and seek to account for them with different resources. See, for example, MacFarlane (2014, section 5.5).

The problem for the incompatibility thesis is that they don't. For example, Benton (2012) argues that the key diagnostics that support the knowledge account of assertion also apply to *transparent* predictions. In particular, Moorean profession of ignorance is just as bad with transparent predictions as it is with past-directed assertions like (6).

(9) * She will win but I don't know that she will.

Against this, Weiner (2005) insists that predictive assertion is compatible with such Moorean denials. However, at the critical point in Weiner's argument at which Moorean data are discussed, it is clear that he has performative predictions in mind:

> Suppose that after Aubrey asserts [*that the French will attack at nightfall,*] Pullings asks, "How do you know that the French will attack at night fall?" and Aubrey responds,
>
> (10) I don't know they'll attack at nightfall – we haven't intercepted their orders – but my prediction is that they will.
>
> (Weiner, 2005, p. 235; square brackets are my insertions and Weiner's example numbering is replaced with mine)

Performative predictions are not probative in this context, since our question is precisely whether transparent predictions behave like them or in some other way. In sum, Benton's observation that (9) has the distinctive badness of Moorean denials strikes me as strong as any in this literature, so it is admitted into evidence as far as the present discussion goes.

This behavior of transparent predictions also sharply distinguishes them from "hedged assertions" (Benton and Van Elswyk, 2018). Consider this example as an illustration:

(11) She won, I think, but I don't know for sure.

There is no reason to think that assertions about the future *have to be* hedged, and their incompatibility with Moorean denials helps emphasize that.[9]

[9] A reviewer for *Ergo* identifies a much more promising way to appeal to hedged assertions. One might think that (i) *performative* predictions are hedged assertions and (ii) what I called "transparent predictions" are simply ordinary assertions. This proposal innovates over much of the literature I engage with here by obviating the need for a special theory of prediction. I have some faith in the first claim: While its development would be very different from what is to follow, there would be important connections between the resulting theories. I am much less concessive about the second claim. My discussion is founded on the strong intuition that *some* predictions involve neither explicit hedges nor markers of performativity – not even ones that are inherited

Transparent predictions also behave like assertions in other important respects. As with assertions, it is erroneous to make transparent predictions only on the basis of purely statistical evidence. While Williamson (2000, p. 245) relies on past-directed examples (e.g., *your ticket did not win*), it is just as bad – Weiner's (2005) intuition notwithstanding – to assert *Your ticket will not win* on purely statistical evidence, absent any sort of hedge.[10]

Taking a more general perspective, it would be bizarre if a conceptual barrier existed whereby simple declarative sentences such as *it will rain* just could not be used to make assertions.

I said that there would be a puzzle at the end of this discussion, and so far not much seems puzzling about these observations. Taken together, they guide us toward a surprising conclusion: Performative predictions are not assertions, and transparent predictions typically *are* assertions. It follows that there is no uniform relation between predictions and assertions: They are independent speech acts, in the sense that a single act can be both, one, or neither. I think this *is* the correct moral and, yes, not much of a puzzle, in light of the observations. But the observations are puzzling because not everyone will find this view congenial. Moreover, they do guide us toward an outstanding puzzle: How should we understand the speech act of prediction so that it's distinct from assertion but also clear that one and the same act can be *both* a prediction and an assertion?

9.3   The Future Discovery View

The key case I relied on when rejecting the future content hypothesis immediately suggests an alternative view. I repeat the case here with its original numbering:

(4)   Simona takes a test at 9 AM, then leaves for vacation. The test is graded instantly but Simona has not let her friends know the outcome. One of her friends goes on to say, "I predict that she passed."

---

from the surrounding context. This judgment may not be universally accepted, but it is sufficiently clear and strong to warrant theorizing on it.

[10]   Quick dialectic check: Although I am using Weiner as a foil, he would agree that the incompatibility thesis is false and that transparent predictions are assertions. However, the reasons I am offering for that are strictly incompatible with Weiner's outlook. He doesn't take incompatibility with Moorean denials to be even diagnostic of assertion.

The most distinctive feature of (4) is that although the time of the event is in the past, the question whether Simona passed isn't settled until a time that follows the prediction. That fact appears to play an important role in explaining why the final utterance in (4) is a prediction.

We could stretch this insight to form a new view (*NB*: not *my* view). The *discovery view* agrees with the future content view that prediction includes a future element. However, it diverges by claiming that what has to be future in a prediction that p is the time of discovery – that is, the time at which the question whether p is settled. Here is a slightly more precise statement.

THE FUTURE-DISCOVERY ACCOUNT OF PREDICTING. A speech act a with content p is a prediction if and only if

(D0) a is an assertive.
(D1) The truth-value of p is not settled by the evidence that is collectively available to the participants to the conversation.
(D2) The question whether p will be settled by forthcoming evidence.

It is difficult, and perhaps even impossible, to analyze the phrase "settled by evidence" as it occurs here. Still, without attempting to define it, we can try to illuminate it. Belief states are often viewed as closing off inquiry on some subject matter. According to this view, acquiring a belief that p is relevantly similar to adopting a plan: It involves some degree of close-mindedness about further deliberation on p (Friedman, 2019). In the belief case, this close-mindedness is only appropriate when one's evidence is strong enough to warrant closing deliberation. So, to make sense of what it is to be "settled by evidence," we can think in terms of whatever level of evidence is strong enough for someone to acquire that warrant.

Setting aside the details of how this insight could be developed, it is evident that the discovery view classifies the speech act in (4) as a prediction. It has the features of assertives (i.e., commitment to truth and a word-to-world direction of fit), and it meets D1 and D2. The collective evidence leaves it open whether Simona passed the test, and in the provided context it is reasonable to assume that the conversational participants will find out whether she did indeed pass. A similar treatment applies to the preschool object-in-a-box example: When a child answers *It's a toy car!*, her expression counts as making a prediction because the current evidence does not settle the contents of the box and because the class will soon discover what is in the box.[11] Surprisingly, the discovery view even accounts for the tape delay example in (3), without any additions involving surrogate timelines. What makes Elena's speech act a prediction is that the time at which the relevant conversational participants will find out whether Steph made the free throw lies in the future.

Benton and Turri (2014) object that the discovery view – which they interpret somewhat differently than I do – attaches the wrong subject matter to predictions.

> The primary problem with the [Discovery] view is that it mischaracterizes what our predictions are about. When we make the prediction, "Boston will win the series in five games", it doesn't seem to us that we're making a prediction about what we'll learn about the outcome of the series. Rather, it seems to us that the truth of our prediction depends solely on the outcome of the series. (*B&T*, p. 1861)

B&T are correct in emphasizing the importance of subject matter. However, not every version of the discovery view gets the subject matter of predictions wrong – and specifically the view in DO–DI–D2 doesn't. The kinds of views that are affected by *B&T*'s objection are those that claim *I predict that it will rain* is approximately synonymous with *I predict we'll discover that it will rain*. But the version of the theory just sketched makes no such claim. Instead, it claims that future discovery is a necessary condition for predicting, which is compatible with it not being reflected in the content of the speech act.

B&T advance a second, independent objection:

> Late in life, Edwin Hubble lobbied for the Nobel Prize Committee to make work in astronomy eligible for the Nobel Prize in physics. At the time of Hubble's death, the Committee hadn't re-classified work in astronomy. Suppose that on his deathbed Hubble said, "I predict that the Committee will make work in astronomy eligible for the Nobel Prize in physics." Hubble's prediction isn't falsified by the fact that he died before learning that the Committee did re-classify astronomy. (*B&T*, p. 1861)

B&T's reasoning is that, according to the future discovery view, Hubble's speech act counts as a prediction only if Hubble got to find out whether

---

[11] This example also helps illuminate why condition DI needs to refer to the collectively available evidence, as opposed to the individual evidence. Suppose that one child already knows what object is in the box because she peeked ahead of time; when she says *It's a toy car!* her utterance should still count as a prediction.

the Nobel Prize reclassified astronomy. But he did not get to find out, so his speech act does not count as a prediction.[12]

This objection succeeds against versions of the discovery view that make it a necessary condition that the *speaker* will find out. But, here again, we must be careful to note that it does not strike against every version of the discovery view. The discovery view formulated here – though somewhat vague about what it is for evidence to be forthcoming – does not state this requirement. It only demands that the question be answered at some point relative to some body of evidence that is suitably related to the community in which the prediction takes place.

With that said, there is an immediate generalization of *B&T*'s second objection that targets every version of the discovery view that includes a constraint like D2. Some predictions concern events that future evidence is not guaranteed to settle. Here is an example borrowing from an unrelated discussion in Dummett (1959):

(12)   A city will never be built here.

If a city is built on the relevant spot, someone will indeed find out. But if no city is ever built on the relevant spot, no one will find out.[13] Despite that, someone who uttered (12) ought to be counted as making a prediction – both by direct intuition and by the voiceover test.

The generalization in the neighborhood is that predicting that p does not require that it be settled that the question whether p will be conclusively answered at all. It does not have to be settled for the speaker, for the addressee, or for anyone else.

Another, related reason for concern is that some predictions target conditional claims.[14] Consider the following statement:

[12]   *B&T* say that the prediction isn't "falsified" but I think it is not charitable to interpret them to mean this. Whether the prediction is true or false is not at issue here, but rather whether the speech act is to be classified as a prediction. The reason *B&T* talk about the prediction being "falsified" is that they interpret the discovery view as claiming that *I predict that p* entails *I will discover that p*. I have already objected to that part of their view, but I think this objection is instructive when reinterpreted along the lines that I present here.

[13]   The case might be spelled out so that someone can find out even if no city will never be built on that site. What matters to my argument is that the case *can also* be set up so that no one will find out.

[14]   I say "predictions that target conditional claims" instead of "conditional predictions" because the latter might be interpreted as analogous to conditional assertion, which I do not intend to discuss here. A conditional assertion is an assertion that is made under a condition. If the condition is not satisfied, no assertion takes place (see Goldstein, in press b, for a recent discussion of the theory of conditional assertion). By analogy, a conditional prediction ought to be a prediction that is made under some condition, so that the condition is not satisfied if no prediction has taken place. It is an interesting question whether there are conditional predictions in this sense, but I won't tackle this question here.

(13)   If we put cats on a spaceship, they would find a way to survive

The discovery view fails to classify conditional predictions as predictions, and for the same reasons why it fails on potentially unsettled predictions like (12). Namely, it cannot be settled that the question concerning the content of the prediction will be answered, because conditional predictions weigh on conditional questions. If the antecedent of the conditional question is not satisfied, then there is no expectation that the conditional question will be conclusively answered.

9.4   The Proper Expectation Account

Benton and Turri leverage their criticisms of the future content and future discovery views into an alternative account. They maintain that the speech act of prediction is characterized by its constitutive norms – drawing on Williamson's (2000) defense of the knowledge account of assertion. In particular, predictions are characterized by a norm that requires the speaker's credence to have a particular kind of structure and a particular relation to the speaker's evidence.

Williamson characterizes assertion in terms of core rules (the "constitutive rules"), on the basis of an extended analogy between the rules governing speech acts and the rules governing games.[15] Following and expanding on Unger (1975), Williamson suggests characterizing assertion as the unique speech act whose constitutive rule is:

KNOWLEDGE ACCOUNT OF ASSERTION. One may assert p only if one knows p.

---

[15]   Williamson appropriates the phrase "constitutive rules" from speech act theory (e.g., Searle 1969), but emphasizes a critical respect that is underappreciated in the speech-act theory canon. For Searle, a constitutive rule r for practice π is that if r is not obeyed, then participants are not engaging in π. According to this conception, constitutive rules both define a practice and state necessary and sufficient conditions for it. Williamson emphasizes that there is a critical conceptual space between defining a practice and stating necessary and sufficient conditions for it.

> Constitutive rules do not lay down necessary conditions for performing the constituted act. When one breaks a rule of a game, one does not thereby cease to be playing that game. When one breaks a rule of a language, one does not thereby cease to be speaking that language; speaking English ungrammatically is speaking English. Likewise, presumably, for a speech act: When one breaks a rule of assertion, one does not thereby fail to make an assertion. One is subject to criticism precisely because one has performed an act for which the rule is constitutive.

> Williamson is right. The "travel" rule in basketball is part of a rule-based definition of the game of basketball. But if a player travels during a game, they are still playing basketball.

B&T follow a similar playbook in their normative account of prediction. According to these theorists, prediction is the unique speech act subject to:

PROPER EXPECTATION RULE FOR PREDICTION. One may predict p if and only if one properly expects p.

It is interesting and unusual that *B&T* state their norm in terms of a biconditional. It is standard protocol to state norms for speech acts as necessary conditions for permissibility – not as necessary *and sufficient* ones. This protocol arises because if the force of the permission modal *may* is left unspecified, a performance of a speech act might be classified as impermissible for reasons that have nothing to do with the constitutive norms for that speech act. Having acknowledged this point, however, it's reasonably clear what *B&T* have in mind. They mean, as far as *constitutive* requirements go, proper expectation is the only standard: One may predict p only if one properly expects p; any other form of impermissibility must result from violations of principles that are not constitutive of prediction. To see why this might work, consider an analogy: The game of chess could be characterized in terms of a biconditional pinning down the set of permissible moves at any point in a game. Such a biconditional might not rule out rude behavior, but it would not follow from that omission that rude behavior is permitted during chess matches. The job of the biconditional is to pin down permitted behavior only *as far as the rules of chess go*.

Perhaps the most urgent clarification concerns what it is to "properly expect" something. According to *B&T*, the mental state of expectation is primitive. They gloss it as follows:

> ([M]ere) expectation is a mental state of slight commitment, which requires regarding a proposition as more likely than not. (p. 1862)

One expects *properly* when one's expectations are, in some sense, sanctioned as correct by one's evidence:

> One's mere expectation that p will be "proper" when one's credences are apportioned to one's evidence, namely when one's evidence makes p more likely than not-p. (p. 1862)

It is particularly instructive to understand how *B&T*'s proper expectation norm relates prediction to assertion. As they highlight (p. 1865), the proper expectation account makes it possible for overlap to occur between predicting and asserting. At the same time, the proper expectation account explains why not all predictions are assertions: Predicting is a game that can be played for a cheaper price than asserting (i.e., by subjecting oneself to lower epistemic standards). In some contexts – when the information about the most urgent subject matter does not quite meet the epistemic standards for assertion – a speaker might wish to play the cheaper game only.

The proper expectation account threads nicely through our motivating puzzles. It does not demand that the contents of predictions be in the future, so it can account for the evidence that doomed the future content view. Likewise, it does not demand that future discovery be on the horizon. For that reason, it is immune to the criticisms we raised against the future discovery view. Someone who predicts that a city will never be built on this spot might well possess evidence that favors this claim over its negation.

Though the proper expectation account marks a striking advance in our understanding of prediction, it has some problems that suggest we should look for a refinement.

Consider first what the proper expectation view predicts about present-directed certainties. Suppose I am staring out my window and I see heavy rain. Obviously, I meet the conditions for properly expecting that it's raining. The credences that are appropriate to my evidential state all favor raining over the alternatives. But it does not seem plausible to say that I can predict that it's raining.[16] The attempted performative prediction *I predict that it's raining* is infelicitous (or, in the right context, an attempt at a joke). I can, of course, assert that it's raining – but in this case the voiceover heuristic suggests that I'm not, after all, predicting.

(14) A: It's raining.
   Voiceover: * That prediction turned out to be right.

B&T gesture toward an account of the infelicity of such predictions within their theory. They propose that the existence of strength relations between speech acts that are somewhat parallel to strength relations between contents. It is a basic Gricean point that (cooperative) assertion is governed by a "assert-the-stronger" rule. It can be defective (because it's uncooperative) to assert that one believes it's raining when one knows it's raining. Similarly, assertive speech acts might be governed by a "perform-the-stronger" rule:

> If you're going to perform an assertive speech act, you should perform the strongest assertive that your evidence permits (and no stronger).

---

[16] This case is reminiscent of a case discussed in von Fintel and Gillies (2010) to illustrate the evidentiality of epistemic *must*. Despite the different theoretical domain, there seems to be a connection between the requirement of "indirectness" that von Fintel and Gillies discuss for *must* and the parallel requirement that appears to be operative in prediction.

So, the account goes, I cannot predict that it's raining because I can assert that it's raining. Because assertion is the stronger (i.e., more demanding) assertive speech act, that's what I should perform.

This reasoning fails for two independent reasons. First, "perform-the-stronger" operates as *B&T* expect it to only when it applies to incompatible speech acts – speech acts that cannot be performed simultaneously. Part of what motivates the "assert-the-stronger" rule is that any one assertion can be an assertion of only *one* content. But a key claim of the present discussion is that prediction and assertion are not incompatible: One and the same speech act can be *both*. Since they are governed by compatible constitutive rules, there is no metaphysical or normative barrier to performing an act that is subject to both sets of rules.

Perhaps *B&T* presuppose that though they are governed by compatible constitutive rules, one can never perform both speech acts with a single event of utterance. I don't see a reason to accept this argument. Two basketball teammates might engage in a competition about who can score more free throws with their off hand during a professional game. If so, their free throws would be simultaneously subject to both the rules of basketball and the rules of their game-within-the-game. Indeed, this point is familiar from the theory of speech acts itself. A mainstream view of performative utterances, such as *I promise to clean my room*, is that they involve two, overlapping speech acts: a promise to clean my room and another speech act such as an assertion, or a declaration, that I promise to do so (Searle and Vanderveken, 1985, p. 4, and, more extensively, chapter 7).[17]

A second problem with *B&T*'s account of why one cannot predict past and present certainties is that, much like the maxim of quantity that it mirrors, "perform-the-stronger" requires a fully cooperative context. As Mitchell Green (1995) notes, Grice's maxim of quantity seems suspended in certain contexts of strategic conversation – for example, if I am testifying in a court setting.[18] While the strategic context still requires a substantial amount of cooperation, there need be no presumption that one must be informative to the point that one must always assert the stronger of two

[17] A reviewer notes that an interesting theoretical perspective on this point emerges from the "semanticized" analysis of performatives in Condoravdi and Lauer (2011). Condoravdi and Lauer make a strong case that performative utterances are in the first instance assertions. On my reading, however, Condoravdi and Lauer are generally neutral on the ontological question of whether multiple speech acts are associated with a performative.

[18] See also Asher and Lascarides (2013). Furthermore, recent work in philosophy of language, such as Camp (2018), draws attention to the fact that noncooperative contexts are probably the norm, rather than outliers to be excluded from the analysis.

(relevant) propositions. The fact some inferences traditionally associated with the maxim of quantity still seem to go through in such contexts is evidence that they aren't entirely based on the kinds of reasoning outlined by Grice.

Something similar should also hold for the "perform-the-stronger" rule. Since this rule is based on the insight that we should maximize the informative upshot of our speech acts, it ought to be suspended in contexts that, for whatever reason, are less than fully cooperative. And yet it is still bad in such contexts to make predictions about things that one is certain of. Even in the courtroom, I cannot predict p when I and my interlocutors share direct, conclusive evidence in favor of p.

Reflecting on such cases leads to another concern for the proper expectation account. Though I have argued at length (and concur with *B&T*) that there can be predictions about the past, their distribution is limited in ways that the proper expectation account does not address. One can predict past and present eventualities only if there is some reason to believe that one will find out what that answer is. Suppose that, a few decades out of high school, I am looking at the photo of a basketball team I played on back then. The photo reminds me of my teammate Sam, who was a passionate, committed player and a remarkable athlete. It is odd for me to say:

(15) *? I predict that Sam still plays basketball to this day.

But the reason why it is odd need not be that I don't have a proper expectation. I may have excellent evidence that people with Sam's skill, passion, and commitment tend to stay active as players.

What I suggest is that the extent to which (15) is licensed depends on the degree to which we have reason to expect direct evidence. This is the kind of phenomenon that the discovery view gets right. If we lack a reason to expect that we will find out, (15) sounds bad. However, if we imagine modifying the context to suggest that we will (or might) find out, the status of the prediction improves. For instance, suppose I am about to attend the twenty-year reunion of the basketball team; I expect to learn what Sam ended up doing. In such a context, (15) may well be a flawless utterance.

A third concern, which for now I will leave a little vague, is that the proper expectation view says too little about the relation between predicting and theoretical prediction. In Section 9.7, I will highlight that if we accept my proposal, we can draw some links between theoretical prediction and the speech act of prediction. I do not think that the story I will tell then generalizes plausibly to the proper expectation account.

As a last remark about the proper expectation view, I note a point of detail. *B&T* say that an expectation is proper when the evidence supports p over $\neg p$. This is too strong. I can nondefectively predict that Spain will win the World Cup without being willing to take the Spanish team over the field. The norm does not capture this behavior, because it requires my evidence to support the proposition that Spain will win more strongly than its negation. The norm ought to be weakened so that one can predict that p as long as evidence supports having greater credence in p than in the relevant alternatives. This observation is not an objection to the proper expectation account since it can be addressed with an easy tweak. Instead, it is best taken as a reason to redefine what counts as a proper expectation. Toward that goal, we can say that one *properly expects* that p when (i) one's credence in p is greater than one's credence in the alternatives and (ii) one's evidence supports these inequalities. In the remainder of this chapter, I will use *proper expectation* in this more generous sense.

9.5   The Synthetic View

I propose an account of predicting that synthesizes elements of both the discovery view and the proper expectation view.

> SYNTHETIC VIEW. Prediction is the unique speech act $\mathcal{A}$ that is governed by the rule that one may perform $\mathcal{A}$ with content p in context c only if:
>
> s1. The contextual evidence in c does not settle whether p.
> s2. It is possible, as far as contextual evidence goes, that evidence that settles the question whether p is forthcoming.
> s3. One properly expects p.

Both conditions s1 and s2 appeal to a notion of "contextual evidence." This could be taken to be the common knowledge of the participants in the conversation. Alternatively, in a more flexible sense, it might be taken as some body of evidence that is salient in context. Under both conceptions, the contextual evidence is not solely determined by the speaker's own epistemic state. In fact, under the flexible interpretation, there might be no connection at all between the contextual evidence and the speaker's evidence – roughly as in "exocentric" uses of epistemic modals

(Egan et al., 2005; Stephenson, 2007) . I will entertain both conceptions in the following discussion, though I will use the common knowledge interpretation as a default.

One point that deserves highlighting is that the sense of possibility in s2 should be a "thick" one. For every unsettled question Q, there is a smidgen of epistemic possibility that Q will be settled in the future. So, it cannot be that any degree of possibility is enough to meet s2. That would trivialize s2, since it would follow that whenever s1 is satisfied, so is s2. Since we are already demanding satisfaction of s1, s2 would be idle. For s2 to not be idle, the relevant sense of *possible* should be closer to *seriously possible*. I won't attempt to analyze this concept of serious possibility, relying instead on general linguistic competence to evaluate individual applications of the theory.

It is possible to weaken clause s3 to the claim that one simply expects p, by dropping the propriety condition. There is a strong intuition here, which s3 accounts for, that one ought not to predict against one's evidence. However, that intuition might be accounted for by claiming that propriety is a normative requirement fir the mental state of expectation. It won't matter to my analysis whether we think of propriety as built into the analysis of the speech act of predicting, or as a separate requirement for mental states of expectation.

The synthetic view threads with ease through the desiderata we accumulated up to this point. Recall from Section 9.3 that we took *B&T*'s first objection to demand that a discovery-based account of predicting should separate the discovery component from the content of the prediction. At that point, I noted that this goal can be accomplished by letting future discovery be a *necessary* condition of predicting and keeping claims about discovery out of the content of prediction. The synthetic proposal also implements something similar to this blueprint, but in a normative setting. According to the synthetic proposal, *normatively* correct prediction (i.e., prediction that complies with the constitutive rules) requires the possibility of future discovery. Thus, we are twice removed from the original proposal: The synthetic view requires less (i.e., serious possibility of future discovery vs. future discovery). Moreover, the sense of "requires" is different. For the original discovery view, future discovery was a necessary condition of prediction. In the context of the synthetic view, the relevant requirement is normative: The possibility of future discovery is a requirement of *permissible* prediction.

The synthetic view also deals handily with *B&T*'s Hubble example. Future discovery need not be up to the speaker. All that is necessary for something to count as a prediction is that future discovery be possible in light of the contextual evidence. In Section 9.3, I noted some related challenges to the Hubble example. For instance, I noted that the naïve future discovery view fails with predictive utterances such as the following:

(16)   A city will never be built here.

The synthetic view handles this by merely requiring that evidence settling *p* might become available. In the city case, we know that if the prediction is true, we will never find out. In contrast, if the prediction is false, the target epistemic state might potentially be informed about it. Very much the same treatment can be extended to predictions of conditional contents. Suppose I predict that if Liz runs, she will win. It is typically not the case that we are guaranteed to find out whether this prediction is correct, but the hybrid view merely requires that this be possible. Indeed, it is possible unless we are certain that Liz doesn't run, or that if Liz runs she won't win. In both of these exceptional cases, the prediction would intuitively be defective.

Discussion of such cases naturally draws attention to the status of those predictions that occur in contexts in which it is settled that we will never find out either way. Suppose we will never find out whether the number of stars is infinite, and it is common knowledge that we won't. The synthetic view predicts that one cannot meet the norm when one predicts that the number of stars is finite. A speaker might well be making a prediction, but they would be making a defective one. I take this to be the correct characterization of the case. It does seem that it is in some sense defective to make such a prediction, even if one had some evidence for it and if one apportioned credence to the evidence in the correct way. The synthetic proposal explains this defectiveness without relying on any additional norms. Those who disagree with me on this verdict might still accept a version of the synthetic view that scratches requirement s2.

Let us move on to the constraints I used to critique *B&T*'s account. First, I mentioned the case of present-directed certainties that are settled by one's direct evidence. I considered a case in which I am staring out of a window at a rainstorm and noted that in such case I cannot felicitously predict that it's raining. The synthetic view explains this as a violation of s1. Second, in the case of the high school basketball photo, the prediction plausibly violates clause s2. In the initial version of the case, we are not given any reason to expect that we will find out. In the variant in which we imagine that we are preparing to attend a reunion, we can felicitously perform the prediction. After all, it is now possible (indeed, likely) that we will find out whether Sam still plays basketball. In general, the synthetic view predicts – correctly in my view – that the appropriateness of predicting will covary with whether there is enough reason to think that we will discover.

Let us stress test the synthetic view one more time. What does the view predict about cases in which an agent wrongly believes that they violate the standards for prediction? Consider a small variant on Simona's exam case: Simona's friend Louise wrongly believes that her evidence settles that Simona passed. As it happens, that is not true: Louise's evidence does not settle that Simona passed. Louise says, *I predict she passed*. This utterance seems defective. But did Louise violate a norm of prediction? It would seem not: The synthetic norm is entirely insensitive to Louise's beliefs on the matter. Here we should fall back on the idea of "secondary propriety" that is sometimes discussed in connection with rules of assertion.[19] The idea is that our behavior (generally speaking) is governed by a meta-norm according to which if an agent is subject to rule *R*, then the agent ought to act in such a way that they know, or at least have enough evidence to suspect, that, they do not violate *R*. For example, in a high-stakes basketball game, it might be irresponsible to run too close to the sideline, even if one is actually inbounds. As far as the rules of basketball go, of course, the only thing that matters is whether the agent is inbounds or out of bounds. But as far as our overall evaluation of the agent goes, her walking too close to the line might be defective – perhaps even deserving of blame. In a similar way, that behavior might be irresponsible, and thus defective, when one does not know that one is complying with the norm – and indeed Louise does not she is complying with the norm.

As a final point of evaluation, I note that the synthetic view may be somewhat weakened to suit alternative theoretical frameworks. Mona Simion and Christoph Kelp have recently challenged Williamson's "constitutive rules" approach to speech acts.[20] According to Simion and Kelp, if some activity is governed by a set of constitutive rules, then an agent cannot systematically violate a (significant) majority of those rules without being seen as ceasing to engage in that activity. But, they argue, one can violate the knowledge norm systematically and still engage in the practice

---

[19] See Williamson (2000, pp. 256–257), DeRose (2002), and Weiner (2005, p. 236). Lackey (2007) argues against the idea of secondary propriety. I find Lackey's arguments striking but not inescapable, though I won't face the escaping challenge here.

[20] Kelp and Simion (2018) and Simion and Kelp (2020). These papers draw on, and aim to strengthen, related arguments by Maitra (2011).

of assertion. As an example, they cite a thinker who under the spell of an evil demon is transformed so that the near totality of her beliefs are mistaken. This hapless victim might still assert things, but those assertions would be systematically false. I have some doubts about the success of this challenge,[21] but the ecumenical point I want to stress is that one can grant the challenge and still tell a story about constitutive rules in a lighter sense. This is exactly what Simion and Kelp do to make sense of the connection between knowledge and assertion. They propose that the generation and distribution of knowledge is an essential part of the *function* of assertion. This might be seen as "constitutive" in a lighter sense: It is essential to refer to knowledge in the specification of the good functioning of an asserting agent. This lighter sense of constitutivity is also a plausible fallback for the synthetic view.

9.6 Predicting and Asserting

Where does the synthetic view leave us when it comes to the relationship between prediction and assertion? Suppose, for definiteness, that assertion is governed by the knowledge rule. Then, prediction and assertion are governed by compatible norms, so that it is metaphysically and normatively possible for a single act a to be both. *A fortiori*, the same is true for norms that set standards for assertion that are weaker than knowledge.[22]

It is critical to this result that, even though someone who asserts p must know the content of their prediction, S's knowing that p is compatible with the existence of contextual uncertainty about p – uncertainty of the sort that is required to license prediction. For example, if "unsettled by contextual evidence" is understood in terms of compatibility with common knowledge, then all that is necessary for the norms to be simultaneously satisfied is that (i) the speaker knows p, (ii) but it is not common knowledge that p among the conversational participants and (iii) it is compatible with common knowledge that an answer to the question whether p is forthcoming.

---

[21] I think that the agent we imagine when we try to imagine someone whose beliefs are nearly totally false is, in fact, not someone whose beliefs are nearly totally false. And if it was, even ordinary conversations with them would sound like conversations with bad chatbots.

[22] This applies to all the weaker norms we have considered – specifically, the truth-norm advocated by Weiner (2005), or the reasonable belief norm of Douven (2006) and Lackey (2007), or the context-sensitive norm of Levin (2008) and Goldberg (2015).

At the same time, the relative weakness of the synthetic norm explains why predictions need not always be assertions (and in this respect it behaves in exactly the same way as *B&T*'s norm). In some contexts, the best one can do is predict without asserting.

9.7 Predicting and Theoretical Prediction

I conclude with some more speculative thoughts about what my proposal suggests about the relation between predicting and theoretical prediction (henceforth T-prediction). By T-prediction, I mean what is described in statements such as:

(17)   Special relativity predicts that a twin in a high-speed rocket, as viewed by her Earth-bound sister, will have a slower-ticking clock.[23]

A large literature on T-prediction in confirmation theory focuses on explaining why prediction appears to provide greater confirmation than accommodation (see Barnes, 2018, for a survey). The puzzle is that this appearance seems to conflict with key tenets of Bayesian confirmation theory. I will set these important questions about the epistemological significance of T-prediction aside.

What is of present interest is the concept of T-prediction that emerges from these discussions and how it might be related to predicting. For example, here is the opening of Maher (1988) – one of the most influential articles on prediction and accommodation:

> It is widely believed that if a piece of evidence for a theory was known at the time the theory was proposed, then it does not confirm the theory as strongly as it would if the evidence had been discovered after the theory was proposed. (p. 273)

Maher seems to be presupposing a definition of T-prediction that links it with discovery.

> p is a theoretical prediction of T iff p is a piece of evidence for T that is not discovered by the time that T is first proposed.

This would seem to be good news for a theory of the speech act of prediction that gives future discovery a role – and, therefore, good news for the

---

[23] https://physics.aps.org/synopsis-for/10.1103/PhysRevLett.113.120405

synthetic view. But in what sense are they connected? As noted in the introduction to this chapter, theoretical predictions are not acts, but rather propositions that are suitably related to theories. This difference in ontology means, among other things, that they are not subject to the kinds of norms that govern speech acts.

The upshot is that if a normative theory of the speech act of prediction is correct, a single analysis cannot simultaneously capture both predicting (the speech act) and T-prediction.

Coming to this realization need not mean that no connection can possibly be drawn between these concepts. A lack of connection between the two senses of *prediction* would be a remarkable surprise, given that many other languages are similar to English in that they have one word that applies to both. The translations of *prediction* into Spanish (*predicción*), Italian (*predizione*), French (*prédiction*), and German (*Voraussage/Vorhersage*) are all flexible in the same way as the English word.

My proposal is that the term *prediction* is polysemous. This polysemy helps explain why there seem to be connections between its different senses and, at the same time, why T-prediction is not simply reducible to a more general kind. The philosophical and linguistic consensus is that polysemy is a different phenomenon from (pure) lexical ambiguity.[24] Polysemy and pure (lexical) ambiguity are two different ways in which a word may have multiple meanings.[25] Slicing concepts somewhat crudely, we say that pure (lexical) ambiguities are cases in which a word is associated with multiple unrelated meanings. The hackneyed example of ambiguity is *bank* (financial institution vs. edge of the river), but consider also the English use of *date* (fruit vs. time vs. outing involving two people). Pure ambiguities might well be, and generally are, historical accidents. By contrast, polysemous expressions have multiple, conceptually connected meanings. An example of polysemy in this sense is the word *book*, which can refer both to the intellectual product (what one assigns in a syllabus) and to its physical copies (what students buy at the bookstore).[26]

---

[24] Hawthorne and Lepore (2011); Sennet (2016); Viebahn (2018).
[25] A terminological note: Some authors use "ambiguity" as a term for the large category of ways in which words might have multiple meanings. Others use "ambiguity" for what I refer to as "pure lexical ambiguity." I have chosen to never use "ambiguity" without modifiers. Instead, I contrast "polysemy" with "pure lexical ambiguity" or "pure ambiguity."
[26] I avoided saying that polysemous expressions have multiple, "related" meanings to dodge an important objection. As Sennet (2016) notes, the ecclesiastical and the ornithological meanings of "cardinal" are related – both originate from the name for the color. However, "cardinal" patterns in fundamental ways like an ambiguous expression.

Because the meanings of polysemous expressions are non-accidentally connected, it is often the case that the patterns that drive the polysemy are replicated across a variety of analogous expressions. For example, Viebahn (2018) notes that the polysemy of *book* has natural analogues in other polysemous expressions that can be used to denote intellectual products: *Speech*, *piece*, and *play* are all examples. We see a similar pattern with *prediction*: This is not the only speech act that has a theoretical counterpart. We speak of the *questions* of physics, biology, etc., just as if we speak of the predictions of such theories.

The hypothesis that *prediction* is polysemous would nicely explain why the dual interpretation is preserved in a variety of languages.[27] After all, instances of polysemy, but not instances of ambiguity, typically travel across languages in just this way.

In addition, there are more directly linguistic reasons to think that the term *prediction* is indeed polysemous. Several linguistic tests attempt to drive a wedge between polysemy and pure lexical ambiguity (Sennet, 2016; Viebahn, 2018). These tests are not perfectly sharp – some polysemous terms might fail some of them – but I will argue that they are dialectically useful despite their imperfection.

First test: Polysemous expressions sound better than purely ambiguous ones in coordinated conjunction contexts. Suppose that Anna wrote a book and sold the rights to a publisher, while Lars sold his copy of *War and Peace* to the used bookstore. Note that (18) is fine, if a little clever.

(18)   Lars and Anna each received money for a book.

Now suppose that Anna received credit for turning in a paper while Lars received a line of credit from his financial institution. It is not felicitous, except perhaps as an unfunny pun, to say:

(19)   & Lars and Anna each received credit today.

Prediction intuitively aligns with the polysemous terms. Suppose that the meteorologist correctly predicted that a hurricane would hit the coast today; suppose also that mainstream climate science T-predicts increased frequency of hurricanes and that today's hurricane clinched the correctness of that (grim) prediction. In such a context, the following is perfect"

---

[27] "In the case of ambiguity, we would not be surprised to find two utterly different words in other communities, but in the case of polysemy we would. A standard piece of linguistic lore is that with ambiguity two words are in play but with polysemy only one with a variety of connected semantic potentials" (Hawthorne and Lepore, 2011, p. 471).

(20)   The meteorologist and climate science each got a prediction right today.

Second, pure ambiguities cannot be felicitously linked in patterns of ellipsis, but at least some polysemies can. Contrast these sentences:

(21)   a.   Geoff is healthy and the food he prepares for his family is, too.
         b.   * Lars got credit and Anna did, too.
         c.   Einstein predicted that stars near the sun would be deflected and his theory did, too.

The elided *healthy* in (21-a) does not have the exact same meaning as the one that occurs in the first conjunct. In one case, *healthy* refers to Geoff's physical status; in the other, it refers to the properties of the food he prepares. But the ellipsis goes through just fine, plausibly because *healthy* is polysemous. By contrast, (21-b) supports only a reading in which Lars and Anna got the same kind of credit. Finally, (21-c) shows that predictions pattern, once again, with polysemies and not with pure ambiguities.[28] The critical point is that the multiple interpretations of *prediction* are systematically unlike the multiple interpretations of a purely ambiguous expression.

Back in Section 9.4, I mentioned that the proper expectation account does not forge a connection between predicting and T-predictions. I noted then that it would be valuable, though perhaps not decisively so, to have an account that created such a connection. In this concluding section, I have added two important claims in support of that model. The first claim is that connection cannot take the form of single definition encompassing both kinds of prediction. Much more plausibly, the connection is well captured by thinking of *prediction* as a polysemous expression. We should then

---

[28]   Many clear cases of polysemy fail this test. Suppose that Anna is trying to identify a book for her book club, while Lars is trying to find something to stabilize the table. Notice the badness of the ellipsis:

     * Anna thought of a book and Lars did, too.

This behavior should convince us that the category of polysemous expressions may itself be dishomogeneous with respect to some of these tests. This does not undermine my main point. There may be a nonbinary spectrum between pure polysemy and pure ambiguity, but *prediction* systematically patterns in ways that are unlike pure ambiguity.

expect the existence of a fundamental core connecting the two meanings of *prediction*. The second claim is that the discovery views and the synthetic view can capture this connection. As we saw in the quote from Maher, future discovery seems to be a critical element of T-predictions. Since it is also a critical element of the discovery view (and of my synthetic view, albeit in modified form), it is a a natural candidate to be the common element that links the two meanings of *prediction*.

CHAPTER 10

Assertion Troubles

Does future-directed discourse impose special constraints on a theory of assertion? It is tempting to answer *no*. After all, theories of assertion operate at a level at which differences between special subject matters are irrelevant. Assertions about patio furniture do not teach us anything we could not have learned by focusing on assertions about playground locations in Canada.

But the future is no ordinary subject matter. Many philosophers since Aristotle have believed that future contingent claims are semantically *sui generis*, in ways that would inevitably impact the theory of assertion.[1] While extracting semantic theses out of Aristotle requires significant interpretive work (for which I refer the reader to Jones, 2010), the modern tradition that his remarks inspired is much more sanguine. Łukasiewicz (1970, p. 126) writes:

> I maintain that there are propositions which are neither true nor false … All sentences about future facts which are not yet decided belong to this category.

Following Williams (2008a), I refer to this type of view as the *Aristotelian indeterminacy view*. At its core, it is the idea that intuitions to the effect that the future is open are reflected in the semantics by violations of the principle of bivalence: Future contingents express propositions that are neither true nor false.

This commitment exposes the metaphysics to constraints coming from the theory of assertion. In this chapter, I run through my own version of a well-trodden argument to the effect that it is impossible to reconcile the Aristotelian indeterminacy picture with plausible facts about assertion.

---

[1]   In addition to the inevitable reference to sections 6–9 of Aristotle's *De Interpretatione*, the semantics and epistemology of future contingents interacted extensively during the Middle Ages with theological issues, concerning, for example, the omniscience and omnipotence of God. For surveys and discussion of the medieval problems, see Normore (1982), Øhrstrøm (2009), Øhrstrøm and Hasle (2015), and Knuuttila (2015).

Despite the long history of the problem of future contingents, the idea that a specific problem arises in applying a theory of assertion to future contingent propositions seems to have appeared only relatively recently. One of the first authors to think about assertion in this theoretical context is Lewis (1986a). Lewis argues that if the branching metaphysics were right, it would make no sense to make assertions about the future or wonder what it will bring.

> If there are two futures, and both are equally mine with nothing to choose between them, and one holds a sea fight and the other doesn't, what could it mean for me to say that *the* future holds a sea fight? Not a rhetorical question: we have three options. (1) It is false that the future holds a sea fight; because "the future" is a denotationless improper description. (2) It is true that the future holds a sea fight; because "the future" denotes neither of the two partial futures but rather their disunited sum, which does hold a sea fight. (3) It is neither true nor false that the future holds a sea fight; because "the future" has indeterminate denotations and we get different truth values on different resolutions of the indeterminacy. (Lewis, 1986a, p. 207)

According to Lewis, none of these options can be made to work: The mere fact that assertions about the future have a point is a major problem for the Aristotelian picture of indeterminacy and for the branching metaphysics.[2]

Since the publication of Lewis's discussion, assertion has come to occupy a central place in theorizing about the future. For example, Belnap and Green (1994) give a central role to *the assertion problem*, as do Belnap et al. (2001). The very phrase *the assertion problem* has become tightly associated with a semantic and pragmatic program that supposedly goes hand in hand with the branching metaphysics and with the Aristotelian conception of indeterminacy. Concerns about assertion show up, in various guises, in more recent literature. MacFarlane (2003) opens his influential discussion of future contingents with this paragraph:

> Suppose that the world is objectively indeterministic. In some possible futures, there is a sea battle tomorrow. In others, there is not. How should we evaluate an assertion (made now) of the sentence "There will be a sea battle tomorrow"?

This focus on assertion continues in the most recent literature as well.[3]

---

[2] See also Wilson (2014), which amplifies Lewis's critique in the context of Everettian quantum mechanics.

[3] A representative sample includes Besson and Hattiangadi (2014), Borghini and Torrengo (2013), MacFarlane (2008, 2014), Green (2014), Sweeney (2015), Stojanovic (2014), and Weiner (2005).

One thing we should do right off the bat is ditch the phrase *the asser-tion problem* – with its associated presupposition that there is just one problem. Instead, we can identify a few distinct challenges involving the relationship between assertion and future-directed contents. What they have in common is a rough structure: some constraints on assertion are pitched against assumptions about future claims. These assumptions seem to follow from the idea that the future is open. Together, the constraints and the assumptions entail unpalatable consequences. A typical example of such an unpalatable consequence is the conclusion that no future contingent claims are assertible. This is evidently trouble, since some of of these claims at least appear to be unproblematically assertible to us. If we accept that, something has to go. The menu of possible choices is not especially varied: Either we abjure (i) the constraints on assertion, or (ii) the idea that the future is open in a way that has implications for bivalence, or perhaps (iii) the intuition that some future contingent claims can be legitimately asserted.

The goal of this chapter is to spell out some of these arguments in detail. The arguments presented here connect the premise that the future is open with the unpalatable conclusion that no future contingent claims are assertible. In Section 10.1, I distinguish two inequivalent ways in which "assertible" is used in this literature and correspondingly, two kinds of assertion problems. Section 10.2 and Section 10.3 each develop a version of the "assertion problem." I argue that the second version is the centerpiece of a powerful argument against Aristotelian indeterminacy. That argument is completed in Sections 10.4–10.6 by closing off some escape routes.

10.1   Two Notions of Assertibility

One reason why there is a plurality of assertion problems is that "assertible" is a technical term that gets used in somewhat different ways by different philosophers.

In one, slightly inappropriate, sense, what is said to be assertible or unassertible (in a context) are linguistic strings. To say that a string *s* is assertible (in *c*) is to say that *s* is a proper vehicle of assertion. In this sense, *Joe is drinking coffee* is assertible (regardless of whether it's true), but *jirkasaa inking bllll* is not. For Belnap and Green (1994) and Belnap et al. (2001), the assertion problem is how to avoid the implausible claim that sentences like *Joe will drink his espresso at 9 AM* are not assertible in this sense – how to avoid them being sorted as inappropriate *qua* vehicles of assertion.

In the other sense, what is said to be assertible (or unassertible) are the contents of assertion – that is, propositions. To count as assertible, a proposition must have some key property, and it is the job of the theory of assertion to characterize that property. It could be *truth*, it could be *being known by the speaker*, or it could be something else entirely. This notion of assertibility links naturally with the literature on the rules of assertion introduced in Chapter 9, and indeed I will use that theoretical framework to expand on it.

Having drawn the distinction between two notions of assertibility, we need terminology to keep track of it. I reserve the label *assertible* for the second, content-directed sense. For the first, string-directed notion, I use the made-up technical term *sayable*. The content-directed sense should strike us as primary: If what is asserted is a proposition, what is *assertible* should be, in the first instance, a proposition.

10.2 The Original Assertion Problem

The original version of the assertion problem (Belnap and Green, 1994; Belnap et al., 2001) arises from a tension between the claim that future contingent sentences are appropriate vehicles of assertion – and hence "sayable" – and some constraints on what it takes to be sayable.

Consider this string:

(1) x is a shoe

Unlike entirely ill-formed strings, (1) might be a sayable string in the right kind of context. Imagine a context so heavily constrained that x must be assigned a unique value. When contextual constraints fix the value of all open parameters in a string, Belnap and Green say that the string is *closed by context*. Alternatively, (1) could be sayable if the domain of eligible referents for x is uniform with respect to the relevant property. If the domain of eligible referents for x consists solely of shoes, (1) is sayable (and plausibly true); if it consists solely of hats, it is also sayable (but plausibly false). Belnap and Green call this *closure by constancy*. For Belnap and Green, there is no other way to close an open sentence, which means that there are no other ways to make an open sentence sayable. If an open sentence cannot be closed by context or by constancy, it is unsayable.[4]

---

[4] Let me register some mild discomfort with this terminology: "Closure by constancy" *is* a form of closure by context, insofar as it is part of context's role to narrow down the range of eligible referents for an open variable.

The next step into the argument involves an extension of this style of thinking to strings that express future contingent propositions, such as the following:

(2)   The water will boil.

Superficially at least, (2) does not have any free variables, so it might be unclear why it should be viewed as open.[5] Belnap and Green (1994) treat it as open because they include the parameters in the point of evaluation among those that need to be fixed for a sentence to be sayable. Among the relevant parameters is the world of evaluation (or, in branching time terminology, the *history* of evaluation). Belnap and Green's concern is that a branching metaphysician cannot account for how this parameter is closed by either context or constancy. If there are many worlds, each of which has equal claim to contain our future, it is an arbitrary action to select any one of them (except in very special contexts). Moreover, based on the definition of a future contingent, this world parameter will not be closed by constancy.

Let us package all of these considerations together into a single argument:

SATURATION. For any context c and sentence A, A is sayable in c only if the world parameter of a point of evaluation appropriate for A is closed by context or by constancy.

NO CONSTANCY. If the future is open, for any context c and any A that expresses a future contingent in c, the world parameter for A is not saturated by constancy.

NO CONTEXT. If the future is open, the world parameter for A is never closed by the context of utterance.

∴ If the future is open, no future contingent sentences are sayable.

This argument is logically valid, so if we reject the conclusion, we must reject at least one of its premises.

I believe there is strong reason to deny the "no context" premise, as I will explain in Chapter 11. However, this argument is flawed in a more basic way. It's entirely unclear why we should find its premises plausible, and for that matter it's unclear why we should feel embarrassed by its conclusion. This is because a "sayable string" is a technical construct that is intuitively opaque and lacks a clear role in the theory of meaning.

---

[5] In the selection semantics I advocate, there is at least one free variable for modal bases, though this is evidently irrelevant here.

An additional problem is that no justification is provided for extending the initial ideas about open variables, which are bits of the object language, to parameters of evaluation, which are bits of theoretical apparatus. I am not denying that a sensible distinction can be drawn between those strings that a would-be asserter would consider using and ones that they would not. Instead, the main issue is that this notion classifies the strings that are uttered to assert future contingent claims as proper vehicles of assertion. The English declarative *Chloe will have some soup* meets the relevant criteria. It is much less plausible to claim that some strings classified as declarative according to their clause type are nonetheless ineligible as vehicles for assertion because of some technical constraints involving the saturation of the contextual parameters in the formal semantics. For all these reasons, I set aside versions of the assertion problem that turn on what the notion of a "sayable string" is.

10.3 The Normative Assertion Problem

A more compelling version of the assertion problem must involve the less technical, content-driven notion of assertibility. I formulate one such problem in this section by appealing to theories of the normativity of assertion. The idea of formulating assertion problems in terms of rules of assertion is clearly presented by Besson and Hattiangadi (2014), to whom this section is indebted.

The literature on norms of assertion relies on a fruitful methodology in philosophy of language. According to this methodology, our most reliable data are (i) judgments of acceptability, or felicity, of various speech acts in context and (ii) judgments of acceptability of inference patterns in context. This methodology recommends against relying on direct judgments about truth-value. The reason why implicature-based explanations of linguistic phenomena work, when they do, is that the data the implicature theorist seeks to explain are not marked as requiring a semantic explanation.

As we saw in Chapter 9, much recent work on assertion has given such rules an extra job. Normative constraints are involved in an effort to *define* the speech act of assertion. In this sense, the rules are thought of as *constitutive*. To buy into this style of theory, one needs to make two separate commitments: (1) to be willing to think of assertion as having norms and (2) to think of those norms as contributing to a characterization of the speech act.

These two commitments are separable. Many types of acts are governed by rules, without those rules playing any role in defining those acts. As a simple example, note that defenders of the knowledge *account* of assertion – the thesis that the knowledge rule is constitutive of assertion – derivatively and non-constitutively endorse the truth norm.   After all, anyone who abides by the knowledge norm must also abide by the truth norm. As another example that is not internal to the philosophy of language, consider the rule that pedestrians must cross roads on marked cross-walks. There is no activity that is defined by this rule – except for the trivial activity of *properly crossing the road when one is on foot.*

Unlike in Chapter 9, the present discussion of assertion problems for future contingents only requires engagement at the less committal level of non-definitional normative constraints. I aim to establish that standard constraints on assertions yield implausible verdicts when combined with the Aristotelian picture. The only thing that matters to this argument is that those constraints hold.

Suppose that assertion is governed, in this weaker sense, by some version of the truth norm:

CANONICAL TRUTH RULE. One may assert **A** only if **A** is true.

Our semantic framework as presently constructed does not have a truth predicate that is wholly unrelativized. To connect the truth rule with the semantic framework we have developed, we need to state it in terms of whichever truth predicate is assigned the job of connecting the semantics with the theory of speech acts. In the case of the broadly contextualist framework deployed here, this is the notion of truth at a context.

CONTEXTUALIST TRUTH RULE. One may assert **A** in c only if **A** is true in c.

For truth-relativists such as MacFarlane (2014, section 5.3), the truth predicate that interfaces with the pragmatics is relativized to two context parameters: the context of utterance and the context of assessment. Relativists must then state rules of assertion and retraction in terms of this doubly relativized truth predicate. As MacFarlane (2014, pp. 103–107) elaborates, however, relativists needn't go for an especially distinctive class of rules of assertion. They can just simulate, in their richer environment, what their non-relativist rivals say in their less expressive setup.

REFLEXIVE TRUTH NORM. One may assert **A** in context c_U only if **A** is true as uttered in c_U and assessed at c_U.

When it comes to specifying a truth norm, relativists agree with their contextualist frenemies. What distinguishes the relativist framework from a conceptual and empirical point of view are the distinct norms for *retraction* (see MacFarlane, 2014, section 5.4).

RELATIVIST RETRACTION. An agent in context c_A must retract an assertion of **A** made in context c_U only if **A** is true as uttered in c_U and assessed at c_A.

While my discussion focuses on the contextualist truth norm as a baseline, I will check in with the relativist position at various points throughout the argument.

How do the rules of assertion bear on the metaphysical question of Aristotelian indeterminacy? Let **A** be any sentence that can be used in context c to state some contingent matter of fact about the future. For example, this might be the sentence *This coin will land heads on its next toss*. Suppose that **A** is the proposition that A expresses in c. Suppose also that the rules of assertion require at least truth of the content that is asserted. Then the Aristotelian indeterminacy view faces significant theoretical pressure. Recall that it is crucial to the Aristotelian indeterminacy view that claims about the future are neither true nor false. This is encoded by the commitment to a framework in which an assertion of a future contingent proposition **A** made by uttering some sentence A in c can be true only if A is settled true (i.e., inevitably true) in c. More precisely, we understand settled truth as a property of sentences in context: A is settled in c iff A is true at all objectively possible futures. Putting these ideas together, we reason:

CONTEXTUALIST TRUTH NORM. One may assert **A** in c only if **A** is true in c.

SETTLEDNESS. If **A** is a future-contingent in c, **A** is true in c only if **A** is settled true in c.

CONCLUSION. If **A** is a future-contingent in c, one may assert **A** in c only if **A** is settled true in c.

COROLLARY. If **A** is a future-contingent in c, asserting **A** in context c is not normatively correct.

There are a few easy ways to avoid this conclusion for those who deny Aristotelian indeterminacy. Some of those who deny that the future is open in any sense can escape by claiming that settledness and truth do collapse on each other, because the relevant notion of settledness is trivial: Only what is true is settled.[6] These theorists also maintain that the corollary is only true in the trivial sense that it is a material conditional with a false antecedent.[7]

An alternative response is to hold that the relevant sense of the phrase "open future" is not strong enough to support the assumption that everything that is true is settled true. When properly construed, settledness is a kind of necessity, and necessity is a stronger property than truth. This assumption imposes on the concept of truth at a context a demand it cannot bear.

This critique strikes me as convincing, but I do not think it is available to the defender of Aristotelian indeterminacy. The proponent of Aristotelian indeterminacy endorses a link between future contingency and the status of being neither true nor false. This link is automatically a link between settledness and truth: If future contingent propositions are neither true nor false, the only other propositions that are left to be simply true are those propositions that are settled true and those that are settled false.

Accepting every premise in the argument plus the idea that the future is open leads to an intuitively implausible consequence. After sketching a similar argument, (Besson and Hattiangadi, 2014, 259) conclude:

> [The Aristotelian indeterminacy view], together with orthodox accounts of assertion, predicts that we will judge assertions of future contingents to be incorrect. However, most of the time, we are willing to accept sincere, flat-out assertions of future contingents as correct.

I think this is essentially right, with the further clarification that "correct" means that the relevant assertions are not guaranteed to be in violation of the rules of assertion.

The menu of responses that are available to the supporters of Aristotelian indeterminacy is surprisingly small. Since they accept the connection between truth and settledness and since the argument is valid, they must choose between (i) denying that normatively correct assertion requires truth or (ii) accepting the conclusion of the argument under a nontrivial interpretation. In my view, neither path is sustainable.

---

[6] More explicitly, suppose that to say that **A** is settled in c is to say that **A** is true for each objectively possible future of c. Now consider a theorist who believes that a unique possible world is determinately actual. For such a theorist, the universal quantification in the notion of settled truth will be a trivial quantification over a single world, so settled truth will collapse on truth at a world.

[7] The reader who has read Chapter 8 can probably predict that I don't think the natural language conditional is the material conditional. Here, however, I am just abusing the natural language Conditional to state a philosophical principle.

10.4   Against Concessive Solutions

Faced with the normative assertion problem, it might be tempting to just give in and accept its conclusion. This appears to be the preferred strategy of MacFarlane (2014, p. 231):

> It is better simply to bite the bullet here. If I assert, "I'll arrive on the 9:30 train," and you challenge me "Even if there is a strike or accident on the rails" then I must do one of the following:
>
> (i) Retract my assertion.
> (ii) Back up my assertion by asserting that there will not be a strike or an accident.
> (iii) Clarify that what I meant – what I asserted – was not the proposition that I would arrive on the 9:30 train, but something weaker: that I would arrive on the 9:30 train, barring strikes, accidents, or other rare and unpredictable mishaps; or that I would very likely arrive on the 9:30 train.
>
> I cannot concede that there might be a strike or accident while standing by the unqualified assertion that I will arrive on the 9:30 train.

I think this bullet is best left unbitten. The position that MacFarlane outlines in this passage is an assertion analogue of skepticism about the future. Epistemological skepticism about future contingent contents is the view that we cannot acquire any knowledge of them. MacFarlane's bullet-biting strategy entails that no future contingents are ever asserted in compliance with the rules of assertion. This seems to fly in the face of the fact that we happily, regularly, and unapologetically assert them.

Of course, the claim that this is a widespread practice is compatible with it being normatively incorrect. Cars should stop for pedestrians on the Chicago street I currently live on – it's the law. But they don't. The difference between this case and the case of assertions about the future is that our practice of making claims about the future does not even *appear* wrong to us. For instance, provided that I have the right kind of evidence, an assertive utterance of *it will rain tomorrow* doesn't get close to the level of defectiveness of an assertive utterance of known falsehoods, or even of vague assertions about borderline cases. MacFarlane's skeptical stance demands some kind of explanation of why our practice is so wildly at odds with the rules of assertion, but he doesn't offer such an explanation in his discussion.

It would be extraordinary if the class of future contingent propositions turned out to be wholesale unassertible. The class is large and diverse in its subject matter. Moreover, some of its contents are supported by excellent evidence. Indeed, some of these contents should strike us as so probable that they warrant higher confidence than we have in many ordinary contingent claims about the present or past. For example, it might be a future contingent whether this crystal statuette will break if I drop it from the tenth-floor balcony. And it seems reasonable for me to have higher confidence in that claim than I have in the proposition that Stephen Curry was born in Ohio – which, by the way, I am perfectly willing to assert.[8]

In addition to these general considerations, there is a reason specific to MacFarlane's framework to reject the conclusion of his reasoning. MacFarlane's system features two sets of normative constraints on assertions: rules for *making* assertions and rules for *retracting* them. One critical component of the relativist program is that retraction rules are not mirror images of the rules for making assertion. Recall the relativist retraction rule from Section 10.3. Consider Sarah's Monday utterance of *I will come to your office before 4 PM*. The relativist predicts that Sarah is not just violating the rules of assertion; she is also violating the the rules of retraction many times over. She violates the relativist truth norm by asserting something that was not true as uttered in Monday's context and assessed from that same context. Additionally, she violates the retraction rule at every point between when she makes the assertion and 4 PM on the next day. To comply with the norm, as long as she has not retracted that assertion, Sarah ought to retract it until it turns out to be true (if it turns out to be false, it is agreed by all parties that she ought to retract it). In one sentence: Not only should the assertion never have been made, but it also should be retracted at every point in the interval starting with the utterance time and ending with the event time.[9]

---

[8]   Dialectical note: I am not arguing here from the suspicious-looking principle that if **A** is more likely than **B**, and **B** is assertible, then so is **A**. It is enough for this argument to rely on the weaker claim that we should find it surprising and implausible that *every* future contingent that is more likely than some assertible things should be unassertible.

[9]   I owe this point to a commentary on MacFarlane (2014) delivered by Mark Schroeder at the 2016 Central APA. Schroeder also noted then that the relativist position appears more plausible against an earlier picture of retraction that MacFarlane (2005) developed. In that context, MacFarlane formulated the assertion rule as the claim that a speaker in context of assessment c_A ought to retract an assertion of **A** made in context of utterance c_U if **A** is untrue at c_U and c_A *and if one is challenged to back up the assertion.* A speaker who isn't challenged hasn't violated any norms. The problem is that the bit I italicized has disappeared from the new norm of retraction. Indeed, for some of the intended applications of relativism (e.g., epistemic modality) we desire normative pressure to retract one's assertion whether or not one is actually challenged.

There is another problem with the argumentation I quoted from Mac-Farlane. Toward the end of that quoted passage, he notes that a speaker cannot accept:

(3)   I will arrive on the 9:30 train but there might be a strike.

His suggestion is that the unacceptability of (3) should make biting the bullet on the unassertibility of *I will arrive on the 9:30 train* more palatable. But how so? If we think that *there might be a strike* contextually entails *I might not arrive by 9:30*, then (3) is dangerously close to:

(4)   I will arrive at 9:30 but I might not arrive at 9:30.

This statement is very close to the structure *will* A & *might not* A. In the terminology of Chapter 6, it is a *future might contradiction*. I argued there that FMCs generally sound contradictory, and plausibly that they sound contradictory for the same reason that epistemic contradictions do. But if that's true, the explanation for the defectiveness of (3) has nothing to do with the unassertibility of future contingents.

Finally, as Alessio Santelli (in press) points out, there is a serious difficulty with MacFarlane's "clarification" strategy [item (iii) in the bit I quoted]. It is almost never the case that I assert propositions such as that I will likely arrive on the 9:30 train. We can see this by considering how this "content deformation" strategy interfaces with probabilistic inferences we might derive from someone's assertion. Suppose I say *I will have dinner tonight*. Knowing, as you do, that I am generally reliable on such matters, you come to ascribe high credence to what I said – the proposition that I will have dinner. But your credence falls short of certainty: I am reliable, but not infallible on such matters. If I instead assert the proposition that I will *likely* have dinner, then that reasoning is fallacious. You shouldn't come to a non-extreme credence in what I asserted. Your credence should be maximal: You should be certain that it's likely that I will have dinner. Deforming the content must also deform our probability judgments in ways we never detect.

A nice dramatization of this point involves interpersonal propositional anaphora (I owe this point to Iacona, unpublished manuscript). Consider this dialogue:

CHILD: I will have dinner tonight.
PARENT: I hope so.

What the parent hopes is evidently that the child will have dinner. She does not hope that it's likely that the child will have dinner, nor does she put her hope in some other reformulated claim. What the child says is that they will have dinner.

For these reasons, then, we ought not be comfortable with accepting the conclusion of MacFarlane's argument. In fairness to MacFarlane, he is not entirely wedded to this bullet-biting strategy. As a fall-back option, he suggests that "those who simply rebel at the idea that asserting a future contingent is always impermissible" (MacFarlane, 2014, p. 232) might have another option.

I do simply rebel, so I'm all ears. The alternative MacFarlane hints at consists of the exploration of an alternative postsemantics. According to (a contextualist version of) this alternative postsemantics, if A is settled true in c, then A is true in c; if A is settled false in c, then A is false in c. In any other case, it is indeterminate. Crucially, the alternative postsemantics is silent on the status of A when it is neither settled true nor settled false. We might say in this case that it is *indeterminate*. Thus, the alternative postsemantics "leaves it indeterminate whether p should be asserted at c, and indeterminate whether an assertion of p made prior to c should be retracted at c" (MacFarlane, 2014, p. 232). This option is in the spirit of the view I develop in Chapter 11. Notably, this view renounces one of the key tenets of the Aristotelian indeterminacy. It is a core part of the Aristotelian picture that if a proposition is not settled true, then it is not true. Once we adopt this postsemantics, we can no longer suppose that the openness of the future is correctly modeled by a failure of bivalence.

10.5   Weaker Rules

Might we block the normative assertion problem by rejecting the idea that truth is required for normatively correct assertion? One path toward this conclusion would be to reject the entire framework of rules of assertion. Another path would be to claim that, whatever those rules might be, they do not require truth.

Influential accounts of the latter kind are advocated by Douven (2006, 2009), who proposes a "rational credibility" norm, and by Lackey (2007), who states that the norm of assertion is that it is reasonable for one to believe A. Here I discuss how the dialectic looks if we adopt Lackey's norm, but very much the same things could be said under Douven's account.[10] According to Lackey, the norm of assertion has this general shape:

REASONABLE TO BELIEVE (RTB) NORM. One may assert **A** in c only if it is reasonable for one to believe **A** in c.

Strictly speaking, the RTB and truth norms are independent: Each can be satisfied while the other is violated.

However, within the domain of future-directed discourse, it seems easier to satisfy this norm than it is to satisfy the truth norm. After all, it is reasonable to believe things that are not true, and one might suppose it reasonable, in the right circumstances, to believe things that are neither true nor false.

I doubt this strategy will work. Much of the argument turns on what it means for it to be reasonable for one to believe **A**. To sustain a sufficiently strong norm of assertion, "reasonable" must be a strong enough property. For example, "reasonable" cannot mean something like "compatible with one's evidence." More paradoxical sentences might be compatible with one's evidence, yet they are the paradigm of sentences whose unacceptability ought to be explained by an account of the normativity of assertion. More generally, one would have to avoid any account in which both a proposition and its negation could turn out to be reasonable.

Claims of the form ⌜**A** is reasonable for α on evidence **E**⌝ must mean something at least as strong as this: The reason for α to believe **A** is stronger than any reason to believe its negation, and not overridden by any reasons that are available to α. But if it means anything like this, it is hard to see how someone who endorses SETTLEDNESS can make sense of it. Something counts as a reason to believe **A** if it's a reason to believe that **A** is true. But when it comes to future contingents, under SETTLEDNESS, a reason to believe that **A** is true should be a reason to believe that **A** is settled. This seems to provide the basis for a reformulation of the argument.

---

[10] Lackey is motivated by a phenomenon she calls *selfless assertion*: cases in which a speaker asserts **A** even if they do not believe **A** – and thus do not reasonably believe it. One might assert **A** and fail to believe it, yet it might be reasonable for one to believe **A**. Be that as it may, both norms are weaker (i.e., less demanding) than any norm that requires asserters to know what they assert, and they are logically independent of norms that require asserters to only say the truth. After all, it may be reasonable for one to assert something that is not true, and there may be truths that are not reasonable for one to believe.

RTB NORM. s may assert $\|A\|$ in c only if it is reasonable for s to believe $\|A\|$
  in c.

BELIEVED SETTLEDNESS. If it is reasonable for s to believe $\|A\|$ in c, it is
  reasonable to believe $\|\mathit{Settled}\ A\|$ in c.

CONCLUSION. s may assert $\|A\|$ in c only if it is reasonable for s to believe
  $\|\mathit{Settled}\ A\|$ in c.

This conclusion is a bit weaker than the conclusion of the argument
against the truth norm. Intead of deriving that all future contingents are
unassertible, the argument concludes that it is impermissible to assert **A**
when it is not reasonable for one to believe that **A** is settled. But even
that conclusion should strike us as problematic. When it comes to future
contingents, it is quite often the case that we lack a belief in their settledness.

The revised conclusion does depend on a slightly different, and more
substantive, premise than in the original formulation of the argument.
According to BELIEVED SETTLEDNESS, it is only reasonable for one to believe
A in c if it is reasonable for one to believe that **A** is settled. An Aristotelian
indeterminist must maintain that reason to believe **A** in c has to be a
reason to believe that **A** is true in c. Moreover, the Aristotelian indeterminist
maintains that **A** is true in c only if **A** is settled true in c.

Summing up, if we interpret "reasonableness" weakly, it cannot be at the
core of a norm of assertion; if we interpret it more strongly, it will generally
not be reasonable for us to have beliefs in future contingent propositions.
On either path, a RTB norm won't help the Aristotelian indeterminist.

In addition to these considerations, some other worries strike directly at
the explanatory completeness of weak normative standards such as the RTB
norm. For one thing, it is part of the standard mission of theorizing about
the rules of assertion that they provide an account of Moorean assertions,
such as:

(5)   It is raining but I don't know that it is.

The standard, knowledge-based account of the badness of (5) is that, under
the knowledge norm, someone who felicitously asserted (5) would have
to (i) know that it is raining and (ii) know that they don't know this. By
factivity of knowledge applied to (ii), they would have to not know that it
is raining, which contradicts (i).

This argument does not work for "reasonable to believe": $RB(\mathit{rain})$
and $RB(\neg RB(\mathit{rain}))$ may well be consistent unless we adopt additional
principles about what it means to rationally believe something. Any such
additional principles would also make it more difficult to square the view

with the Aristotelian indeterminacy picture. For example, Kvanvig (2009) proposes an account of Moorean contradictions under the "justification" norm of assertion – the norm according to which "the propriety of an assertion is a function of one's justification for the content of the assertion." Though different in detail, the justification norm faces a similar worry as the RTB norm concerning how to account for the infelicity of Moorean assertions. Kvanvig accounts for the infelicity of Moorean assertions as follows:

J TO JK. If s is justified in believing **A**, then s is justified in believing s knows **A**.

From this, you can reason as follows:

 (i) If you are justified in believing (5), then you are justified in believing you know it;
 (ii) distributing across the conjunction JK(*rain*) and JK(¬K(*rain*));
 (iii) if JK entails J, J(¬K(*rain*));
 (iv) but presumably one can't be justified in believing contraries.

My point here is that the defender of Aristotelian Indeterminacy must deny J TO JK and thus cannot borrow Kvanvig's account of Moorean assertions. Although there are concepts of justification in which one can be justified in believing what is neither true nor false, one cannot know what is neither true nor false. And if one cannot know what is true nor false, we should probably say that one should not be justified in believing that one knows it.

I'll consider one last type of norm, albeit briefly. One might entertain the view that the rules of assertion are separately sensitive to truth and falsehood. Belnap and Green (1994) propose that the normative status one incurs by asserting **A** is such that if **A** is true, one deserves credit; if **A** is false, one deserves discredit. When I assert a future contingent such as *it will be sunny*, what I assert is neither true nor false; as a result, I neither deserve credit nor deserve discredit. If my assertion turns out to be true, I shall get the credit; if it turns out to be false, I shall get discredit.

This view does a better job than a truth norm because it sorts assertions of future contingents as having a pending, rather fully settled status. However, I think this goal is best reached with a slightly different picture. Although I suggested earlier that future-talk was *sui generis*, it is unlikely that the speech act of assertion is best characterized in ways that treat future discourse as special. However, the "bifurcated" proposal structures the norms of assertion in terms of the twin notions of credit and discredit precisely to create the space that distinguishes gappy sentences. Only future contingent assertions get to take advantage of the fact that one's levels of credit and discredit may vary over time. Furthermore, unlike the standard truth norm, it is unclear how the proposal relates to epistemic norms such as the knowledge norm of assertion.

Most importantly, the proposal is incomplete. Although it's plausible that a general notion of goodness of an assertion might lie on a scale with more than two positions, some of the distinctions we want to draw really *are* binary distinctions. Either an assertion was permissible in context or it wasn't. The bifurcated proposal would have to be completed with some account of that distinction as well. At first sight, either permissibility should go with asserting the true, or it should go with asserting the not false. In the former case, we are forced back into the assertion problem: All assertions of future contingents are impermissible. In the latter case, we are forced to endorse the twin implausible consequence that all assertions of future contingents are permissible. Neither is a happy place.

10.6   Non-normative Conceptions of Assertion

This style of argument generalizes to some degree to non-normative accounts of assertion. In this section I sketch some reasons to think these accounts are just as hard to combine with the Aristotelian picture of indeterminacy. Consider Stalnaker's theory of assertion – arguably one of the most prominent non-normative theories. According to Stalnaker (1978), the essential effect of assertions is to add the asserted content to the common ground – the set of mutual presuppositions between the participants of a conversation. Now, nothing in the account essentially requires that one assert truths. In the right context, I might assert *Santa Claus will bring Nino three presents*. Ordinarily, such an assertion adds to the common ground the proposition that Santa Claus brings Nino three presents. We do not demand that the common ground consist exclusively of true propositions because assertions are involved in pretense, as well as fictional and hypothetical discourse. Here is Stalnaker making just this point:

> [The] actual world in which a discourse takes place need not be compatible with the context of that discourse, which is just to say that some things presupposed by a speaker may in be in fact false. This may happen for a number of different reasons. A speaker might be presupposing something false simply because he has a false belief, either about the subject matter of

the discourse, or about the discourse itself. He might presuppose something false in order to deceive, or because of some mutually recognized pretense. Sometimes the most effective way to communicate something true is to presuppose something false. (Stalnaker, 1998, p. 7)

This is all well and good. However, we must note two additional things.

The most important point is that Stalnaker's theory is not incompatible with there *being* norms of assertion. Stalnaker's analysis competes with theories in which norms *characterize* assertion, but it is perfectly compatible that assertion, once characterized in terms of its essential effects, also happens to be subject to norms. If it's independently plausible that there are norms of assertion and that they are roughly along the lines of the truth norm, or the reasonable belief norm, then all the arguments of the previous sections apply. In fact, it is reasonable to think that anyone who accepts a version of Grice's Maxim of Quality accepts that assertions are subject to epistemic norms of some sort.

What if one denies that there are norms of assertion altogether? In that case, we would rely on judgments about what speech acts ordinarily achieve and aim to achieve. The typical point of assertions is to convey some information or, as it is sometimes put, to zero in on the actual world.

> The reasons people talk to each other are of course varied and complex, but it seems reasonable to assume that there are some kinds of purposes that are essential to the practice, and that are the principal reasons for speech in the most straightforward kinds of conversation. In a simple exchange of information, people say things to get other people to come to know things that they didn't know before. They utter certain noises with the expectation that someone hearing them will thereby acquire certain particular information. (Stalnaker, 2002, p. 703)

Once we grant this, the assertion problem resurfaces. Asserting future contingents is no different from asserting present or past claims. If the point of uttering *Obama was the president of the United States in 2009* in 2016 is to zero in on the actual world, the point of uttering *Obama will be the president of the United States in 2009* in 2008 should plausibly be the same. But if truth requires settledness, as the proponent of Aristotelian indeterminacy demands, then assertions of future contingents must be understood to pattern with fictional and hypothetical assertions. This is unexpected: Assertions of future contingent claims look like ordinary assertions, not parts of some related make-believe practice.

CHAPTER II

Thin Red Lines without Tears

Thinking about assertions of future contingents spells trouble for branching metaphysics and for the Aristotelian picture of indeterminacy. But perhaps not all is lost for those who want to preserve a robust sense of the openness of the future. This chapter explores the prospects for an alternative model – a sophisticated version of the *thin red line* picture criticized by Belnap and Green (1994).[1]

The central idea of the thin red line view is that although there are many objectively possible futures, there is exactly one actual future (Malpass and Wawer, 2012, p. 117). The sophisticated spin on this idea is that if the future is genuinely open, then it is objectively indeterminate which of the objectively possible futures is the thin red line. It might be indeterminate whether the coin will land heads because it is indeterminate whether the actual future is a heads future or a tails future. For this picture to get off the ground, we must reject the link connecting the claim the future is open with respect to **A** to the claim that **A** is neither true nor false. This rejection frees us to endorse bivalence: It might be that it is indeterminate whether **A**, but it is determinate that **A** is true or false.[2]

Perhaps this sounds like philosophical lawyerese, but the benefits of this sort of view are diverse and far reaching. One benefit is that this move allows us to think more clearly about the relationship between semantics and metaphysics. Another is that it connects smoothly with the selection semantics: Once we combine selection semantics with the sophisticated thin red line picture, the standard objections against thin red line approaches are easily dealt with.

---

[1] For contemporary work on thin red line metaphysics and some of its linguistic implications, see Borghini and Torrengo (2013), Iacona (2013), and Malpass and Wawer (2012). The view that is presupposed here is not exactly like the views developed by these authors, but there certainly is much that the views have in common.

[2] See Hirsch (2006), Barnes and Cameron (2009), Barnes and Cameron (2011), and Barnes and Williams (2011). All these theorists are working off a theme from McGee and McLaughlin (1995).

11.1 What Is the Open Future Hypothesis?

We need to backtrack. I have talked a little casually about the idea that the future is open, but have not considered carefully what that amounts to. Unfortunately, the literature is not especially cohesive in how the phrase "open future" is used. We must join a terminological debate. The central aim of the game is to identify the most useful way, or ways, of using this phrase. To be sure, what I am looking for here is not a *theory* of the open future, but rather a useful pre-theoretical characterization of what we are talking about when we say that the future is open. My discussion relies on the insightful discussion of Torre (2011), whose general conclusions about how to frame the debate I find especially congenial.

In thinking about the "open future" intuition, it's undesirable to cast too tight a net. For instance, the openness of the future should not amount to the semantic fact that future contingent propositions are neither true nor false. In Chapter 10, I articulated some worries to the effect that this view cannot be squared with our discursive practice. But even setting those worries aside, linking the openness of the future with the idea of truth-value gaps would be a highly technical way of interpreting the intuition. The openness of the future intuition should be more readily available to pretheoretical reflection.

Furthermore (and echoing Besson and Hattiangadi, 2014), if the openness of the future amounts to the failure of bivalence, then Lewis's attempt to account for it in counterfactual terms (within the perfectly bivalent divergentist framework of Lewis, 1979, 1986a) would be motivationally incoherent. After all, if openness just *is* non-bivalence, there is no accounting for it in a bivalent framework. A final worry is that other kinds of truth-value gaps exist (i.e., other kinds of claims that are neither true nor false), the present characterization fails to capture what is distinctive about the openness of the future: Even if openness had something to do with failures of bivalence, it could not just be *identified* with it.

We don't want to cast our net too widely, either. Some intuitions about the future are readily taken at face value by virtually every participant. For example, it is widely accepted that there is a prevalent asymmetry of causation: Effects (usually) occur no earlier than their causes. Similarly, it is common to recognize epistemic asymmetries between past and future (Albert, 2000). We inquire into the future primarily by reasoning and through some rational imagination capacity (more about this in Chapter 12), but in the case of the past many more methods are available to us. Neither of these observations is strong enough to characterize the open future hypothesis. What we want is a cluster of intuitions that are initially powerful, yet also somewhat controversial.

Perhaps the key observation is that in an indeterministic universe the past is nomically necessary, but the future is not. In other words, given the present and the laws governing our universe, the past is fixed but the future is not. But this, too, is a problematic way of carving the relevant distinction. According to some conceptions of the laws of nature, if the laws are too weak to fix the future on the basis of the present, they are also too weak to fix the past on the basis of the present (Lewis, 1979; Markosian, 1995; Torre, 2011). Furthermore, the idea that the future is open does not appear to immediately contradict determinism. As Iaquinto and Torrengo (2018, chapter 2) put the point, indeterminism could be something that explains the openness of the future but does not seem useful as *definitional* of it.

With these constraints in mind, I suggest the idea that the future is open comes down to a complex of three intuitions. First, a *metaphysical parity* intuition along the lines of the one discussed in Chapter 2: There are several possible futures, such that we cannot tell which of them is ours. Second, an intuition about ability: Agents such as ourselves can affect the future but cannot affect the past. Third, a semantic intuition: Contingent propositions about the future are in some sense unsettled, but propositions about the present and past are not. This third intuition comes *close* to the Aristotelian indeterminacy picture, but stops short of equating unsettledness with a truth-value gap.

For the purposes of the present discussion, I set aside the asymmetries of ability. These are heavily involved with other debates that would take us into a whole new territory without actually addressing the questions concerning future discourse and thought that motivate the present book.[3]

I will *not* set aside either the metaphysical parity intuition or the semantic intuition. These come together in the single most famous puzzle about future discourse: Aristotle's sea battle puzzle. Having skirted the puzzle for more than ten chapters, it is time to face it head on. The sea battle puzzle pitches two separate intuitions against each other.

The *prior unsettledness* intuition is that assertions of future contingent propositions appear *unsettled* at the time at which they are made. Suppose that on Monday, Themistocles receives excellent (but not completely

---

[3] For a hot-off-the-press discussion of how the asymmetries of ability might relate to the open future hypothesis, I recommend the discussion in Boylan (in press b).

conclusive) evidence that the Persians will attack by sea. On the basis of that evidence, he says:

(1)   There will be a sea battle tomorrow.

In fact, at the moment of Themistocles's assertion, it is objectively unsettled whether there will be a sea battle on Tuesday. It seems unsettled whether Themistocles's assertion was felicitous. And it seems unsettled not because we don't know enough, but because the underlying reality is somehow indeterminate.

This judgment is in some tension with the *posterior settledness* intuition. From Tuesday's point of view, the normative status of Themistocles's assertion of (1) appears settled. If the sea battle occured, Themistocles's assertion was accurate and he was within his rights to make it. And if it didn't, the assertion awas inaccurate and he shouldn't have made it.

The two intuitions appear to be in direct contrast with each other. Either Themistocles's assertion was defective at both times or it was defective at neither of them. The sea battle puzzle is how to reconcile these contrasting intuitions.

11.2   Metaphysical Indeterminacy

The traditional interpretation of Aristotelian indeterminacy suggests that the unsettledness of a future contingent proposition consists of its being neither true nor false. In contrast to the Aristotelians, Ockhamists maintain that we ought to double up on our stock of truth predicates. There is truth in the actual future, whatever it may be, and *determinate truth*. (The latter is close to the concept of historical inevitability associated with the Peircean future.) The problem with this Ockhamist line is that it is not clear why we need two concepts of truth. Truth-in-the-actual-future seems to be doing virtually all of the explanatory work except for accounting for parity intuitions. There is no point in appealing to a second concept of truth that accounts for parity intuitions and nothing else.

There is a third option: The indeterminacy, or openness, of the future consists of there being indeterminacy in regard to which of the many worlds that agree on the history until now is the actual future. What it is to be indeterminate in this sense is not further analyzed, although it can be further illuminated and justified. This view strives to simultaneously uphold bivalence (unlike the Aristotelian view) and the parity intuitions. Unlike Ockhamism, this approach stops short of the claim that we need two concepts of truth.[4] The indeterminacy concerning which world is actual filters up to the truth predicate. Suppose that **A** is indeterminate; then it is indeterminate whether **A** is true and it is indeterminate whether **A** is false. The view does, however, recognize a distinction between truth and determinate truth.

To illustrate the view, consider again Themistocles's utterance of (1). In the context of this utterance, (1) is indeterminate because it is indeterminate whether the actual future contains a sea battle. This condition arises because it is indeterminate which future, and hence which world, is actual. The root of this indeterminacy is that "our world" – us and our surroundings – fails to settle which of many different continuations is actualized. (This talk of "actualized" worlds comes from the metaphysics of ersatz possible worlds.) Here is how Barnes and Williams put the basic view:

> If it is fundamentally unsettled whether p, there are two candidate representations for actualization – the abstract world which represents that p and the abstract world that represents that $\neg p$. Neither of these are determinately correct, but neither is determinately incorrect, because in reality it's simply unsettled whether p or rather $\neg p$ obtains. (Barnes and Williams, 2011, p. 115)

I am going to call this sort of position *bivalent indeterminacy*.

Bivalent indeterminacy can be invoked to account for a variety of related phenomena. Barnes and Cameron (2009) use it as a basis for a non-relativist treatment of some of the intuitions in the sea battle puzzle. It is worth contrasting their explanation with MacFarlane's. MacFarlane-style relativists account for the prior unsettledness intuition by appealing to the postsemantic prediction that the proposition expressed in the original context by *there will be a sea battle* is neither true nor false as uttered in the context c_{Monday} and assessed at c_{Monday} itself. At the same time, they account for the posterior settledness intuition by claiming that *there will be a sea battle* is either true or false (as the case might be) as uttered in the context c_{Monday} but as assessed in the context $c_{Tuesday}$. Once these postsemantic facts

---

4   The roots of this option lie in the vagueness literature: McGee and McLaughlin (1995), Dorr (2003), and Barnes and Williams (2011). The view has been applied to the indeterminacy of the future by Hirsch (2006), who ascribes the view to Rashi (a Talmudist scholar from the eleventh century AD) and by Barnes and Cameron (2009) and Barnes and Cameron (2011). These authors all agree that the relevant sense of indeterminacy must be a primitive. For some challenges and alternatives to the conception of metaphysical indeterminacy presupposed by these authors, see Skow (2010), Wilson (2013), and Torza (2017).

are plugged into the appropriate normative constraints, predictions about the appropriateness of the two assertions emerge.

This dialectic looks different from the perspective of the bivalent indeterminist. The bivalent indeterminist's key observation concerning prior unsettledness is that it is indeterminate (i.e., not determinately true and not determinately false) at the initial time that there will be a sea battle (Barnes and Cameron, 2009, p. 297). The key observation about the posterior settledness intuition is that, at the later time, it is determinately true or determinately false that there was a sea battle. Neither Hirsch (2006) nor Barnes and Cameron (2009, 2011) spell out in detail how these facts about determinacy interact with the theory of speech acts. My aim in this chapter is to develop these metaphysical ideas in the context of some standard theories about context sensitivity in the philosophy of language.

11.3 Context, Content, and Indeterminacy

How should we represent the linguistic context of Themistocles's utterance of *there will be a sea battle tomorrow*? Proponents of the branching metaphysics often work under the assumption that they must renounce the standard conception of context. Let's see why.

According to the Lewis-Kaplan conception of context, we ought to distinguish between two ways of thinking about context. Contexts may be conceptualized as concrete situations of utterance (Lewis 1980). Alternatively, they may be conceptualized as abstract records of the parameters needed to interpret indexicals and other context-sensitive expressions (Kaplan, 1989b). The concrete context is the kind of thing you might find yourself in if the surrounding conditions allowed for human life. The abstract context is the kind of thing you'd set up if you wanted to program a computer to keep track of how certain context-sensitive expressions depend on features of context. To disambiguate these two contexts, I will refer to the first as the *situation of utterance*, reserving the word *context* for the abstract notion.

When things go smoothly, simple determination relations exist between these. A concrete situation of utterance s determines an abstract context c. Among the parameters that are recorded by c is a world – the world of the context – so c (and hence s) determines a unique world.[5]

---

[5] There is no inverse determination relation: A world can belong to multiple abstract contexts (e.g., one in which I am the speaker, and one in which you are the speaker). Moreover, the same context could be associated with different situations of utterance if we assume that situations – which are concrete events – carry additional details that are not represented by the contexts.

Graphically:

```
situation of utterance ↦ abstract context ↦ world
```

Those who think that the open future intuitions are not rooted in purely epistemic facts must believe that a concrete situation of utterance does not determine a world. In other words, they must break one of these determination relations.[6]

The branching metaphysics breaks the second of these relations: Situations of utterance determine contexts, but contexts don't determine a unique world. The idea is that a situation of utterance s is a concrete chunk of the branching reality. Once we pick out this concrete chunk, we cannot uniquely select *the* world that s belongs to: s must belong to multiple worlds, so the context corresponding to s must determine a variety of worlds. [MacFarlane (2014) makes this move explicit in on p. 77 of *Assessment Sensitivity*.] It is this aspect of the picture – more so than the idea of a branching reality – that creates the problems outlined in Chapter 10. If context determines a bundle of worlds, but the valuation function wants an individual world, the natural move is to supervaluate. And if we supervaluate, we will end up with a violation of bivalence at the postsemantic level.

The alternative is to break the first determination relation. The guiding idea is this: If it is indeterminate which world is actual, it is indeterminate which classical context the utterance is located in.[7] More specifically, if situation s belongs to multiple worlds, then instead of saying that s determines a single "indeterministic" context, we should say that it determines a plurality of classical contexts – one for each "world" of the context" choice.

In Chapter 2, I drew diagrams like Figure 11.1. In the case of branching models, we can read the model (minus the valuation function) off the diagram. However, according to the position I advocate, this relation between diagram and model is not quite so strong. Diagrams constrain,

---

[6] In yet another approach, Boylan (in press b) suggests treating the indeterminacy of the future as a different kind of model. Perhaps instead of evaluating at world points, we should be evaluating at coarser objects (such as sets of worlds). Within this picture, abstract contexts behave in exactly the same way under indeterminacy assumptions as they would under determinacy. In turn, the very idea of abstract contexts as determining a possible world would be considered misguided. I haven't yet had the chance to think through the implications of this model of indeterminacy, so I am not able to give it the space it deserves here.

[7] Variants of this point are made in Sweeney (2015) and Cariani and Santorio (2018). Wilson (2011) offers this sort of picture as an interpretation of Saunders and Wallace (2008). Sweeney seems to think that this option is not available to the *B*-theoretic branching theorist. I think it is, even if I reject *B*-theoretic branching, for the reasons described in Chapter 10. The version I develop here builds on the proposal in Cariani and Santorio (2018).

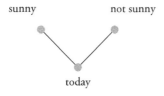

Figure 11.1   Basic branching diagram

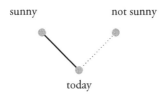

Figure 11.2   One thin red line.

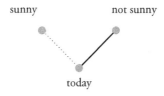

Figure 11.3   … and another

but do not determine, models. The kinds of models that the selection semantics needs are better diagrammed by Figures 11.2 and 11.3, in which we distinguish a privileged future. The semantics of the future needs contexts to mark a thin red line. In these diagrams, it's thick and black, but it's there.

The main idea of this chapter is that if we accept the bivalent indeterminacy view, we are best served by thinking of context (in the abstract sense) as classical, but not determined by the situation of utterance. Although it is indeterminate which context the assertion takes place in, under the semantics for future discourse I developed in the first three parts of this book, basic future-directed sentences, such as bare predictions, are *content-determinate*. In each of the contexts that compete for the status of "actual context," they express the same proposition.[8]

11.4   Indeterminate Normative Statuses

Given the possibility of multiple contexts associated with a single situation of utterance, we need to ask about the normative status of assertions of future-directed sentences. It is most informative to start with the truth norm in its contextualist formulation, as seen in Chapter 10.

CONTEXTUALIST TRUTH NORM. One may assert **A** in c only if **A** is true in c.

Suppose that is indeterminate whether some assertive utterance u of *it will rain* takes place in context c_1 or context c_2. Choose the two contexts so that they disagree about whether *it will rain* is true. In these cases, I propose that it is *indeterminate* whether the truth norm is satisfied. The indeterminacy in truth-value filters up into indeterminacy about the assertion's normative status.

Investigating this view forces us to face a theoretical choice point. In a perfectly classical setting, for each assertion there is exactly one situation of utterance and exactly one context. But now consider this idea idea from the nonclassical perspective we are investigating. There is, indeed, one situation of utterance, but corresponding to it are a plurality of contexts. We must then take one of two options: If assertions have their contexts essentially, then there is one situation of utterance, but several assertions (each of which has its own context and its own normative status). The alternative is to think that assertions do not have their contexts essentially, but instead are mapped one-to-one onto situations of utterance.

The second approach provides a better fit with common sense and retains a more homogeneous relationship between assertions and other kinds of actions. Adopting the second line requires us to bridge an important gap. Each assertion is conceptualized as a single act – a single object of evaluation – and evaluation is relativized to a parameter – the context – that is left indeterminate by the situation of utterance. We need a theory of about the normative status of the assertion *simpliciter*.

---

[8] This is true of any Boolean combination of bare predictions. However, this might fail in more complex fragments of the language. For example, *will*-conditionals are not guaranteed to be content-determinate.

One possibility – though not the one I will endorse – is a kind of permissivism. This view is inspired by von Fintel and Gillies's discussion of "cloudy contextualism" for epistemic modals. Working on a different topic and under very different theoretical constraints, von Fintel and Gillies entertain the thesis that epistemic modal sentences might be context-indeterminate. For each assertion α whose vehicle is an epistemic modal sentence, there is a "cloud" (without the poetry: a set) of contexts $\mathcal{C}$ such that for each context $c \in \mathcal{C}$, it is indeterminate whether c is the context of α.[9]

The present interest of this proposal lies in how von Fintel and Gillies resolve the problems of normative status. They claim that if it is indeterminate which context in $\mathcal{C}$ is the context of assertion α, then the truth norm (or any other norm) is satisfied if and only if it is satisfied according to *at least one of the contexts in* $\mathcal{C}$. By contrast, it is much harder to hold on to an asserted epistemic modality claim one has put in play, as von Fintel and Gillies also think that one ought to retract if the truth norm is violated according to at least one of the contexts in the cloud. This fits an important element of their motivation. According to von Fintel and Gillies, bare epistemic possibility claims are easy to assert and easy to give up.

However well this view might work in epistemic modal discourse, it does not work well for future-directed discourse. One is not licensed to assert propositions that go against all of the evidence, even if those propositions aren't entirely ruled out by the class of historically possible worlds. In general, unqualified assertions about the future are not *that* cheap.

Here, then, is the natural alternative: If (i) it is indeterminate which context in $\mathcal{C}$ is the context of some assertion α, and (ii) if the contexts in $\mathcal{C}$ disagree about the normative status of α, then the normative status of α is indeterminate. If the normative status of an assertion depends on which context it was made in, and it is indeterminate which context it was made in, then the assertion's normative status is indeterminate.[10]

---

[9] Their system differs from mine in many respects. An important one is that it is crucial to the entire debate that epistemic modals are not content-determinate. More specifically, the contexts in the cloud generally disagree about which proposition is the content of an assertion of *the keys might be in the drawer*. The contexts I am considering do not disagree about the content of assertions of *it will snow tomorrow*.

[10] This move does not just apply to the truth norm. In principle, and with the right kind of epistemological work in place, it might apply to the knowledge norm as well. It seems initially possible to be in a state toward **A** such that one doesn't determinately know **A**, but if **A** were true, one would determinately know **A**. The coherence of a concept of knowledge with these features would need to be defended. But if one could be in such a state, it seems that one could

11.5   The Lifting Argument

I want to offer a more formal argument in favor of lifting indeterminacy of context into indeterminacy of normative status. I formulate this argument in a version of the logic of indeterminacy. My argument consists of some premises that collectively guarantee the thesis that indeterminacy in truth-value must be lifted, under the truth norm, into indeterminacy of normative status.[11] This argument is carried out in a formalized version of the metalanguage with a few added symbols.

Let D be an operator for determinate truth in the metalanguage. Set, as a baseline, the idea that D is a normal operator whose logic is at least as strong as the logic KT. Assume further that in the intended application, there is no higher-order indeterminacy. If it's determinate that it will rain tomorrow, it's determinate that it's determinate. And if it's not determinate, it's determinate that it's not indeterminate. This will allow us the luxury of strengthening the logic of the operator all the way to $S5$. This strengthening reflects the idea that the indeterminacy that interacts with future discourse (if indeed there is an indeterminacy of this kind) is fundamentally different from the indeterminacy that some theories associate with vague discourse.

Define an *indeterminacy* operator I in the usual way:

INDETERMINACY. $I(\varphi) \equiv \neg D(\varphi)$ & $\neg D\neg(\varphi)$

I use 'φ' as metametavariable (!) ranging over sentences of the metalanguage. It will be convenient to have available some other symbols and abbreviations:

(i)   Let $\text{cloud}(u)$ be the cloud of contexts associated with u.
(ii) Let c_u be a complex definite description referring to the context of an utterance u. The guiding idea in the background is that if the cloud of contexts associated with u is a proper cloud (i.e., if it includes more than one context), then the reference of c_u will be indeterminate as between the members of $\text{cloud}(u)$.
(iii) Let asserts denote a three-place relation between a speaker, a proposition, and a context.

---

be in such a state toward propositions that are indeterminate in truth-value. Then it would be indeterminate that one would know **A**, and if it were indeterminate that one knows **A**, it would be indeterminate that one has met the norm of assertion. I develop this view in Cariani (in press).

[11]   Similar arguments could be constructed for, say, the knowledge norm if one accepts the possibility of indeterminate knowledge statuses. For thoughts on this possibility, see Dorr (2003), Caie (2011), and Jerzak (2019).

(iv) Let sat denote a relation between a person, a proposition, and a context. Intuitively, this is the relation that holds if the norm(/norms) of assertion is satisfied by the speaker's assertion of the proposition in context.

These are the assumptions my argument relies on:

TRUTH INDETERMINACY. $I(\text{true}(\mathbf{A}, c_u))$

CONTEXT BRIDGE. $(\forall c \in \text{cloud}(u), (\text{asserts}(s, \mathbf{A}, c))) \supset$
   $D(\text{asserts}(s, \mathbf{A}, c_u))$

CONTENT DETERMINACY. $\forall c \in \text{cloud}(u), (\text{asserts}(s, \mathbf{A}, c))$

TRUTH NORM. $\text{sat}(s, \mathbf{A}, c) \equiv [\text{asserts}(s, \mathbf{A}, c) \supset \text{true}(\mathbf{A}, c)]$

Call these *the assumptions*. Informally, the first assumption says that it is indeterminate whether **A** is true in the context of utterance. This assumption, which we're exploring in this entire chapter, is essentially non-negotiable in the context of this argument (although it may be subject to all kinds of external objections). The second assumption states that if all the contexts in the cloud agree that the speaker asserted **A**, then it's determinate in the context of utterance that the speaker asserted **A**. The third assumption states that the contexts in the cloud do agree that the speaker asserted **A**. The last assumption is a formalization of the truth norm: The norm of assertion is satisfied with respect to speaker s, proposition **A**, and context c if and only if c contains an assertion by s of **A**; then **A** is true in c. (Note that c is implicitly universally quantified in this statement.)

With this work in place, we can state:

Fact 11.1 *The assumptions entail $I(\text{sat}(s, \mathbf{A}, c_u))$.*

(A proof of this fact appears in the appendix at the end of the chapter.) Informally, when the assumptions are satisfied, it is indeterminate whether the truth norm is satisfied or violated.

Because the argument is valid, the only path of resistance involves rejecting the assumptions or elements of the setup. While I might be overly optimistic, I see only one element of the setup that gives me pause. I have introduced the definite description c_u; it is an implicit part of the picture (though I should emphasize not one that shows up in any of our official assumption) that c_u's reference is indeterminate. The potential cause of concern here relates to foundational problems with indeterminate identity, brought out by a famous argument introduced by Gareth Evans (1978). I won't chase this thread of argument in here, or even present Evans's argument. Instead, I will say very quickly that many responses to it are possible, and that the one that best fits the present theoretical framework is made by Williams (2008b).

The upshot is that the lifting argument provides important support for the idea of lifting of indeterminacy of semantic statuses to indeterminacy of normative statuses.

11.6   Assertion Problems Solved

In Section 10.3, I formulated a normative version of the assertion problem for future contingents. Here it is again:

CONTEXTUALIST TRUTH NORM.   One may assert **A** in c only if **A** is true in c.

SETTLEDNESS.   If **A** is a future-contingent in c, **A** is true in c only if **A** is settled true in c.

CONCLUSION.   If **A** is a future-contingent in c, one may assert **A** in c only if **A** is settled true in c.

COROLLARY.   If **A** is a future-contingent in c, asserting **A** in context c is not normatively correct.

Assuming that my view is correct, the argument must fail somewhere, since may view entails that future contingents have indeterminate normative statuses.

As I anticipated in Chapter 10, the assumption to be rejected is SETTLEDNESS. Because contexts are classical Kaplanian contexts, the truth of **A** in c does not require that **A** be settled in c. It is possible for a future contingent sentence to be true in c even if **A** is not settled in c. To amplify this point somewhat, this is possible because, while there is no world that the situation corresponding to c determinately belongs to, c itself must determine a single world.

What might fail is an analogue of settledness for situations of utterance – something like this:

SITUATION SETTLEDNESS.   If the future is open, **A** is true in situation of utterance s only if **A** is settled in s.

But the theory built here does not leverage this notion of "truth in a situation" in any interesting way. What *does* have significance is the notion of truth at a context – and for that notion, settledness fails.

In light of our discussion so far, we can say more about the normative status of an assertion of **A** given a situation of utterance. If the future is open with respect to **A** in a given situation, then an assertion of **A** in that situation will have an indeterminate normative status. That indeterminacy might resolve itself with time. In more detail, consider the metalinguistic statement:

(i)   Assertion α made in c_u with content **A** was accurate (= met the norm of assertion).

For simplicity, let us again focus on the case of the truth norm. At the time of c_u, the reference c_u is indeterminate. If Monday is the day before an indeterministic flip of a fair coin, and on Monday someone asserts *the coin will land heads*, the status of the assertion is equally indeterminate. However, on Wednesday (i.e., post-coin flip), the set of worlds that are candidates for actuality has shrunk. In concert with this shrinkage, the set of contexts that are eligible referents of c_u also shrinks. If on Wednesday the coin has landed heads, (i) is now true, since the assertion has met the relevant norm with respect to the eligible cloud of referents for c_u on Wednesday. More generally, normative statuses that were initially indeterminate turn determinate over time.

As noted at the beginning of the chapter, here we build on a version of the "thin red line" view (Belnap and Green, 1994; Malpass and Wawer, 2012; Borghini and Torrengo, 2013). At the core of the thin red line views is the idea that there determinately is a unique actual future, yet the many possible continuations of the present are ontologically on a par. To this standard picture, the bivalent indeterminacy metaphysics on which I built my theory of context adds that the thin red line is itself indeterminate – an important difference between this picture and standard proposals in the spirit of the thin red line. Standard versions of the thin red line picture must address the metaphysical question: "What distinguishes the thin red line from the other objectively possible worlds?"[12] The proponents of bivalent indeterminacy are exempted from having to address this particular challenge, since their position is precisely that nothing does.

11.7   Objections against TRL: Belnap and Green

It does not often happen that a philosophical doctrine gets a memorable name by authors who are dead set on refuting it. But this might just be

---

[12]   See the penetrating discussion of Borghini and Torrengo (2013, pp. 114–115) for more on how constrained the thin red line theorist is.

what Belnap and Green (1994) did with their discussion of the thin red line views. The literature offers many inequivalent formulations of this doctrine. Here is how Belnap and Green introduce it:

> It is tempting to hold that there is a distinguished history, the thin red line, which we might call TRL. TRL represents the actual history, the one and only actual history in all of *Our World*. If you metaphorically stand outside *Our World*, you will see it clearly marked. One may posit a TRLwithout shifting from an objective to a subjective construal of indeterminism (a contrast discussed in Section 2), and we shall understand the TRL proposal in this objective way. The proposal succeeds in avoiding the assertion problem by postulating a "history provided by the context of use" in addition to the "moment provided by the context of use." This permits future tense sentences to be closed by context. (Belnap and Green, 1994, p. 379).

To state the thin red line thesis more concisely and within the framing of the present discussion, it amounts to the view that even if the worlds that agree with our past and present are objectively on a par, there is nonetheless a unique world that is singled out as distinctive – perhaps as the "actual" future.

MacFarlane (2003) worries that the concept picked out by this characterization is incoherent. Either there isn't an objectively marked-out world or, if there is one, then the objectively possible futures are not on a par after all.

> The non-red branches in the tree are supposed to represent objectively possible futures, but their non-redness indicates precisely that they will not be the continuations of the history that includes the utterance in question. Looking down on the tree of branching histories from above, God can see that given the past and the context of utterance, only one continuation remains in play: the one marked with the thin red line. In what sense, then, are the others really "possibilities"? (MacFarlane, 2003, p. 325)

The bivalent indeterminacy account explains why this line of thought fails. It may well be that some unique world contains our future, but it could be objectively indeterminate which world this is. Although it would be hard to explore the boundaries of the thought experiment of God looking down at the tree of worlds, it is consistent to imagine that God would not be able to see a thin red line at all. An argument for the consistency of this position comes from an analogy between the bivalent indeterminacy view and similar views concerning the problem of the many. It seems consistent to say that it is indeterminate which aggregate of molecules corresponds to the city of Chicago, while at the same time insisting that there is an aggregate of molecules that is the city of Chicago. Under this position, it is unlikely that God will be able to tell which aggregate of molecules is the city of Chicago, after all.

One possible way of interpreting the indeterminacy here is as having to do with the gap between the metaphysics and the semantics. Consider a plausible way of thinking about referential indeterminacy: It is not implausible to think that the referent of the word "Chicago" is indeterminate between various aggregates of molecules. Even if that were so, we wouldn't change the semantics of proper names to allow *Chicago* to refer to a different kind of object – say, a plural object. Instead, we submit that the referent of *Chicago* is indeterminate among the eligible referents.

Returning to future discourse, it may well be that our world matches what the branching metaphysics says it is. Even if that is so, the semantic apparatus needs a unique "world of the context." If reality looks like Figure 11.1, we run the semantics twice: once with the model corresponding to Figure 11.2 and once with the model corresponding to Figure 11.3. The best way of putting this point is to emphasize the Kaplanian distinction between situations of utterance and contexts. The metaphysical import of PARITY is that for each situation of utterance s and eligible world w, it is not determinate that s uniquely belongs to w. That is compatible with the semantics that adopts as input a richer representation of reality.

Nevertheless, Belnap and Green (1994) levy some more specific charges against TRL accounts. Their main argument is a dilemma. Either we interpret the thin red line as an *absolute* feature of reality or we interpret it as *flexible* one. It is *absolute* if it is fixed independently of our position in time. It would be absolute if it were fixed *sub specie aeternitatis* – in MacFarlane's terms, if God could see it by looking down at the tree of branching worlds. It is *flexible* otherwise. For example, the thin red line would be flexible if two moments on different sides of a branching fork were associated with different thin red lines. Belnap and Green think that both construals of TRL are incoherent, albeit for different reasons.

To make their argument more vivid, consider this scenario. Suppose that I will, in fact (i.e., as a matter of what happens on the thin red line), teach my regular course load in the coming academic year and that if I do, I will not have time to write a book. Right now, it is possible that I will get a fellowship and be released from teaching. Importantly, this alternative possibility is not marked as the absolute thin red line (i.e., as my actual future). This is, according to (Belnap and Green, 1994, p. 379), precisely where a problem arises. On the basis of this scenario, the following should be an acceptable discourse:

(2)   It is possible that I will not teach my regular course load. And in that case I will go on to write a book.

Belnap and Green think there is a problem in interpreting this discourse. They reason as follows: (i) The semantic function of *will* is to return us to the absolute thin red line; (ii) for that reason, even if *will* occurs embedded in a possibility operator, it should shift us back to the thin red line, (iii) but in the thin red line I do not write a book.

It might be easier to appreciate this point through an analogy. For Belnap and Green, the TRL incorporates, in addition to a metaphysical view, a semantic assumption to the effect that *will* works very much like the temporal indexical *now*. No matter how far shifted we are in temporal evaluation, *now* returns us back to the time of utterance, as in this Kaplan-inspired example:

(3)   Someone who will be a billionaire in 2066 is now in diapers.

Similarly, no matter how far displaced we might be in terms of which world we are evaluating at, *will* must return us to the thin red line. Under this assumption, we cannot correctly derive the truth-conditions of the first sentence in (2):

(4)   It is possible that I will not teach my regular course load next year.

This objection is quite persuasive if we add to the absolute thin red line view the semantic assumption that *will* involves an indexical effect of returning us back to the absolute thin red line.

However, this is not the view I developed here. The selectionist framework described in Parts II and III of this book does not assign to *will* the semantic function of returning the evaluation to an absolutely set thin red line. I will have more to say about this shortly, but for now the moral is that this horn of Belnap and Green's dilemma does not apply.

The other horn of the dilemma concerns the *flexible* thin red line. If the thin red line were flexible, it ought to be modeled as a function $\text{TRL}(\cdot)$ that inputs moments w_t and outputs a world – the thin red line at that moment. Nested inside this horn of the dilemma, Belnap and Green set up a sub-dilemma. A flexible theorist must commit one way or the other on this property:

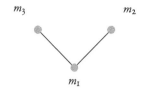

Figure 11.4   Basic branching diagram

CONVERGENCE. If two moments m_1 and m_2 belong to the same world (in their terminology, "lie on the same history"), then TRL(m_1) = TRL(m_2).

Either way, Belnap and Green think there will be trouble.

Suppose a flexible thin red line theorist accepts CONVERGENCE. Notice first this key constraint on any viable TRL picture:

TRL-CENTERING. For all w and t, w_t is a moment on TRL(w_t).

This contraint expresses the natural thought that for any moment m, the thin red line at m must go through m itself.

Now suppose (without loss of generality) that m_2 follows m_1 on one branch, and that another branch goes through m_1 that does not contain m_2 but contains m_3 instead. Figure 11.4 depicts this possibility. Then CONVERGENCE will entail:

TRL(m_1) = TRL(m_2) and TRL(m_1) = TRL(m_3)

Hence, by the transitivity of identity:

TRL(m_2) = TRL(m_3)

But this final entailment contradicts TRL-CENTERING: Whatever the thin red line at m_2, it cannot contain m_3, because it must contain m_2, and m_2 and m_3 are not on the same branch.

This reads to me like a convincing argument against CONVERGENCE. The problem is that Belnap and Green argue that rejection CONVERGENCE is also problematic. They claim that CONVERGENCE requires foregoing these inferences (which we encountered at the end of Chapter 1 and again in Section 5.4):

will will A $\models$ *will* A

A $\models$ *was will* A

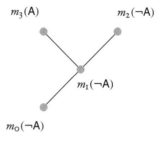

$m_3(A)$ $m_2(\neg A)$

$m_1(\neg A)$

$m_0(\neg A)$

Figure 11.5   Diagram for not rejecting CONVERGENCE

These inferences might fail because when we stack two temporal expressions, each one of them will shift the time of evaluation, and hence shift the relevant moment, and so potentially shift the TRL. Figure 11.5 shows a model based on this structure.

In Figure 11.5, each moment is labeled with $\neg A$ or A according to how the model's valuation function treats A. Suppose that at any given point, the truth or falsehood of A depends only on what happens at that point. The model in Figure 11.5 features two worlds (or "histories" in the preferred terminology of Belnap and Green). The first, call it w, corresponds to the sequence of moments $\langle m_0, m_1, m_2 \rangle$. The second, call it v, corresponds to the sequence $\langle m_0, m_1, m_3 \rangle$. Finally adopt these further assumptions: (i) *will* is a linear tense operator (for illustration's sake); (ii) $\mathrm{TRL}(m_0) = \mathrm{TRL}(m_2) = w$; but (iii) $\mathrm{TRL}(m_1) = \mathrm{TRL}(m_3) = v$. Then *will*($A$) is false at m_0: On m_0's thin red line w, there is no future point at which A holds. But *will will*(A) is true at m_0: On m_0's thin red line, there is a point (m_1) such that the thin red line *at that point*, i.e., v, contains a future point (m_3) at which A is true.

The convergence assumption might have ruled out this structure for $\mathrm{TRL}(\cdot)$ and guaranteed that no such shift happens. But we are just working under the assumption that it is false.

I agree with Belnap and Green that there are significant problems with the idea of a relative thin red line. However, I also believe that the selection semantics framework sidesteps all of these concerns while also accounting for what made the idea of a relative thin red line plausible in the first place. It represents a middle ground of sorts between the absolute and flexible versions of the thin red line.

To explain this point further, note that two things in my framework might deserve the label *thin red line*. The *contextual thin red line* is the designated world of *c* (for any context *c*). The *selectional thin red line* is whatever world is the result of selecting out of a set of historical possibilities from the perspective of a world of evaluation. The contextual thin red line is absolute, provided that we are given a context. This sense does not exactly match the original sense of "absolute TRL" I entertained earlier: It is not set *sub specie aeternitatis* but by context. In particular, if it is metaphysically indeterminate which world is actual, there will be multiple contexts with their own thin red lines. However, the contextual thin red line does have one of the key semantic features of an absolute thin red line: Once you fix a context, no operators of the language can shift it.

The contextual thin red line, together with the semantic package I advocated in Parts II and III, avoids the problems Belnap and Green posed for the absolute thin red line. Their criticism of absolute thin red lines depends on the assumption that *will* tracks back to the thin red line, much like *now* tracks back to the present time. However, nothing in our account assigns this role to *will*. That is, *will* is not an indexical that tracks back to the thin red line, but instead is evaluated *via* a selection function whose input is the world of evaluation. Sometimes that selection function takes the absolute thin red line as input, and typically when it does, it will return that input thin red line. This happens, in particular, when *will* does not occur embedded under devices that shift the world of evaluation away from its contextually set value.

In the specific case of (4) (repeated here),

It is possible that I will not teach my regular course load next year.

the selection semantics delivers the expected truth-conditions even if the thin red line, as we stipulated, is one in which I do teach my regular course load. Let w_{teach} be such a world, and let us consider the truth-conditions we predict for (4) under the semantics in Chapter 7. These truth-conditions are given in (5), assuming that f_h is the historical modal base for *will* in (4) and $f_\diamond$ is the modal base for *it is possible*:

(5) $[\![(4)]\!]^w = \exists z \in f_\diamond(w), \exists e(v(I \text{ teach regular load}, e, \textbf{sel}(z, f(w))) =$
   $1 \ \& \ \tau(e, \textbf{sel}(z, f(z))) \subseteq \text{EXT}(\{now\}))$

Informally, this says that there is a world z such that z's future contains an event amounting to my teaching of my regular load. There is nothing strange or unusual about these truth-conditions.

As for the arguments against flexible TRL, they are made moot by the fact that our choice of thin red line is not flexible. Admittedly, our framework does allow for the definition of a relative TRL – namely, whatever is the output of the selection function. However, it would be incorrect to model this sort of flexible TRL in terms of a unary function on moments. Our selection functions take two inputs: a set of worlds and an individual world. Ahead of fixing which world we are selecting *from*, we cannot determine our "relative TRL." As a result, the CONVERGENCE premise cannot even be properly formulated within this framework. Finally, both of the allegedly problematic inferences for the relative thin red line without CONVERGENCE are valid in the semantics developed in Chapter 7.

11.8　Objections against TRL: MacFarlane

MacFarlane (2014) also rejects thin red line views, although on the basis of rather different considerations: "The Thin Red Line view yields bizarre predictions about merely counterfactual retrospective assessments of future contingent claims" (p. 2019).

Consider the by-now-no-doubt-very-familiar diagram in Figure 11.6. It represents three possible contexts: c_0 is located at a pre-branching point on Monday; c_1 and c_2 are both after the branching node and occur on Tuesday.

Like Belnap and Green's flexible approach, MacFarlane models the thin red line picture in terms of a unary function TRL($\cdot$). Unlike Belnap and Green, MacFarlane takes TRL to be a function of context. The thick line in

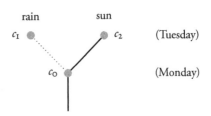

Figure 11.6　Three-context basic branching diagram

Figure 11.6 represents TRL(c_0). Suppose that in context c_0 on Monday, Jake assertively utters:

(6)   Tomorrow Berkeley will be sunny.

MacFarlane asks us to imagine assessing Jake's assertion from the perspective of c_1 and c_2 on Tuesday. Things look good from c_2's perspective, but not from c_1's. The thin red line picture predicts Jake's Monday assertion was accurate because in the thin red line world it was, in fact, sunny. But that is odd: The rain is pouring on your head, right as you are busy congratulating Jake for his true assertion that it would be sunny.

That's a bad verdict. But MacFarlane goes on to make a key point:

> A proponent of the Thin Red Line could perhaps meet the objection by saying that the Thin Red Line is different for each of the two observers. But this would amount to taking the TRL function to be a function from a context of use and a context of assessment to a world. Because the view would give a semantic role to contexts of assessment, it would be a version of a relativist view, not an alternative to one. (MacFarlane, 2014, p. 211)

This argument also fails according to my proposal. According to the view I advocated toward the end of Section 11.6, the thin red line is itself indeterminate and the diagram in Figure 11.6 misses out on the key reason why. There were *already* two contexts on Monday: one whose continuation was on the sunny branch and one whose continuation was on the rainy branch. Branching made the difference between these two contexts tangible, but the distinction was there all along.

11.9   Conclusion

The sort of obstacles that Belnap and Green, on the one hand, and MacFarlane, on the other hand, envisioned as standing in the way of the thin red line view do not seem to apply to the present proposal. I have proposed that, should one want to insist on the intuitions that I think lie at the core of the idea of the open future, then the preferable option is to adopt a model in which contexts are classical (in the sense of determining a possible world). The indeterminacy concerning which world is actual filters up into indeterminacy as to which classical context is to be associated with a situation of utterance. Furthermore, it filters up into indeterminacy as to whether the norms of assertions are satisfied by utterances of future contingent claims.

Appendix: Proofs

Fact 11.1 The lifting argument

Assumptions

TRUTH INDETERMINACY. $I(\text{true}(\mathbf{A}, c_u))$
CONTEXT BRIDGE. $(\forall c \in \text{cloud}(u), (\text{asserts}(s, \mathbf{A}, c)))) \supset$
   $D(\text{asserts}(s, \mathbf{A}, c_u))$
CONTENT DETERMINACY. $\forall c \in \text{cloud}(u), (\text{asserts}(s, \mathbf{A}, c))$
TRUTH NORM. $D(\text{sat}(s, \mathbf{A}, c) \equiv [\text{asserts}(s, \mathbf{A}, c) \supset \text{true}(\mathbf{A}, c)]$

Claim: The assumptions entail $I(\text{sat}(s, \mathbf{A}, c_u))$.

Proof. We run two reductios, and then we appeal to the definition of the indeterminacy operator to finish off the argument. For the first reductio, assume

(i) $D(\text{sat}(s, \mathbf{A}, c_u))$

Applying the K axiom for D on the left-to-right direction TRUTH NORM principle after instantiating with c_u yields:

(ii) $D[(\text{sat}(s, \mathbf{A}, c_u)) \supset D[\text{asserts}(s, \mathbf{A}, c_u) \supset \text{true}(\mathbf{A}, c_u)]$

Here we can detach the consequent by modus ponens for $\supset$, and then by another application of the K axiom for D derive:

(iii) $D[\text{asserts}(s, \mathbf{A}, c_u)] \supset D[\text{true}(\mathbf{A}, c_u)]$

Together, CONTEXT BRIDGE and CONTENT DETERMINACY entail:

(iv) $D(\text{asserts}(s, \mathbf{A}, c_u))$

This and (ii) entail:

(v) $D(\text{true}(\mathbf{A}, c_u))$

However, (iv) contradicts something that follows from TRUTH INDETER-MINACY – namely, $\neg D(\text{true}(\mathbf{A}, c_u))$. Because we are considering a determinacy operator that does not allow for higher-order indeterminacy and because our background logic is classical, *reductio* is valid, so we conclude that $\neg D(\text{sat}(s, \mathbf{A}, c_u))$.

For a parallel reductio, assume:

(v) $D\neg(\text{sat}(s, \mathbf{A}, c_u))$

From the K axiom for D and the TRUTH NORM, deduce:

(vi) $D\neg(\text{true}(\mathbf{A}, c_u))$

That entailment must conflict with:

(vii) $\neg D\neg(\text{true}(\mathbf{A}, c_u))$

But (vii) is in turn entailed by TRUTH INDETERMINACY. As a result, by reductio, this branch of the argument entails $\neg D\neg(\text{sat}(s, \mathbf{A}, c_u))$. Together, the two reductios entail our conclusion that it's indetermiante whether $\mathbf{A}$ is true in c_u.   □

PART V

Future Cognition and Epistemology: Some Themes

CHAPTER 12

Imagining and Simulating the Future

I believe that we know many things about the future. Here are some examples of things I know. That, in one hour, my body still will contain blood. That, as of tomorrow, none of my grandchildren (if I am to have any) will be born. That Lori Lightfoot will be the mayor of Chicago in July 2020 (this is ahead of me at the time of this writing). No doubt some future events result from such complex factors that they are altogether impossible to forecast to a degree that would be sufficient for knowledge. The local weather two years out is inaccessible to our knowledge in a way that the local weather two years ago is not. Even so, complexity might limit how much knowledge of the future we can accumulate, but it is not, in principle, a barrier to foreknowledge.

The idea that we have substantial, though limited, knowledge of the future stands in direct opposition to the rather common view that the future is intrinsically unknowable. Many skeptics about the future do not want to deny us knowledge altogether – they are not all-out skeptics. They think instead that there are specific barriers to knowledge when it comes to future-directed claims, with the possible exception of necessary propositions about the future. I won't try to refute this kind of future-directed skepticism. Instead, in this chapter and the next, I investigate what knowledge of the future must be like, assuming that it is possible.

In tackling these questions, I will assume that the future is not metaphysically indeterminate. This assumption is the exact opposite of the assumption I operated under in Part IV. An objection might be raised that because of this, I am missing out on the most significant reasons for skepticism about the future. (I consider what to say in response to these challenges in Cariani, in press.) Maybe so. But while I grant that the possible metaphysical indeterminacy poses important challenges to an epistemology of the future, many difficult questions concerning the possibility of knowledge of the future arise independently of any indeterminacy.[1]

One type of threat to the possibility of foreknowledge stems from a broad commitment to empiricism. Peter Carruthers (1990) suggests – plausibly in my view – that the core commitment of empiricism is a rejection of knowledge claims "except where we can provide at least the beginnings of a naturalistic account of the processes through which that knowledge is acquired" (p. 67). It is on this basis that empiricists find it initially problematic to speak of innate knowledge or of substantive *a priori* knowledge. Commitment to this tenet of empiricism also provides an initial challenge to human foreknowledge. The fact that the future does not causally impinge on us seems to make it initially difficult to provide a minimally naturalistic account of how we acquire knowledge about it.[2]

One cannot evade this challenge by rejecting empiricism or Carruthers's proposed characterization of empiricism. Perhaps some kinds of knowledge cannot be reconciled with the naturalist requirement. Nevertheless, that naturalist requirement plausibly governs an important subset of our knowledge: *empirical* knowledge. A much more modest thesis is that purported knowledge of the future cannot qualify as empirical knowledge without "the beginnings" of a naturalistically acceptable account of its origin. Then the lingering problem is that the bulk of our purported knowledge about the future – such as my knowledge that it will snow in Chicago next year – may well be empirical. From this point of view, empiricist strictures about what sorts of knowledge are possible are irrelevant to the argument: Enough trouble arises if it turns out that empirical knowledge of the future is impossible.

My aim is to put together such beginnings. The first step is this: If the contents of future claims are modal contents, then the epistemology of the future is a chapter of modal epistemology. In turn, the cognitive science of

---

[1] For examples of difficult epistemological puzzles about the future without any indeterminacy assumptions, see Hawthorne and Lasonen-Aarnio (2008) and Dorr et al. (2014).

[2] This issue also rises to maximal prominence in the context of naturalistic theories of knowledge. In his classic "A Causal Theory of Knowing" (1967), Alvin Goldman notes that a causal connection requirement seems to put future-directed knowledge out of reach. If knowing **A** requires some causal connection from the truthmakers of **A** to one's mental state, Goldman reasons, and if there is no backward causation, then there is no knowing future contingents. In an effort to save the possibility of knowledge of the future, Goldman weakens the theory so as to allow knowledge in cases in which there is a common cause of the future event and the present belief. Today's devastating injury to our star player will cause us to lose tomorrow's match and also causes us to believe now that we will lose that match. That's enough to meet the causal requirement with respect to the proposition that we will lose that match. While Goldman himself abandoned the causal theory of knowledge in favor of the more general reliabilist framework, these problems are quite general.

future judgment is a chapter of the cognitive science of modal judgment. This fits well with the motivational idea for this project – that there is a fundamental connection between future modality and counterfactual modality. Given the strength of that link, it is extremely natural to suppose that there might be equally deep connections at the level of thought.

Filing future judgment under the category of "modal judgment" is not enough, however. Substantive modal knowledge may be just as problematic for a naturalist as foreknowledge. To meet the naturalistic constraint on empirical knowledge, we must develop some preliminary understanding of the faculties that allow us to acquire modal knowledge. My strategy will be to put together a view of empirical knowledge of counterfactual claims by means of a selective literature review, and then explore how its extension to future discourse might go. Specifically, I start by considering the claim that a distinctive way of making counterfactual judgments involves *mental simulation*. I understand mental simulation to be the mental process whereby thinkers engage their imaginative faculties to come to judgments about some state of affairs. Typically, the target state of affairs is not one that is causally upstream from one's judgment. The idea that an imaginative capacity is crucial to counterfactual judgment has been discussed by many authors.[3] Instead of providing an exhaustive map of this literature, I will focus on some theoretical highlights that establish a baseline view about counterfactual epistemology. I will then use this view to investigate whether similar cognitive and epistemological claims could be made in the case of future judgment.

12.1 The Simulation Heuristic

All the basketball analysts had predicted that the Golden State Warriors would reach the 2019 NBA finals and win another title, their third in a row. Golden State did reach the NBA finals, but a unique stroke of injury misfortunes took out critical players. Undermanned, they lost to the Toronto Raptors. Everyone who followed these events – everyone except for some Raptors fans – judged:

(1)   If Golden State had not faced injuries, they would have won.

---

[3] Kahneman and Tversky (1982), Williamson (2008), Kroedel (2012), Balcerak Jackson (2018), and Strohminger and Yli-Vakkuri (2019).

Philosophical attention to counterfactuals like (1) has largely focused on their truth-conditions. Meanwhile, a parallel literature in cognitive psychology has explored the mechanics of counterfactual thinking without going through the intermediate step of first developing their semantics.[4] This research focus is structured around a complex cluster of problems.

One is the *hypothesis choice problem:* Why do people tend to explore some counterfactual scenarios as opposed to others? To continue with our basketball example, suppose one is thinking about the conditions under which they would judge that Golden State would have won the finals. Why consider the specific hypothesis in the antecedent of (1)? Why does that particular antecedent seem to be a more natural choice than some competing ones (e.g., *if the Raptors star players had been injured, …*)?

Closer to my present interests is the *enrichment problem:* What kinds of situations do people envisage when they entertain a counterfactual scenario? Someone who entertains the counterfactual in (1) typically imagines a situation in which the injuries never happen and those players go on to play during the finals. Evidently, this is not the *only* way of filling out a scenario that is consistent with the antecedent of (1). Perhaps all the Golden State players are healthy but they decide to go on a backpacking trip to New Zealand during the finals. Or maybe they play but someone on the opposing team experiences a sudden skill leap. From the psychological point of view, it is valuable to ask: How do people enrich the antecedent of a counterfactual to flesh out the hypothetical scenario beyond what is explicitly stipulated by the antecedent itself?

Even once we have filled out our hypothetical scenario, we do not have a counterfactual judgment. Related to the enrichment problem is the *evaluation problem:* What features of a hypothetical scenario do people rely on in determining whether to accept or reject a counterfactual? Suppose I do fill out the antecedent of (1) so that all the Golden State players are healthy, not on a backpacking trip, and so on. What kinds of methods do people deploy in reaching counterfactual conclusion under such a fully fleshed-out antecedent scenario?[5]

---

[4] Perhaps the most prominent example of this kind is the work by Kahneman and Tversky (1982), discussed later in this section. For a more recent example of this approach, within the "mental models" theoretical paradigm, see Johnson-Laird (1983) and Byrne (2007).

[5] The enrichment and evaluation problems finally make contact with semantic theories of counterfactuals. Mainstream semantic analyses of counterfactuals invoke the idea of a minimal modification of actuality that is required to accommodate the antecedent (consider for instance, Stalnaker, 1984; Lewis, 1979). If these semantic insights are on the right track, it seems plausible that counterfactuals like (1) ought to be evaluated by minimally modifying some representation of the actual world. Of course, the observation that there is a parallel question in semantics does not mean that the psychological question is settled.

A pioneering contribution to the cognitive science of counterfactual thinking is the work on the "simulation heuristic" done by Kahneman and Tversky (1982). Among other things, Kahneman and Tversky propose a novel approach to the evaluation problem for counterfactuals. They suggest that people often make counterfactual judgments by running *mental simulations* of scenarios (hence the name "simulation heuristic"). This involves forming a representation of actuality, including a representation of those tendencies, forces, and laws that govern its dynamic development. Given a representation like this, a simulating agent would intervene on it to accommodate the effect of one or more counterfactual suppositions. Finally, they would rely on the dynamic principles in their model to come to a determination about counterfactual outcomes. Here is their basic description of the heuristic:

> There appear to be many situations in which questions about events are answered by an operation that resembles the running of a simulation model. … The starting conditions for a "run" can be left at their realistic default values or modified to assume some special contingency; the outcomes can be left unspecified, or else a target state may be set, with the task of finding a path to that state from the initial conditions. A simulation does not necessarily produce a single story which starts at the beginning and ends with a definite outcome. Rather, we construe the output of simulation as an assessment of the ease with which the model could produce different outcomes, given its initial conditions and operating parameters. Thus, we suggest that mental simulation yields a measure of the propensity of one's model of the situation to generate various outcomes. (Kahneman and Tversky, 1982, p. 201)

Despite this lucid abstract description, Kahneman and Tversky's experimental illustrations of the simulation heuristic are not very detailed. Even worse for our purposes, they do not seem to target the motivational idea laid out in the preceding quote. Consider their lead experiment:

> Mr. Crane and Mr. Tees were scheduled to leave the airport on different flights at the same time. They traveled from town in the same limousine, were caught in the same traffic jam, and arrived at the airport 30 minutes after the scheduled departure of their flights.
> Mr. Crane is told that his flight left on time.
> Mr. Tees is told that his flight was delayed, and just left five minutes ago.
> Who is more upset?
> Mr. Crane   Mr. Tees
> (Kahneman and Tversky, 1982, p. 203)

Kahneman and Tversky report that 96 percent of (student) participants judged that Mr. Tees was more upset.

The theoretical argument that is invited is something like this. Participants' degree of acceptance for the proposition that X is upset is proportional to the closeness and availability of antecedents A such that they accept *if A, X would have made his flight*. The closeness of these antecedents is constructed by the "reverse simulation" process. Start from the counterfactual conclusion that "X made his flight" and reverse-engineer an antecedent that suffices to support it. For Mr. Tees, this antecedent might be *if we had arrived just a bit earlier*. For Mr. Crane, it might be *if we had arrived on time*. Mr. Tees's antecedent is intuitively closer to the actual course of history than Mr. Crane's. Hence, Mr. Tees ought to be more upset.

Set aside concerns you might have as to whether the experiment does support this argument. My worry is that the experiment bears only on the hypothesis choice problem and not on the concerns about enrichment and evaluation highlighted by Kahneman and Tversky in their general description of the simulation heuristic.

Despite these argumentative shortcomings, Kahneman and Tversky's discussion of the simulation heuristic has been extraordinarily influential. The idea that people simulate alternative possibilities appears in a variety of disconnected literature threads. Indeed – a sign of true success – the idea of mental simulation shows up in a variety of incompatible versions.

Besides counterfactuals, Kahneman and Tversky (1982) entertain, but do not develop, a handful of other applications of the simulation heuristic – all relevant to my project in this book. These include (i) how people make predictions, (ii) how people assess (conditional and unconditional) probabilities, and (iii) how people form judgments of causality. Notably, the role of simulation in causal judgment has received significant attention in recent literature, especially in connection with the high-powered causal modeling framework (Gerstenberg et al., 2015; Icard et al., 2017).

More recent research in psychology and neuroscience has taken the simulation idea well beyond these initial domains. A growing body of research in cognitive psychology and neuroscience has emphasized connections between anticipating the future and remembering the past (Schacter et al., 2007). Thus De Brigard (2014) develops within the philosophical literature the provocative thesis that the primary role of memory is not remembering what was, but rather simulating what *could have been*. According to DeBrigard, memory is part of a larger cognitive system that enables us to both anticipate the future and reconstruct past facts from more basic bits of information that we can store and retrieve more efficiently (see also the more recent epistemology-focused development in Aronowitz, 2019).

In this same theoretical framework, Szpunar and McDermott (2008) and Szpunar (2010) explore the concept of episodic future thought. We think of memory in connection with the past, but, Szpunar argues, there are relations that we bear to possible future events that mirror the relations that we bear to remembered events. Just as people have episodic memories of events (memories of events experienced from the first-person point of view) they have states that are akin to episodic memories, but concern future states of affairs. Such states are experienced as "mental simulations" of the future.

Another application of the simulation paradigm concerns so-called mindreading. Not to be confused with the similarly named school of magic tricks, mindreading is the study of how people figure out what others are thinking. A prominent hypothesis in this arena (though by no means the only one) is the simulation theory. [See Goldman (1992) for its presentation and Spaulding (2016) for a critical review.] According to the simulation theory, we form beliefs about what others are thinking by simulating being them.

12.2   Simulation and Counterfactuals

That all sounds interesting, but exactly how are mental simulations supposed to work in counterfactual judgments? Imagine that one evening Sara was burdened with work and left her office late. This caused her to miss the train. You want to know: Would Sara have been late leaving her office had she not missed the train? According to the simulation hypothesis, when people are faced with this question, they set up a kind of mental model of the situation.

Presumably these models are mental objects that stand in some kind of structural relation to the systems they represents.[6] A model of Sara's situation might start off as an accurate representation of those real elements the thinker assumes to be relevant to the counterfactual judgment. It is inviting, initially at least, to suppose that these simulation models are nonsymbolic in nature. One possibility, for instance, is that one's simulation model of Sara's home journey takes the form of mental imagery of some sort.

---

[6] Mental simulations are not always conceived in this way. At one end of the spectrum, mental modelers have suggested that people construct mental models corresponding to certain types of sentences. For instance, people evaluating a conditional of the form (*if* A)(B) attempt to construct a mental model of the situation corresponding to A & B (Johnson-Laird, 1983; Byrne, 2007). I won't be addressing this type of view, despite its significant influence in cognitive psychology.

Understood this way, simulation models are mental analogues of simulations we might carry out in the external world. Instead of mental imagery, an isomorphic simulation could have relied on Lego bricks to represent bits of Sara's environment. These models, whether mental or external, might represent the factors that are relevant to the target question that's guiding inquiry: potential obstacles Sara might encounter, the distance between the office and the train station, the initial position of the train, etc.

Crucially, the models need some temporal dynamics – principles that would regulate their evolution at each tick of the model's clock. In the model of Sara's journey home, with each tick of the model's clock, the train gets closer to the station. More generally, the model's dynamic principles specify how prior states evolve into new ones. A standard dynamic principle (for simple cases of mental simulation) is to the effect that things will evolve in agreement with the thinker's "naïve physics" engine. This is the cognitive system that is responsible for people's ability to form expectations about the relative motions of macroscopic objects (Battaglia et al., 2013).

An important element of simulation as a vehicle for conditional judgment is that a simulation might be altered by tinkering with its initial conditions. Pleasibly, one can tweak the model's initial condition while holding fixed its dynamics as a way of reaching counterfactual judgments. For example, fixing a model of the situation surrounding Sara's journey home, one could explore what would happen if Sara left her office at earlier or later times. It is natural to interpret these interventions as probing counterfactual hypotheses.

Thus, Williamson (2008, chapter 5) proposes that mental simulation is, in some sense to be clarified, at the core of our ability to make counterfactual judgments. Williamson's leading examples involve simulations that are even more basic than the complex case of Sara's journey home. Imagine a spherical boulder rolling down a smooth hill and getting trapped in a bush halfway down. We easily form the counterfactual judgment *if the boulder hadn't been there, the rock would have rolled all the way to the bottom.* The hypothesis we are entertaining is that we form judgments like this by creating mental simulations that rely on our our naïve physics engine.

In such extremely simple scenarios, such simulations unfold in linear patterns – e.g., the boulder rolls down to the bottom. If the target of a simulation is more complex and the simulation is less than perfectly deterministic, a careful thinker might need to run the simulation multiple times. Matters work similarly for the case in which the thinker approaches the simulation task without a specific initial scenario, but with a range of such scenarios. The result of these multiple simulations might be a probability distribution over possible outcomes of the simulation, as opposed to a binary (yes/no) answer.

An important point of emphasis for Williamson is that learning counterfactuals does not *require* mental simulation. One can learn the contents of counterfactual contents by virtually any other epistemic pathway. Testimony is a prime example. A reliable expert might inform me that *If Archduke Franz Ferdinand had not been shot, there would still have been a global war*. Suppose the expert is right, and that nothing spooky is preventing me from acquiring counterfactual knowledge from this testimony (no defeaters are available, the causal pathways that make the counterfactual true are roughly as the testifier imagines them to be, etc.). In such a case, it is natural to say that I learned (i.e., came to know) a counterfactual content from testimony.

Neither is it the case that mental simulation is the only *generative* source of counterfactual knowledge. (A source of knowledge is generative if it creates new knowledge, as opposed to merely transmitting it.) For one thing, some epistemologists maintain that testimony can also be a generative source of knowledge (Lackey, 1999, 2008).[7] For another, some counterfactuals can evidently be learned by deductive inference, which can in the relevant sense be generative. One might acquire knowledge of the counterfactual *if I were to wear a blue dress, I'd be wearing something blue* in just this way.

Finally, under standard semantic assumptions, counterfactuals whose antecedents are true can be evaluated by directly evaluating their consequents. It is a standard assumption in counterfactual semantics that if a counterfactual has a true antecedent and a non-modal consequent, then its truth depends only on the truth of the consequent at the actual world. Suppose it is true that Edoardo traveled to Paris. Consider inquiring into the truth of this sentence:

(2)   If Edoardo had traveled to Paris, he would have seen the Eiffel Tower.

The truth of (2) depends exclusively on whether Edoardo did, in actual fact, see the Eiffel Tower. On the epistemic side, someone who knows that Edoardo traveled to Paris can learn the counterfactual by learning that Edoardo did see the Eiffel Tower.

Williamson (2008) sums up all of these considerations with a useful slogan: "there is no uniform epistemology of counterfactual conditionals"

---

7   Though Lackey's examples of generative testimony are in the non-counterfactual domain, it is an easy homework exercise to construct cases in which testimony generates counterfactual knowledge.

(p. 152). What he means is that any ordinary cognitive faculty might be relied on in producing counterfactual judgments. Conversely, no cognitive faculty is involved *only* in the evaluation of counterfactuals. Consider the case of simulation: One can just as easily simulate actual events as one can simulate counterfactual ones. For example, a detective might simulate a crime in the process of forming a judgment as to how it, in fact, happened.

If that is true, the pressing question then becomes what special role mental simulation is supposed to play in counterfactual judgment. Surely it is too weak to say that *some* counterfactual judgments are learned by mental simulation. For Williamson, the key hypothesis is the following claim:

> [Mental simulation] is the most distinctive cognitive feature of the process of evaluating them, because it is so much more useful for counterfactuals than it is for most non-counterfactual contents. (Williamson, 2008, p. 152).

This does not sound wrong, but it does sound generic. In what sense is it more useful for counterfactuals than for non-counterfactuals? What makes it more useful? And which non-counterfactuals does Williamson have in mind?

To start, I believe that the important dividing line is not between counterfactuals and non-counterfactuals, but rather between modal and non-modal judgment. As Kahneman and Tversky highlighted, if there is a mental simulation system, we have as much reason to think that it is involved in predictive, causal, and probabilistic judgment. A mental simulation system would have to be involved in forming many judgments about *what could have been.* These are neither predictions nor counterfactuals. Think again about Williamson's boulder. Suppose you saw it get stuck on a bush on Monday. On Tuesday, you learn that overnight there were winds strong enough to eradicate the bush. Through simulation you might form the modal judgment that *the boulder could have rolled to the bottom of the hill.* The idea must then be that simulation is especially "useful" in modal thought generally. But in what sense is it "especially useful"? I want to suggest that it is useful because it allows us to form judgments in the absence of direct evidence.

To substantiate this point, we need an operative understanding of direct evidence. This is difficult because what counts as the correct theory of direct evidence is highly controversial. Here I will sketch a picture that guides my thinking, even though it might ultimately be untenable. Suppose that a belief that **A** is formed by a *direct path* if there is a causal path to the belief from an eventuality **A** is about, whose occurrence in world w

is sufficient to establish that **A** is true in *w*. My belief that Caesar was murdered was generated by a causal path that starts with the actual murder and goes through a tortuous, multi-millennial testimonial chain. For many true non-modal and non-logical beliefs, direct paths are generally available. It is possible, and perhaps typical, to learn that Caesar was murdered by means of a direct path.[8]

What is distinctive in the case of modal and future matters is that direct paths are typically *not* available to a thinker. Plausibly, there is no actual event whose content is sufficient to establish that if Oswald hadn't killed Kennedy, no one else would have. And if there is no actual event, then there cannot be a causal path leading from it to anyone's judgment of that counterfactual. Similarly, we rarely see actual events and states that are sufficient to establish interesting possibility claims, such as the claim that life could have developed on Mars.

The first sense in which simulation might be useful in modal thought is that it provides a nondirect path to forming modal and future judgments that is nonetheless anchored in actual events. The anchoring in actuality is of critical epistemic significance. As Balcerak Jackson (2018) argues, if imaginative faculties (including simulation) are to play any kind of epistemic role, they cannot be entirely unconstrained from actuality and divorced from experience. For Balcerak Jackson, the kind of imaginative faculty involved in modal thought is indeed linked to experience because it is "recreative" – in the sense that it involves the reelaboration of materials that are acquired in experience. This recreative aspect then allows us to get traction on the question of how we might acquire empirical knowledge of modal claims.

There is a second way in which simulation might be especially helpful for modal thought. Even in cases where there are alternative, and more direct, ways of forming a judgment, simulation might be faster and less expensive. This is especially the case when simulation methods are compared to more analytical methods.

Consider an example from the literature on computer simulation: the propagation of a fire across a forest. This scenario is well represented by analytical models involving differential equations. But such analyses based on solving differential equations are computationally expensive, so researchers

---

[8] Direct paths are at the center of some externalist epistemologies, such as Goldman's (1967) causal theory of knowledge. But I shy away from many commitments that a causal theorist would undertake about direct paths: I do not claim that direct paths are privileged over other kinds of paths to belief formation; I do not claim that they are sufficient for knowledge; and I do not claim that they are necessary.

in the field of agent-based modeling (ABM) have devised alternative simulation-based approaches (Wilensky and Rand, 2015, pp. 103–117). A prototypical ABM model might represent a forest on fire as a collection of agents (the fire sparks) and static locations (the trees). Dynamic and probabilistic principles govern the temporal evolution of the model. For example, if a tree is on fire at time t, there is some probability that its neighbors will be on fire at a later time t^+. These principles might in turn be sensitive to various parameters whose values may be left up to the modeler. Once we have an ABM model whose accuracy is good enough for our modeling purposes, we can start relying on it in practical circumstances – perhaps even stop using the analytical model altogether.

Something similar may be true of mental simulation. For it to be both important and useful, it doesn't have to be a pathway to judgments that we would not otherwise reach. Instead, it is sufficient that in enough situations, simulation is faster, more convenient, or easier to use than alternative methods.

12.3   Varieties and Degrees of Mental Simulation

The mental simulation hypothesis I sketched is schematic in important respects. Rips (1986) argues that no way of spelling out the simulationist insight will be satisfactory. Rips distinguishes between a thick – "global" in his words – and a thin understanding of mental simulation. In this global sense, a simulation is a fully fleshed-out model of the relevant domain – a scaled-down version of the complex models we construct to predict complex systems such as the weather. By contrast, in the thinner "local" sense, talk of simulation is just a fancy way of referring to a patchwork systems of heuristics that need not add up to a comprehensive picture of the cognitive system being modeled. Rips finds neither construal to be adequate.

Rips frames the fundamental theoretical opposition along a key battle line. For him, the distinctive idea of the simulation hypothesis is that simulation is essentially nonsymbolic. Simulations operate exclusively on unarticulated mental imagery.

> The important thing is that this sort of reasoning *doesn't* feel like carrying out a derivation in some sort of internal logic or probability calculus. (Rips, 1986, p. 270)

To see how this is a substantive move, let me briefly spell out an alternative hypothesis and see exactly why it is ruled out by this statement.

Suppose that an important part of learning about the world involves forming and maintaining a *causal model* of the world itself, or some chunk thereof. Here, I use "causal model" in the rather technical sense that has been enshrined in the causal inference literature of the last few decades (Pearl, 2000; Spirtes et al., 2000). Start with a set of variables **V**, each representing some way the world might be in some specific respect. In this context, a *causal model* is a directed acyclic graph over **V**. Here is a very simple causal model based on three binary variables, representing Williamson's boulder example:

`pushed-at-the-top?` → `bush-in-the-way?` → `reached-bottom?`

Psychologists have appropriated the theory of causal models, with many claiming that it provides a useful picture of how people in fact reason about causal matters.[9] Much of this psychological work can be carried out by sticking to the claim that causal models merely characterize the functional profile of human causal reasoning, while staying neutral on the more substantive question of whether people actually manipulate causal models as representations. For our discussion, it will be instructive to take that extra step and entertain the view that people precisely manipulate symbolic representations that roughly correspond to causal models. So, let's imagine an agent who makes counterfactual judgments by:

(i) Generating a causal model of the relevant chunk of reality (or perhaps a range of causal models with a probability distribution over them) and

(ii) Intervening on that causal model so as to verify the antecedent of the counterfactual and then

(iii) Checking what effect this intervention has on the consequent.

In a sense, such an agent may be said to be running mental simulations every time they work out the results of some counterfactual interventions on their background model. However, if we stipulate that simulations are completely nonsymbolic, manipulating causal models does not count as simulation-based thinking, because the representations associated with causal models are themselves partially symbolic.

This teaches us that we need to keep in mind two sets of distinctions. On the one hand, Rips's thick/thin distinction deals with whether the simulation provides a sufficiently coherent representation of the simulated reality.

---

9 See Sloman (2005) and references therein.

On the other hand, we can distinguish between conceptualizing simulation as completely nonsymbolic versus allowing symboling elements.

With these distinctions in hand, we can return to Rips's central argument. Let S be any system about which we want to make predictions. Rips argues that in the thick sense, it is implausible that people are capable of performing the simulations required to have a comprehensive model of S, let alone one that is accurate. At the least, we can't do so for many of the systems that might be of potential interest. This qualification is important: Rips is not challenging the idea that we might operate on mental imagery to explore highly simplified scenarios such as balls colliding. His point is that it is implausible to claim that we can manipulate a mental model for evaluating counterfactual thoughts that are of any actual interest. We won't be able to make sense of complex conditional claims such as *if Sara had left earlier, she would not have missed the train* or, worse, *if a Soviet cosmonaut had been the first to the Moon, the space race would have continued.*

To substantiate this challenge, Rips leverages two kinds of findings. The first finding focuses on the limits of a AI engines for spatial reasoning: At the time of Rips's writing, and to some degree even now, these engines are limited in their qualitative simulation capacities to very simple domains.[10] Rips focuses specifically on Forbus's program FROB, which is able to "describe and answer questions about the behavior of balls … bouncing around in a two-dimensional plane [with a line boundary]" (Forbus, 1983). Forbus's system is designed to work with qualitative information about the trajectories of balls, rather than with fully specified quantitative information – say, about their speed, momentum, etc. Even in this relatively tame application, it is hard to obtain something useful from the AI simulation without actually resorting to analytical quantitative models of space. The implicit argument goes something like this: If our best attempts to replicate a simulation-like cognitive system that is capable of elementary spatial reasoning are visibly hampered (without the support of an analytical model), we have reason to think that the human cognitive system is not limited to purely qualitative manipulation of model elements.

This is not a knock-down argument, nor is it presented as such. For one thing, the methodology of investigating human cognition by generating

---

[10] For a description of a simulation-based engine based on more contemporary approaches, see Battaglia et al. (2013). While the intuitive physics engine described in this paper is capable of drawing much more substantive inferences about scene settings than that described in the Forbus (1983) paper from three decades earlier, it also relies on a system with a much stronger symbolic component, a point to which I shall return shortly.

AI systems that replicate some of its functionality is limited. For another, the results obtained by Forbus (1983) do not necessarily speak directly to what different AI systems might be able to do forty years hence. [Again, a comparison with systems such as the one in Battaglia et al. (2013) is instructive.]

As for the second finding, Rips reports an experiment conducted in collaboration with Dedre Gentner concerning the relationships between physical variables in a closed room (Rips, 1986, pp. 271–272). Rips describes this experiment in a somewhat quick fashion, but the central claim is that people's judgments about which variables affect which others are incoherent in ways that are hard to square with the idea that they run a single, global mental model of the room. In particular, the experiment reveals pervasive intransitivity in causal judgments – well beyond the kinds of cases of causal intransitivity that are discussed in the philosophy literature. The argument here is that if people ran a global mental model of the room that had any prayer of tracking the right dependence relationships, they would not end up with such wildly intransitive patterns of judgment.

From these two findings, Rips concludes that the mental simulation that is allegedly involved in counterfactual reasoning cannot properly be the "thick" simulation. But, Rips worries, it cannot be thin simulation either, because thin simulation is nonsymbolic. Moreover, it is a little much to use the term "simulation" for a patchwork assemblage of nonsymbolic rules of thumb. At its heart, thin simulation is just too unspecific to meet the explanatory demands of the cognitive scientist:

> Mental modelers' loose talk about mental simulation or simulation heuristics is of little use unless it can be translated into a plausible psychological mechanism that is capable of doing the simulating, where by "plausible mechanism" I mean one that is framed in terms of the ordinary cognitive vocabulary of elementary information processes – for example, comparison and storage operations. But the best examples we have of how this translation would go … puts these simulations out of the reach of all but the experts in a given domain. Of course, people do make predictions about what will happen in complex physical and social interactions. They plan actions and evaluate the probable consequences. If you like, you can refer to these projections as "simulations based on mental models." But in doing so, you forfeit the claim that "simulation" should be taken literally as a distinct type of reasoning. You have become a figurative, rather than a literal, mental modeler. (Rips, 1986, pp. 273–274)

I am sympathetic to Rips's fiery polemic. Talk of "mental simulation" incurs a conceptual debt. The theory is not complete without a fuller understanding of what sorts of processes and mechanisms are involved.

Insofar as we have some kind of grasp of such processes, it is highly localized and not generalizable to some of the most interesting case.

I am not convinced, however, that agreeing with this much would force one to give up the simulationist insights into future and counterfactual cognition altogether. The key is to accept that the development of the theory of the relevant processes and mechanism is very much a work in progress and, crucially, to renounce the dichotomy between nonsymbolic mental models and symbolic reasoning. There are just *models*, period. Models are simplified representations of complex systems, where the simplifications serve some explanatory or computational purpose. There is no official edict, save for the commitments of some of the original mental modelers, to the effect that modeling must consist exclusively of nonsymbolic manipulation. More generally, there is no contradiction between claiming that people perform some kind of simulation and the idea that they rely on symbolically encoded information. If I am right, then an agent's simulation engine might consist in part – maybe even in a *large* part – of symbolically represented rules.

At this point, one might worry that if an agent's "simulation engine" is entirely symbolic, then running simulation is just a special case of inference. If so, nothing much is gained by calling it a "simulation" or by referring to a type of application of deductive reasoning as the "simulation engine." I would be inclined to agree with this diagnosis if "mental simulation" comprised performing deductions that rely only on symbolically encoded rules (and symbolically encoded premises about the environment). However, proponents of "mental simulation" need not be forced into reducing simulation to inference, either.

12.4   Simulation and Inference

Is mental simulation reducible to inference? Following Aronowitz and Lombrozo (2020c), I argue that, according to most conceptions of inference, simulation does not count as a form of inference. Indeed, I will endorse the thesis that simulation-based judgment is *sui generis*.

Aronowitz and Lombrozo's way of arguing that simulation is not a form of inference is to pin down some characteristic features of inference and argue that simulation-based belief lacks these features. Specifically, they consider arguments that pitch some constraint on inference against some features of mental simulation.

To illustrate this general strategy, let us start with a strong constraint on inference. If this constraint were defensible, it would provide very strong reasons to not assimilate simulation to inference. Unfortunately, it will turn out to be too strong, though its exploration will provide some valuable morals. Suppose that inference, whether inductive or deductive, requires a thinker to explicitly endorse the claim that the conclusion is based on the premises.

EXPLICIT ENDORSEMENT. For a thinker to believe **C** on the basis of inference from $\mathbf{A}_1, \ldots, \mathbf{A}_n$, the thinker must endorse a corresponding basing claim, where a basing claim is something of the form **C** *because* $\mathbf{A}_1, \ldots, \mathbf{A}_n$.

This claim conflicts with the idea of assimilating simulation to inference because, Aronowitz and Lombrozo argue, there are mental simulations in which the thinking agent is unable to identify a propositional basis of any kind for their belief. They offer an example drawn from experiments conducted by Schwartz and Black (1999): Imagine being given two cylindrical glasses, each half-filled with water. The glasses have the same height, but one is larger than the other. Next suppose that the two glasses are about to be progressively tilted from vertical to horizontal position, in such a way that at any given moment the two glasses have the same angle relative to the horizontal plane. Which glass will be the first to spill water? Schwartz and Black (1999), as quoted by Aronowitz and Lombrozo, report that people often answer this question incorrectly if the problem is presented verbally. However, people do better if they are invited to close their eyes and run the experiment in their imagination – i.e., if they are invited to simulate the process. (It turns out that the larger glass will spill first.)

The suggestive moral of this case is that sometimes simulation-based judgment can hit on a correct belief even when analytical thinking seems to fall short. For the purposes of the present argument, we don't expect simulation to perform *better* than inference. It is enough to simply exercise the simulation capacity in which the thinker is incapable of endorsing a corresponding basing claim.

SIMULATION WITHOUT BASING. It is sometimes the case that a thinker can form a judgment that **C** by simulation without being able to endorse any corresponding basing claim.

Taken together, EXPLICIT ENDORSEMENT and SIMULATION WITHOUT BASING entail that there are exercises of the simulation capacity that are not inferences.

As I anticipated, the immediate problem with this argument is that EXPLICIT ENDORSEMENT is too strong. Aaronowitz and Lombrozo point out that if we are after a sense of inference that might be available to nonhuman animals, we have to entertain a sense of "implicit inference" in which one can count as inferring even without explicit endorsement of the basing claim.

That may be right. However, Aronowitz and Lombrozo also note that even if we weaken the constraint on inference, the argument still seems to go through.

AWARENESS. For a thinker to believe **C** on the basis of inference from premises $A_1, \ldots, A_n$, the thinker must be aware that their belief in **C** depends on $A_1, \ldots, A_n$.

SIMULATION WITHOUT AWARENESS. It is sometimes the case that a thinker can form a judgment that **C** by simulation without being aware of any premises on which their belief depends on.

In the glass-pouring example, Aronowitz and Lombrozo suggest that one's belief that the larger glass will spill first might depend on several premises. However, the thinking agent might not be aware of such premises, yet still come to the same conclusion.

I suggest taking their argument one step further: I deny that there are premises that the thinker relies on in the glass-pouring case. This denial means that we need not rely on AWARENESS, but on the much weaker claim that for inference to occur, there needs to be reasoning that operates only on symbolically encoded premises. I grant that the glass-pouring example includes potentially representational states, but those states are not enough to qualify the process as inference. In sum, I advance this argument:

CAUSAL CONSTRAINT. For a thinker to believe **C** on the basis of inference from $A_1, \ldots, A_n$, their belief in **C** must be caused by belief, or some similar attitude, toward $A_1, \ldots, A_n$.

SIMULATION UNTETHERED. It is sometimes the case that a thinker can form a judgment that **C** by simulation without it being caused by any kind of belief.

The basic idea behind this last premise is that in simple cases, the operation of imaginative faculty is describable in terms that make no reference to any specific beliefs. We could describe the behavior of, say, the naïve physics module without describing any specific beliefs that play anything like the causal role of premises.

Perhaps one needs to have certain beliefs to have a naïve physics module at all, either because these beliefs are preconditions of basic physical reasoning or because they are immediate downstream consequences of any such module. Maybe one needs to believe that normal solid objects don't mesh together when they bump against each other. But even if that were the case, those beliefs do not play the causal role that is distinctive of premises in inference. The identity of the whole collection of such beliefs is much fuzzier than the identity of the premises one relies on in inference. Finally, agents who are aware of such beliefs would not plausibly count them as reasons for a verdict reached on the basis of simulation. It seems plausible that at least sometimes simulation comes apart from inference.

12.5 Future Judgment and Inductive Reasoning

Let's take stock. We took note of attempts by Kahneman and Tversky, and then later by Williamson, to link counterfactual thinking with mental simulation. As part of the discussion of Williamson's model, I proposed two senses in which mental simulation might be particularly useful in counterfactual thinking. First, mental simulation might be an accessible indirect path to (empirically grounded) judgment in contexts where direct paths are unavailable. Second, even where other paths might be available, simulation might be, in some sense, more efficient (e.g., quicker, or less resource intensive). Next we considered Rips's argument that once we factor in the complexity of many simulation tasks, there is tension between taking simulation to be useful and taking it to be entirely nonsymbolic. The moral I drew was that simulation must allow for symbolic shortcuts. But even so, leveraging arguments by Aronowitz and Lombrozo, I claimed that mental simulation cannot be reduced to inference.

It is time to return to my main topic. It is inviting to think that everything that was said about counterfactual judgment might be said, with very little change, about future-directed judgment. This extension involves accounting for some minor differences. In the counterfactual case, the simulation takes off from a representation of a hypothetical scenario that need not be actual, or even believed to be actual. In the case of (nonconditional) future-directed judgment, the simulation takes off from an agent's representation of the present circumstances (or from their beliefs about the present circumstances).

Reflecting on future-directed judgment in light of what we said about mental simulation reveals some important points that did not emerge from our consideration of counterfactual judgment. Notably, a very significant chunk of our future-directed judgments are formed by inductive inference. Indeed, it is almost a platitude that inductive reasoning serves as a prime vehicle of future-directed beliefs. It is perfectly ordinary practice to form judgments about some future matters by combining the present facts with the laws (broadly understood to include nonphysical laws). If you know that the patient is not pregnant now, you can judge that she won't give birth in two months.

The question concerning how is it even possible for the bulk of our future knowledge to be generated cannot just be reduced to mental simulation. Instead, we require a balanced combination of simulation and inductive inference. The psychological literature on the cognitive processes and systems that power inductive reasoning is sparse, especially by comparison with the literature on deductive reasoning.[11] In one respect, however, there is near consensus: At least some forms of inductive reasoning involve symbolic manipulation similar, though perhaps not identical, to the kinds of manipulations involved in deductive reasoning.

Once we recognize the importance of inductive inference in the case of future-directed judgment, it becomes obvious that some counterfactuals are supported in much the same way. Many counterfactuals, such as *if she had gotten pregnant today, she would not have given birth in a month*, are typically accessible on the basis of inductive reasoning and are not accessible on the basis of (nonsymbolic) simulation-like processes.

The upshot is this: Future-directed judgment and counterfactual judgment do exhibit some fundamental similarities, but we should not focus on simulation as the distinctive driver process powering both. What is most distinctive about (nondeductive) future and counterfactual thought is the combination of inductive and simulation-based learning. In combination, these processes cover a huge critical swath of future-directed (and more generally modal) judgment. Even without a fully articulated theory of the processes involved, we can at least rest momentarily satisfied with this answer to the question of where empirical knowledge of the future could possibly come from.

---

[11]   See the essays collected in Feeney and Heit (2007) for a starting point.

CHAPTER 13

On the Direct Evidence Inference

Back in Part II, I noted Klecha's observation that the phenomena surrounding the acquaintance inference help justify the modal analysis of *will*.[1] Recall that the acquaintance inference paradigm (Section 3.5) consists of inferences to the effect that certain predicates of personal taste require specific associated experiences.

(1)   a.   That soup tastes disgusting ↪ I have tasted that soup
       b.   That soup tasted disgusting ↪ I have tasted that soup

The crucial phenomenon is that modals and future-directed *will* suppress it:

(2)   a.   That soup must taste disgusting ↛ I have tasted that soup
       b.   That soup will taste disgusting ↛ I have tasted that soup

Anand and Korotkova (2018) helpfully call this phenomenon acquaintance inference *obviation*. In this chapter, I seek to capitalize on some of the insights from Chapter 12 to reflect on how modal judgment can relax demands for evidence.

My route to a view about acquaintance inference obviation will not be direct, but rather quite panoramic. Some related phenomena directly involve a stark asymmetry between future on the one hand and past/present on the other hand. In particular, Dilip Ninan (manuscript). has recently identified a puzzle that reveals a critical asymmetry between past and future judgment. After presenting the puzzle, as well as some strategies for its solution, I argue that the modal nature of future discourse is critical to a satisfactory solution. Since I believe that this puzzle is related to the puzzle of acquaintance inference obviation, I suggest a unified treatment.

---

[1]   The present discussion is largely shaped by Pearson (2013), Ninan (2014), Kennedy and Willer (2016), Willer and Kennedy (2016), and Anand and Korotkova (2018).

13.1   Ninan on the Direct Evidence Inference: Background

Here is Ninan's puzzle:

> Andy is a personal chef to a wealthy entrepreneur, Beth. Andy is making a new dish for Beth's dinner tonight (suppose it is a Friday). Based on his knowledge of the sorts of foods that Beth usually likes, Andy says to his friend Chris:
>
> (3)   Beth will like this when she eats it
>
> Andy finishes preparing the dish, and heads home for the night, before Beth gets back from work to eat dinner. When Beth returns, she eats the dish Andy has prepared, and thoroughly enjoys it. The next morning (Saturday), one of Andy's friends asks Andy, Did Beth enjoy the dish you made for her yesterday? Andy hasn't heard from Beth or anyone else whether or not she enjoyed the dish. I think it would seem odd here for Andy to flat-out assert that Beth liked the dish, i.e. to say,
>
> (4)   Yes, she liked it
>
> In order to make that claim, Andy would need to be more directly connected to the fact that Beth enjoyed the dish in question. For example, Andy would need to have been told by Beth or someone else that she did in fact enjoy the dish. Absent evidence of that sort, it would be better for Andy to hedge in some way, i.e. to say one of the following:
>
> (5)   She probably liked it
>
> (6)   She must have liked it – it was just the sort of thing she usually likes

Let us introduce some abbreviations to streamline the presentation:

early = the time at which Andy prepares the meal
late = the time at which Andy reflects on whether Beth liked it
will like = Andy's earlier utterance of *Beth will like this*
did like = Andy's later utterance of *Beth liked this*

When possible, I combine *earlier* and *later* in constructions such as *earlier time*, used to denote the time of Andy's first assertion. The interpretation of these combinations should be entirely unambiguous. I also occasionally, and abusively, use **will like** and **did like** to refer to the propositions expressed in each of these assertion, as opposed to the utterances themselves. Context will help disambiguate.

A variety of judgments could be extracted from the story of Andy and Beth. The basic judgment is:

ASSERTIBILITY ASYMMETRY. Andy's early assertion of **will like** is felicitous, but his late assertion of **did like** is not.

Even those who doubt this should accept a weaker comparative judgment. It would be preferable for Andy at the later time to utter a modalized claim, such as *she must have liked the dish* or *she probably liked the dish*. There is no similar preference for Andy's future-directed assertion at the earlier time. I find the judgment at the center of ASSERTIBILITY ASYMMETRY to be persuasive, and my argument presupposes this is correct (a more complex argument could be run with the comparative claim instead).

Ninan also introduces a more controversial epistemic judgment:

KNOWLEDGE ASYMMETRY. At the early time, Andy knows **will like**, but at the later time he does not know **did like**.

As we will see, this means that there is a parallel puzzle involving knowledge and the specific epistemic judgment in KNOWLEDGE ASYMMETRY.

13.2   Ninan on the Direct Evidence Inference: The Puzzles

I will eventually argue that the puzzles founded on the asymmetry of assertibility are rather disanalogous from ones founded on the asymmetry of knowledge. But in this section I want to set them up as closely as possible.

Start with the assertion puzzle. There is an evident tension between these five claims:

ASSERTIBILITY ASYMMETRY. Andy's early assertion of **will like** is felicitous, but his late assertion of **did like** is not.
CONTENT SAMENESS. Andy's early assertion of **will like** and his late assertion of **did like** have the same content (call this content **like**).[2]
BASIS SAMENESS. At the early time Andy has exactly the same basis for **like** as he does at the later time.[3]

---

[2]   It is not essential to the argument that these be the exact same propositions. In Section 13.3, I identify a much weaker claim that is still strong enough to get the puzzle through. However, it greatly simplifies the presentation to assume that the propositions are identical.
[3]   In many discussions of this puzzle, this observation is commonly presented in terms of the claim that Andy has the same *evidence*. However, under the Williamsonian thesis that one's evidence is what one knows (Williamson, 2000), it would be incoherent to say that his evidence is the same while also insisting there is a difference in whether Andy knows the relevant proposition. For this reason, I prefer the more psychologically laden terminology of *basis*. At the same time, I will speak somewhat loosely and pretheoretically of the "evidential quality" of a basis, referring to refer to how well the basis supports the target claim.

EVIDENTIAL QUALITY. The evidential quality of that basis does not change between the two times (e.g., no new defeaters, either targeting **like** or the support that the basis provides to it).

STABLE ASSERTIBILITY. For any two times t and t', if (i) **A** is assertible at t for speaker s, (ii) s's basis for asserting **A** doesn't change between t and t', and (iii) the evidential quality of that basis doesn't change, then **A** is assertible at t' for s.

With minimal additional background assumptions, these can be shown to be contradictory. One of these five principles has to go.

Ninan views the assertion puzzle as grounded in a similarly structured puzzle about knowledge: STABLE ASSERTIBILITY fails because of a similar failure at the level of the underlying knowledge states.

KNOWLEDGE ASYMMETRY. At the early time, Andy knows **will like**, but at the later time he does not know **did like**.

CONTENT SAMENESS. **Will like** and **did like** are the same proposition (i.e., **like**).

BASIS SAMENESS. At the early time Andy has exactly the same basis for **like** as he does at the later time.

EVIDENTIAL QUALITY. The evidential quality of that basis does not change between the two times (e.g., no new defeaters, either targeting **like** or the support that the basis provides to it).

STABLE KNOWLEDGE. If one knows **A** at t, one's basis doesn't change between t and t', and the evidential quality of that basis doesn't change, then one knows **A** at t'.

As a handy label, I will refer to the two puzzles together as the *directness puzzles*. Epistemic solutions to the directness puzzles involve the claim that STABLE ASSERTIBILITY fails because STABLE KNOWLEDGE does – for example, because knowledge is a rule of assertion.

If this diagnosis is correct, two surprising epistemological conclusions follow. First, knowledge of future states of affairs is significantly "cheaper" than knowledge of similar past states of affairs. We tend to think of the future as significantly less predictable than the past, and thus future knowledge as much harder to come by than knowledge of analogous past events. But if Ninan is right, in some respects the bar for future knowledge is lower than the bar for knowledge of the past and the present. The second extraordinary epistemological conclusion is that knowledge of the future is fragile in a novel, theoretically transformative way: Merely going through time can bring about knowledge loss.

As anticipated, I seek to give disanalogous treatments to the two puzzles. In Section 13.5, I offer some reasons to block the knowledge puzzle at the very first step, by denying KNOWLEDGE ASYMMETRY, which opens up the possibility of holding on to STABLE KNOWLEDGE. While I prefer a dissolution of the epistemic puzzle, I argue that it is possible to meet the assertibility challenge by denying STABLE ASSERTIBILITY.

13.3   Amplifying the Puzzles

It is helpful to quickly dismiss some initially tempting positions on the puzzles that are either easily refuted or implicitly undermined by arguments I have made in previous chapters.

First in line for quick dismissal is the suggestion that the assertion puzzle is due to the fact that **will like** is not an assertion, but rather some other kind of speech act. As I argued in Chapter 9, if it talks like an assertion and quacks like an assertion, then it is an assertion. That argument won't be repeated here.

According to another resistance strategy, we ought to question whether the same proposition is expressed in the two speech acts – i.e., questioning CONTENT SAMENESS. The anodyne version of the challenge starts from the observation that according to some theories of propositions, the propositions in **will like** and **did like** must differ due to their different structures. For instance, according to the Fregean theory of propositions – with propositions identified in very fine-grained terms as structures of concepts – it is impossible for a modal claim and a non-modal claim to express the same proposition.

This version of the challenge is easily dismissed. It is consistent with such theories that the two propositions are very closely related, and in particular that as a result of this relation (and holding fixed the basis and its quality) early assertion of **will like** is felicitous if and only if late assertion of **did like** is. That biconditional is all that the argument needs. Accepting this biconditional is partially warranted by the fact that the two propositions are plausibly associated with the same intension.

A more aggressive challenge to CONTENT SAMENESS would have us deny that two propositions even have the same intension. This outcome is predicted by those views according to which the modal *will* in *she will like this dish* means something like *probably will* or *normally will* or *inevitably will*. In light of the work of this book, no such meaning is close to correct. Chapter 4 highlights the fatal flaws of these views, such as their inability to predict scopelessness facts as well as their inability to even get the beginnings of a story about the probability of such claims. Ninan (manuscript) relies on similar considerations to block this strategy.

Others may suspect that the directness puzzles are tied to some special feature of some class of aesthetic predicates, much like the acquaintance inference is triggered by predicates of personal taste. However, strictly speaking, *liked* in *she liked the dish* is not a predicate of personal taste, since it doesn't pattern with standard predicates of personal taste when it comes to disagreement, retraction, etc. (MacFarlane, 2014). Instead, it is a verb that *reports* one's aesthetic state.

In fact, the phenomenon is not specifically restricted to some category of aesthetic predicates, however broadly identified. The use of aesthetic predicates is inessential to the generate the past/future asymmetries in question.

Consider this contrast:

> [**Future indirect**] Frozen Lake is an unmanned weather station in north-western Canada. The Weather Center has tracked snow patterns at Frozen Lake since 1900. Since 1900, Frozen Lake has seen snow every winter. Dr. Lee knows all of this. On the basis of the track record, she says:
>
> (7)   It will snow at Frozen Lake next year.

This case is parallel to Andy's early assertion in the Beth case. We expect (7) to be generally judged to be felicitous, since the evidence is just about as good as it can get. We also expect (7) to contrast with an analogous past-directed case.

> [**Past indirect**] Frozen Lake is an unmanned weather station in northwestern Canada. The Weather Center has tracked snow patterns at Frozen Lake since 1900. Since 1900, Frozen Lake has seen snow on every documented winter. However, the 2015 data went missing. Dr. Lee knows all of this. On the basis of the track record, she says:
>
> (8)   It snowed at Frozen Lake in 2015.

(8) is defective in a way that is reminiscent of **did like**. Although Dr. Lee's basis appears to be of equal quality as her basis in **future indirect**, that basis is not sufficient to support the judgment.[4]

---

4   Note some differences between this contrast and the original contrast in the tale of Beth and Andy. The present case cannot be described as a case of assertibility/knowledge loss: (7) and (8) in their respective contexts do not express the same proposition. Second, Dr. Lee's basis is stipulated to be similar, but that similarity does not arise from the fact that it is literally the same basis maintained

13.4   The Available Evidence Account

Epistemic approaches to the puzzles maintain that STABLE KNOWLEDGE fails. That is, knowledge does not supervene on one's basis, even when the evidential quality of the basis is fixed.

According to the *available evidence view*, the supervenience basis must include knowledge that is *available to the agent*. At the earlier time, Andy knows **like** – the proposition expressed by both **will like** and **did like** in their respective contexts – because, epistemically speaking, he can do no better than carry out a piece of causally grounded inductive reasoning. By contrast, at the later time, he does not know **like**. At this point, Andy could do better than rely on inductive reasoning: He could obtain direct evidence. Beth is just a phone call away, and what was good enough earlier no longer cuts it.

Although I emphasized the role of knowledge in formulating my view, it's important to note that the available evidence view does not have to be stated in terms of Andy's knowledge. Start with (a part of) Grice's (1975) maxim of quality:

EVIDENTIAL QUALITY.   Assert **A** only if you have enough evidence for **A**.

Next, observe that what it means for an agent to have enough evidence depends partly on what evidence is available. Thinking in terms of what it is to have "enough evidence" helps make this point more intuitively plausible. What counts as "enough" might depend not just on the evidence one has, but also on other evidence that one might feasibly collect. As an analogy, scoring "enough points" in a game does not depend just on how many point one's team scores, but also on how many points the opposition scores.

So far, so good. But in what sense does the availability of new evidence impair Andy's later knowledge? Surely the available evidence account does not involve the claim that one's evidence must always be based on the best available source. It would be utterly implausible, except maybe for a skeptic,

---

through time. What makes (7)–(8) relevantly parallel to **will like–did like** is that her basis should be just as good for the future-directed judgment as it is for the past-directed one.

Of course, we can find cases that mirror the original case more closely. Suppose that every night Andy cooks two meals for Beth, a risotto and a bouillabaisse. Beth can choose which meal to eat for dinner, and which to take to work the next day. Suppose again that Andy is knowledgeable about Beth's preferences on this matter. It seems that earlier, Andy can assert that she will eat the bouillabaisse for dinner and save the risotto. However, at the later time it is defective for him to assert *she ate the bouillabaisse*.

to require that at any given time, one must have the *best* kind of evidence that's available at that time. The idea has to be more coarse-grained. Perhaps there is a fundamental qualitative distinction between the direct and indirect evidential paths. Recall from Chapter 12 that one's basis for the judgment that **A** is a direct path if **A** is causally downstream from the eventualities that **A** deals with. My belief that *Caesar was murdered* is based on a direct path because there is a long and tortured causal chain starting with his stabbing and ending with my belief.

Here is a first pass at a combination of principles that predicts the right verdict in Beth's story: If at time t, there are direct paths that would settle whether **A** and S base their judgment on an indirect path, then S does not have enough evidence for **A**. Alternatively, if no direct path is available to S at t, then whether S possesses good enough evidence depends only on the quality of their indirect basis.

One notable feature of the available evidence view is that it does not treat the puzzles as fundamentally temporal. What matters is what evidence is available and what sort of path one bases one's judgments on. What initially appeared to be an asymmetry between past and future judgments may turn out to be a superficial reflection of the fact that we usually lack direct access to future eventualities.

Problems for the Available Evidence View

Plausible as it may sound, the available evidence view cannot quite be right. Some past-directed assertions based on indirect evidence are felicitous even if direct evidence is available but not possessed by the speaker. While the theory might be patched to deal with these cases, the deadly blow is that some past-directed assertions based on indirect evidence are infelicitous even without direct evidence.

Stable Cases

One of Ninan's core observations is that not every matching pair of past/future assertions gives rise to an asymmetry of assertibility.

> [**Stable assertibility**] Suppose that at 1 PM Simona tells her colleague Akari that she is going to be at the library at 2 PM to return some books. At 2:30 PM, Jess comes into the office wondering whether the books were returned. Jess asks Akari about them and Akari replies: *Simona returned them.*

Intuitively, even though Akari lacks a direct path connecting her to Simona's returning of the book, she is entitled to make her past-directed assertion.

Likewise, there is no barrier to making an assertion that denies the occurrence of extraordinarily implausible events. I can flawlessly assert, without checking for direct paths, that my brother did not just adopt a family of gorillas in the last six hours. My basis involves judgments about his character, habits, and tendency to avoid extraordinarily pointless – perhaps even cruel – acts.

These examples of stable assertibility pose a problem for the available evidence view: If Akari's lack of access to available direct evidence undermines her knowledge, as the view posits, her past-directed assertion should be undermined, too. Instead, it seems perfectly felicitous. Unfortunately, as we will see, the phenomenon of stable assertibility is quite recalcitrant. None of the most promising views of the directness asymmetry have a very satisfactory account of it.

Divorcing Temporality and Directness

Things get quite a bit worse for the available evidence view once we consider cases that are about the past but that stubbornly demand direct evidence even when none is available. In some such cases, the view crashes spectacularly. To establish this point, Ninan (manuscript) sets up a variant of the tale of Andy and Beth:

> [**Beth's death**] The Death case is exactly like the Beth case, except that Beth dies immediately after eating and enjoying the dish. She leaves no trace of the fact that she enjoyed her last meal. On Saturday morning, Andy learns of Beth's death.

Ninan judges, and I agree, that in this variant of the Beth case, Andy's later assertion of **did like** is defective. Since the story stipulates that Andy can do no better than assert **did like** on the basis of indirect evidence, the fact that it is still not assertible at the **later time** suggests that the available evidence view is wrong.

It is a bit more difficult, though not impossible, to generate cases that are about the future and in which direct evidence might be available. To make this possibility vivid, I will illustrate it with yet another vignette.

> [**Future direct**] Marta's colleague Lorenzo is scheduled to land in Rome from Los Angeles on Tricolor Airline at 5 PM. Tricolor Airline is famous for its reliability and punctuality. Indeed, that particular flight from Los Angeles

to Rome has never been late. It is now noon and Lorenzo has been flying for a few hours already, though Marta hasn't checked for any updates. Marta says to her colleague:

(9)　　Lorenzo will land at 5 PM.

Because the trip has already started, it is possible, although very unlikely, that Lorenzo's plane was delayed leaving out of Los Angeles. If it were delayed, there would now be available evidence that the plane won't arrive at 5 PM. The crucial fact that the evidence is available now depends on the fact that Lorenzo's scheduled departure time has already passed.

Despite that possibility, there is no intuitive problem with Marta's assertion of (9) (assuming that in fact the plane is not late). Sure, there *could be* direct evidence that would settle that Marta's assertion is false, but she is intuitively entitled to her assertion.

These considerations create additional trouble for the available evidence view. One can assert a future-directed proposition on the basis of indirect evidence even if there *could be* direct evidence that would establish its falsehood.[5]

13.5　On Future Normalcy

Ninan proposes a different epistemic account of the directness puzzles – one centered on the notion of an "abnormal" development of a history. As with epistemic accounts generally, Andy is said to know the content of **will like** at the **earlier time** but does not know the content of **did like** at the later time, even if those propositions are identical. However, the strategy differs in mechanics and content beyond this point. Suppose that for one to know **A**, one must be able to rule out certain alternatives to **A**. For Ninan, a past/future asymmetry exists in regard to which alternatives must be ruled out to know something. When it comes to whether one knows some proposition that is about future events, possible worlds whose futures are abnormal are treated as irrelevant. However, for propositions that are about past events, worlds that contain past abnormalities are relevant, which means that they may undermine knowledge.

---

[5]　A defender of the available evidence view might stress that their actual hypothesis is that assertibility depends on the existence of evidence that would settle the matter in each of the two possible ways. But surely the **future direct** case might be modified to account for that wrinkle as well.

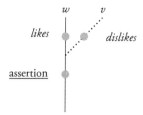

Figure 13.1   Future abnormality

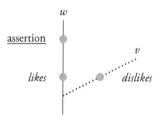

Figure 13.2   Past abnormality

Consider how this strategy might apply to the original Beth vignette. Focus on the **earlier time** and consider a world v that has a similar past to the base world w in the story, but such that Beth dislikes the dish in v.

In the scenario depicted in Figure 13.1, since v has an abnormal future, Ninan's proposal has it classified as irrelevant. By contrast, when the abnormal event is in the past with respect to the assertion, as shown in Figure 13.2, the future normalcy constraint does not apply to v. From the perspective of the **later time**, worlds that were normal up to the **earlier time**, but abnormal between then and the **later time**, must meet the future normalcy constraint (as long as they remained normal after the **later time**).

Ninan develops a formal implementation of this proposal within the relevant alternatives framework (Lewis, 1996). In Lewis's relevant alternatives system, one starts with the idea that s knows **A** in context c if and only if **A** is true at all the relevant worlds (for s in c). The point of the intellectual game is to flesh out a theory of knowledge by specifying the "rules of relevance." Examples of Lewisian rules include the *rule of actuality*, according to which the actual world (in c) is always relevant. Another example is the *rule of reliable method*, which states that if s forms the belief that **A** by a sufficiently reliable method, then the worlds in which the method misfires are classified as irrelevant.

Ninan's proposes adding one more rule to the Lewisian canon: the rule of *future normalcy*. According to this rule, world v is classified as irrelevant for s in c if v contains an abnormality after the time of c. Importantly, there is no matching rule for ruling out past (and present) abnormalities as irrelevant.

The normalcy account threads through many of the extensions I highlighted in Section 13.4. Since it doesn't require a transition, it applies immediately to the transitionless stories involving snow patterns at Frozen Lake. Importantly, it applies cleanly to the gloomy case involving Beth's death: Even if Beth has died and left no trace of whether she enjoyed the dish, nothing rules out an abnormal past in which she did not enjoy the dish (and then died).

Motivational Problems for Future Normalcy Accounts

The normalcy account has some unique advantages over the available evidence view, but it also suffers from some shortcomings. To start, the account relies on what appears to be a magically arbitrary stipulation. If possible abnormalities may stand in the way of knowledge about the past, why shouldn't they also stand in the way of knowledge about the future? Consider the point from the opposite perspective. Suppose there are two brothers: Prometheus, who is tasked with investigating the future, and Epimetheus, who is tasked with investigating the past. If the view is right, Prometheus can restrict future-directed inquiry to normal possibilities, while Epimetheus must always factor in the entire range of possibilities, normal and abnormal. The asymmetry between the two brothers seems arbitrary.

Relatedly, the relevant alternatives apparatus does not do much special explanatory heavy lifting. A solution very much like Ninan's account could be laid out entirely without it. Suppose you started with a stringent knowledge concept $knows_1$, which does not allow for ignoring abnormal futures. Next, define the concept $knows_2$ in such a way that for all propositions **A**, one $knows_2$ **A** if and only if either one $knows_1$ **A** or one $knows_1$ that in all normal futures **A** holds. Finally, stipulate that knowledge is the concept picked out by $knows_2$. It follows that at the earlier time, Andy knows Beth will like the dish, since he knows that in all normal futures Beth likes the dish. However, it also follows that at the later time, Andy doesn't know that Beth will like the dish. Evidently, this disjunctive proposal is not an satisfactory account of the directness puzzles. The challenge for the future normalcy theorist is to explain in which respects the view is more satisfactory than the disjunctive proposal.

Substantial Problems for Future Normalcy Accounts

A more direct problem is the theory's prediction about the **future direct** case. In this case, you have excellent evidence that the plane will land at 5 PM. Nevertheless, in some possible worlds, due to abnormalities in the past, the plane will land at 6 PM. Maybe the plane had a rare technical problem leaving Los Angeles. The future normalcy view seems to predict that this world should count as relevant since its abnormalities are located in the past, and for that reason that my assertion of (9) is defective. But that prediction seems wrong.

This problem can be made more dramatic by considering a variant of this case that was given to me by Paolo Santorio. Suppose that Andy pledges to cook a meal for each member of our department on the occasion of their birthday during the next calendar year. Andy's team will research each of these meals ahead of time to maximize the extent to which the birthday person will enjoy it. Andy and his team are generally remarkably good at this. Now consider *everyone will like their birthday meal.* By analogy with future-directed data in Ninan's example, this a perfectly acceptable claim if made on the eve of the new year – before the meal has been prepared. Crucially, it remains good if you utter it during April of the new year, when some birthdays have already started happening, whether or not you have additional direct evidence that the person liked the meal. Like future direct, the April assertion that everyone will like their birthday meal is partly about the past and partly about the future.[6]

Another problem for the future normalcy view emerges from Ninan's own discussion of **stable** cases, such as my example of Simona's library trip. Ninan tentatively suggests that the future normalcy view can classify them as cases of knowledge (and felicitous assertion) because the possible past abnormalities are ruled out by other criteria under the relevant alternatives picture. In this picture, the role of reliability is codified by the *rule of reliable*

---

[6]   In a quick conversation, Ninan replied to the challenge based on **future direct** by noting that I am squeezing a prediction out of the future normalcy account that the view does not make. Strictly speaking, the future normalcy rule only states that future abnormalities do not undermine knowledge. It does not insist that past abnormalities *do* undermine knowledge – only that they *might* not. This seems right about the view as presented. However, it also means that the view is at best incomplete, since it needs to make predictions about the past-directed cases. Moreover, Santorio's quantified variant makes this move unprincipled, since it relies on the very same kind of judgment that is involved in the basic Beth case.

method sketched earlier, which states that when a belief is formed by a sufficiently reliable method *m*, the worlds in which *m* fails (i.e., the worlds in which it yields a false belief) are classified as irrelevant.

Let us briefly illustrate the rule of reliable method. Suppose that there is a flower in my visual field. There are some possibilities in which my perceptual faculties are mistaken – it's not a flower that I see after all. But because perception is reliable in the base world, those worlds in which I mistakenly believe that I see flower are classified as irrelevant. The rules of reliable methods and future normalcy posit distinct sufficient conditions for irrelevance, but they are not entirely independent: A belief-forming method could be reliable to such an extreme extent that any abnormality in the history of the world is *ipso facto* a failure of the method. Ninan conjectures that this happens in cases of stable foreknowledge: Simona's testimony is so reliable that past abnormalities end up being irrelevant – not *qua* abnormalities, but *qua* failures of a sufficiently reliable method (e.g., trusting a reputable testifier who has no reason to lie).

The implication of this account is that the methods employed in cases of easy foreknowledge are less reliable than the methods employed in cases of stable foreknowledge. Unfortunately, this suggestion does not sit well with the data we have been compiling. In the Frozen Lake variants considered earlier, we made Dr. Lee's indirect evidence as reliable as could be: a perfect regularity which is traceable to a causal mechanism – what causes macroscopic weather patterns at Frozen Lake – and which we have no reason to suppose is being altered. (Well, let's pretend we can forget about global warming.) Surely this is no less reliable than the methods we use in stable cases. Predictions about whether it will snow in a place like Chicago in winter are much less likely to fail than predictions about what an agent will do in the next hour, even if the prediction comes from that agent and even if that agent is sincere.

Problems for All Epistemic Accounts

Problems also arise for all epistemic views of the directness asymmetries, and especially for the core prediction that they involve knowledge loss. Recall that we assumed that at the center of the Beth puzzle is a single proposition, which I labeled **like**. Consider the later time in Beth's case, now focusing on the knowledge ascription:

(10)   Andy knew yesterday that Beth would like the dish.

Is (10) true? If yes, then the following should sound good:

(11)   Andy knew yesterday that Beth would like the dish, but he doesn't
         know now that Beth did like the dish, and the evidence on which
         he bases his belief hasn't changed.

There is something odd about (11), but epistemic accounts appear to sanc-
tion every component of it. In conversation, Ninan suggested a potential
move to push back on (11). Maybe once Andy stops knowing **like**, he doesn't
know the content of (10), and so cannot assert it. This maneuver works
assuming my preferred semantics for *would*.

   However, once we start considering Andy's past-directed *would* judgments, some sharper problems become clear. Plausibly, Andy currently
knows the subjunctive conditional *Bath would have liked the dish if she tried
it*. Furthermore, the story could be amended so that he does know that
she tried it (Beth owns special e-dishes, and through an app on his phone
Andy can check how much food is left on the e-dishes). These conditions
sit poorly with the judgment that Andy does not know that Beth liked the
dish. If that's true, Andy's knowledge is very close to failing to be closed
under counterfactual modus ponens.

   A striking variant of this objection, suggested to me by Matt Mandelkern, starts with acknowledging the plausible truth the following knowledge
ascription in the scenario:

(12)   Andy knows that Beth must have liked the dish

Consider now two big pieces of philosophical orthodoxy.[7] First, *must*-
claims entail their prejacents, so that *Beth must have liked the dish* entails
Beth liked the dish. Second, knowledge is closed under entailment. It then
follows from from (12) that Andy knows that Beth liked the dish. And if
that conclusion is accepted, the assertibility asymmetry cannot be grounded
in the epistemic asymmetry, because there is no epistemic asymmetry.

13.6   The Lexical Account: First Steps

Let's take stock of where we are. There is, I maintain, no epistemic
asymmetry. Andy knows **will like** at the earlier time if and only if he knows

---

[7]   Obviously, these are not uncontroversial. However, enough support for them exists that it's clearly
      a cost of the view to deny them.

did like at the later time. This is compatible both with the nonskeptical take that he knows in both cases and with the skeptical case that he knows in neither case. For the sake of definiteness, and to remind you of my general anti-skeptical tendencies, I adopt the former position – that Andy knows in both cases. My proposal, however, will work for the skeptic as well.

If the asymmetry of assertibility is not grounded in an epistemic asymmetry, then it is plausibly linguistic. That means we must provide a linguistic treatment of it. We can, as always, pray to the implicature gods. But, if I may be curt, I don't see how they might help. Maybe some magic could be performed involving Grice's Maxim of Manner, mandrake root, and dragon teeth, but I haven't been able to cast this particular spell successfully.

A more serious proposal would be to treat the relevant phenomena as presuppositional. Indeed, this is a well-established position when it comes to the acquaintance inference due to works like Pearson (2013) and Anand and Korotkova (2018). In the acquaintance inference case, this amounts to the claim *that chunk of blue cheese is tasty* presupposes that the speaker has tasted the blue cheese or something similar (details, of course, vary between different proposals). In the direct evidence inference case, the move amounts to claiming that *Beth loved the dinner* presupposes that one has direct evidence about the past eventualities one is speaking of.

Unfortunately, there are reasons to avoid a presuppositional treatment. Presuppositions project through *must*; by contrast, as Ninan (2014) points out, neither the acquaintance inference nor the directness requirements do.

(13)   She must have stopped smoking. ($\Rightarrow$ she used to smoke)

(14)   That chunk of blue cheese must be tasty. ($\nRightarrow$ I have tasted it)

(15)   Beth must have loved dinner. ($\nRightarrow$ I have direct evidence of that)

Similar considerations emerge if we consider conditional antecedents.

(16)   If she stopped smoking, someone else smoked this. ($\Rightarrow$ she used to smoke)

(17)   If this chunk of blue cheese is tasty, I will eat my words. ($\nRightarrow$ I have tasted it)

(18)   If Beth loved dinner, I will cook it again. ($\nRightarrow$ I have direct evidence that Beth loved dinner)

Two observations: First, this disanalogy goes through even if we adopt a distinction between "soft" and "hard" presupposition triggers. Soft triggers are supposed to be ones that do not always project in these established ways. But the acquaintance inference and the direct inference *never* project in these ways. Second, it is possible to conceptualize presupposition in such a way that this projection behavior is not constitutive of the category as a whole. Maybe there are different types of presupposition – some giving rise to this projection behavior and some not. If so, the distance between this hypothesis and the view I am about to develop is much smaller.

Let's take stock. We have a growing list of established explanatory patterns that do not quite fit these phenomena. I believe that these systematic failures should lead us toward a radical view: the idea that these evidential constraints are baked in the lexical meanings. This is because meanings are, in fact, complex in a particular way: They encode semantic values (the kinds of things that contribute to truth-values of sentences); they encode (standard) presuppositions; and finally they encode constraints on which type of evidence is demanded by application of a particular predicate.

This idea should probably be the subject of its own book-length discussion, rather than being relegated to the last few sections of the present one. I take solace in the fact that Willer and Kennedy (in press) advocate a version of this idea (with an expressivist twist I won't develop here), in part to deal with the acquaintance inference. Everyone likes a good cliffhanger, so let me end the book by sketching briefly what this theory might look like. Even if all we want is a sketch, we are about to enter fraught dialectical territory. A rich literature already exists on the evidentiality of modals. Though I will attempt to draw the straightest path to some basic conclusions, I want to pause to acknowledge some work that is relevant in a footnote.[8]

Let's start building the account. In a simple, purely denotational view, predicates denote properties, modeled as functions of the appropriate type.

$$[\![\text{died}]\!] = \lambda w \lambda x. \text{ x died in } w$$

$$[\![\text{tasty}]\!] = \lambda w \lambda x. \text{ x is tasty in } w$$

A standard way of encoding presuppositions in this model would be to treat them as conditions of definedness of these functions. Suppose, for the

---

[8] Some of the material that would be most directly relevant to an expansion of the present discussion is in Portner (2007, sections 4.2.2 and 5.3), von Fintel and Gillies (2010), Murray (2014), Matthewson (2015), Korotkova (2016), Winans (2016), Rett (2016), and Mandelkern (2019c). The many references within these works also point to the larger landscape of research on evidentiality.

sake of illustration, that *died* presupposes that its argument lived. Then its partial function meaning would amount to this:

$$\lambda w \lambda x : x \text{ lived in } w. \ x \text{ died in } w$$

This partial function is defined (at w) only within the subdomain of things that lived (in w), and if defined, outputs 1 if the argument is died and 0 otherwise.

Though the dominant approach, the partial function model is not the only model of semantic presupposition available. Some alternative models separate presuppositions and narrow semantic values (understood as contributions to at-issue contents); these are the multidimensional theories of presupposition (Karttunen and Peters, 1979; Sudo, 2012). For example, meanings might be treated as pairs, with the first element being the semantic value and the second element being the semantic presupposition.[9]

(19) $\langle \lambda w.\lambda x.x \text{ lived in } w, \lambda w.\lambda x.x \text{ died in } w \rangle$

This meaning might compose point-wise with the meanings of individual-denoting terms, according to whatever composition rules are appropriate.

From a broader point of view, these multidimensional theories are not restricted to presupposition, but also capture the more general idea that lexical meanings might be rich and complex objects, with many facets and many ways of contributing to communication. In particular, once we model presuppositions in a multidimensional setting, there is no special reason to stop at *two* coordinates. If some element of meaning does not contribute to at-issue content and is not reducible to (standard) presuppositions, we should just treat it as a separate coordinate. Since we have reasons to treat evidential constraints as non-presuppositional dimensions of meaning, that means that we should treat them as additional coordinates.

Before showing how this might work, let me introduce a piece of terminology. Some body of evidence **E** settles whether **A** (relative to some background information **B**) iff **E** either entails or refutes **A** (relative to **B**) – that is, iff **B** ∩ **A** ⊆ **E**. With this concept, the meaning of *died* might now look like this:

(20) $\langle \lambda x.x \text{ died in } w,$
        $\lambda x.x \text{ lived in } w,$
        $\lambda x. \text{ the direct evidence of the speaker of context } c \text{ settles}$
        $\text{whether } x \text{ died in } w \rangle$

---

[9]   This sequence approach has been helpful for those theories that aim to distinguish between different kinds of presupposition – e.g., between semantic and expressive presuppositions.

The first element of the meaning is a contribution to the at-issue content, the second is a presupposition, and the third is a constraint on the type of admissible evidence. Linking the specific evidential constraint to verb meanings allows us to introduce differences between different kinds of verbs. Perhaps predicates of personal taste demand a certain specific kind of direct evidence – say, acquaintance evidence. So here is *tasty* (I use "none" to signify that the presuppositional coordinate is empty).

(21)   ⟨λx.x is tasty,
          none,
          λx. the speaker's acquaintance evidence in c settles whether x is asleep⟩

Things are about to get more complicated. But if developing this theory was just a matter of throwing in one extra coordinate into lexical meanings, they would not be so bad.

13.7 The Lexical Account: Developments

The logical next step would be to theorize about how these evidential constraints project through various embeddings. The principles of projection for evidence-type constraints would also need to be written into their lexical entries. This might look suspicious, but again it seems like a generalization of a standard form that a theory of presupposition projection might take.

Following the playbook of Willer and Kennedy (in press) we might say that negations just inherit the underlying requirements of its arguments. As a result, sentences like

(22)   That is not tasty

(23)   Newton did not die in misery

end up being constrained in the same way as *that is tasty* and *Newton died in misery*.

A preliminary idea about conjunction would be to say that it involves conjoining the evidential requirements of their arguments. Consider this statement:

(24)   That is tasty and Kepler died in misery

The result is that (24) (i) presupposes that Kepler lived and also (ii) is subject to a pair of evidence-type constraints, one per conjunct. In particular,

(24) continues to require acquaintance evidence for its first conjunct and (broadly) direct evidence for its second conjunct. This might work for unembedded conjunctions, but we will shortly see, by considering disjunctions and embedded conjunctions, that things are not quite this simple.

Modals suppress, defuse, or alter these evidence-type constraints, so that when they combine with these predicates the evidential requirement disappears. This behavior is what we wanted to account for why modals such as *must* obviate the acquaintance inference for predicates of personal taste as well as the directness inference for predicates of other kinds.[10]

(25)   That chunk of blue cheese must be tasty

(26)   Beth must have loved dinner

As is crucial to both the account of the phenomena and this book's motivation, these ideas also extend to *will*:

(27)   This tomato juice will be disgusting

(28)   Beth will love dinner

This could be encoded by giving each modal a lexical entry whose third element is a function that reads the evidential constraint emerging from the prejacent and replaces it with a different, more permissive constraint. I'll pause here to note that this is what's critical in accounting for acquaintance inference obviation.[11] This stipulation is also critical in accounting for the obviation of the directness inference by modals, including *will* and *would*, in Beth's case, in **future direct**, in **future indirect**, and in their variants.

Brief victory lap

Let us pause to explore how this analysis might thread through the constraints we've accumulated. In the original story of Andy and Beth, Andy can assert the future-directed claim *Beth will like the dish* because

---

[10]   There are many implementations of this playbook. For example, we don't need to say that *must* wipes out the evidence-type constraints coming from its prejacent. Mandelkern (2019c) argues that *must* generally requires that some argument for its prejacent be salient in context. The picture I am considering allows, but does not require, that this additional constraint be written into the meaning of *must* as part of its evidence-type demands.

[11]   At a high level, this suggestion is pulling the same levers as the presuppositional approaches to the acquaintance inference described by Pearson (2013) and Anand and Korotkova (2018). The main difference is that I deny that this phenomenon is presupopositional.

will suppresses the direct-evidence requirement emerging from *like*. At the later time, Andy cannot assert the past-directed claim because past tense does not suppress direct-evidence requirements. For this reason, STABLE ASSERTIBILITY fails: There are assertibility requirements that are are not fixed by how a speaker related epistemically to the asserted proposition. Instead, these requirements are tied to how the proposition was expressed.[12]

The analysis also makes the right predictions about some of the variants we considered. For starters, it smoothly extends the variant in which Beth dies, as it is treated in the same way as the standard past-directed case. In particular, the assertibility constraint (which is not suppressed by past tense) is not met. Importantly, the reason why the assertibility constraint is not met has nothing to do with whether direct evidence is available, which helps account for the Beth death case. Additionally, the account gives no special place to aesthetic predicates. The account of the Frozen Lake examples is identical to the account that the analysis offers for the story of Andy and Beth.

The analysis also makes the correct prediction in the **future direct** case. Recall that this case was conceived as a verdict about the future (*Lorenzo will land at 5 PM*), which could potentially be undermined by past abnormalities. If the speaker is within their rights to assert *Lorenzo will land at 5 PM* before takeoff, they are still able to do that while the aircraft is in mid-air.

Finally, this type of analysis is a very promising candidate to handle the dynamics of the acquaintance inference. Here I defer to the more extensive discussion by Anand and Korotkova (2018), as well as Willer and Kennedy (in press). The central feature these accounts all share is that: First, they view the acquaintance inference as rooted in *lexical* facts (and in particular, they link it to the semantics of the verb, just as I did here); second, they treat modals as suppressing the inference, again as a matter of how modals deal with evidential constraints pertaining to their prejacents.

13.8 The Lexical Account: Complications

So far, so good. I want to conclude the chapter and the book by highlighting (and inevitably deferring full treatment of) some outstanding problems for this style of account.

---

[12] I take this idea to be commonplace in discussions of evidentiality. My contribution here is to suggest that it's at play in these cases.

First off, both the acquaintance inference and the direct evidence inference can be suppressed without embedding. In the acquaintance case, it is often observed that so-called exocentric uses of predicates of personal taste either do not trigger the acquaintance inference or trigger a modified one (Pearson, 2013; Ninan, 2014; MacFarlane, 2014; Willer and Kennedy, in press).

(29)   That cat food is tasty … though I have never tried it myself!

In the direct-evidence case, we just need to recall a fact that we highlighted earlier: There are cases of stable assertibility. Recall the example of Akari saying *Simona returned the books*, even though her entire relevant evidence is that Simona said she would return them. I can assert confidently that my brother did not just adopt a family of gorillas, without bothering to double check.

Insofar as I have a proposal about these cases, it is that we should decline to theorize too hard about them. But let me hide this point of view behind some fancy language. I suggest – again in agreement Willer and Kennedy (in press) – that we treat evidential constraints as defaults. Sometimes, these defaults are overridden, though the exact dynamics of this overriding are too opaque to be clearly theorized about in terms of precise formal rules. I do plea innocent by association, however, in the sense that I do not know of other convincing systematic explanations of this dichotomy.

A second complication is posed by disjunction. Earlier I said, somewhat casually but also with some foreshadowing, that unembedded conjunction conjoins evidence-type constraints. But it's clear that there is no parallel principle for disjunction. A quick way to see this is by noting that the following disjunctions clearly do not carry any special evidence-type constraints:[13]

(30)   Either it's tasty or it's not tasty

(31)   Either Beth liked dinner or she didn't

Looking at these examples might suggest that perhaps disjunction is like a modal, in that it weakens or suppresses evidence-type constraints. This conjecture is quick to be born and quick to die. This is not what we observe with disjunctions like (32) and (33):

---

[13] Incidentally, this is another way in which these effects do not behave like semantic presuppositions, as *either she stopped smoking or she didn't* still carries the presupposition that she used to smoke.

(32)   Either the pasta is tasty or the salad is

(33)   Either Beth liked the appetizer or she liked the main course

Clearly these examples carry some evidence-type constraints. To properly assert (32), one must have tasted something. It could be the pasta. It could be the salad. Or it could be a magical ingredient that makes anything that it contains it taste great – butter perhaps. And it may be that the speaker is trying to convey that they have evidence that either the pasta or the salad contains the magic ingredient, but they don't know which.

These two reflections suggest that the projection of evidence-type constraints is just as difficult a topic as the projection of presuppositions. They also point to the broad outline of an account that might be on the right track. Let **C** stand in for the contextual information in context c and let $\ulcorner ET_c(\mathbf{A}) \urcorner$ denote the set of worlds that are compatible with the appropriate type of evidence for **A** in c. For example, $ET_c(\mathbf{A})$ might be the set of worlds compatible with the speaker's acquaintance evidence in c. Then say that the evidence-type constraint of **A** *or* **B** is satisfied if and only if:

- $(\mathbf{C} \cap ET(\mathbf{B}) \cap \overline{\mathbf{A}})$ settles whether **B** or
- $(\mathbf{C} \cap ET(\mathbf{A}) \cap \overline{\mathbf{B}})$ settles whether **A**

This projection accounts for why (30) and (31) lack substantive evidence-type constraints, while (32) and (33) have substantial constraints. It also accounts for why the constraints associated with (32) and (33) are substantial but also more permissive than the mere disjunction of constraints.

Finally, these reflections on the behavior of disjunction show that our treatment of the evidence-type constraints associated with conjunction was too simplistic. As Arc Kocurek pointed out to me, *the pasta is not both tasty and not tasty* is just as free of evidence-type constraints as (30). This strongly suggests that conjunction should get a more complex treatment – perhaps something along the lines of what I suggested for disjunction in the previous paragraph (with appropriate modifications). More generally, it suggests that developing this approach will require us to consider with care how evidence-type constraints project through a variety of complex embeddings (propositional attitudes, quantifiers, etc.). The exact formulation of these constraints, as well as whether the whole approach can be made to work at scale, is, as they say, a matter for another occasion.

Bibliography

Abusch, Dorit. 1997. Sequence of tense and temporal de re. *Linguistics and Philosophy*, **20**(1), 1–50.

1998. Generalizing tense semantics for future contexts. Pages 13–33 in Rothstein, S. (ed.), *Events and Grammar*. Vol. 70 of Studies in Linguistics and Philosophy. Kluwer.

Albert, David. 2000. *Time and Chance*. Harvard University Press.

Anand, Pranav, and Korotkova, Natasha. 2018. Acquaintance content and obviation. Pages 55–72 in *Proceedings of Sinn und Bedeutung*, vol. 22.

Aronowitz, Sara. 2019. Memory is a modeling system. *Mind and Language*, **34**(4), 483–502.

Aronowitz, Sara, and Lombrozo, Tania. 2020. Learning through Simulation. *Philosophers Imprint*, **20**(1), 1–18.

Asher, Nicholas, and Lascarides, Alex. 2013. Strategic conversation. *Semantics and Pragmatics*, **6**(2), 1–62.

Austin, John Langshaw. 1975. *How to Do Things with Words*. Oxford University Press.

Bacon, Andrew. 2015. Stalnaker's thesis in context. *Review of Symbolic Logic*, **8**(1), 131–163.

Balcerak Jackson, Magdalena. 2018. Justification by imagination. Pages 209–226 in Macpherson, Fiona, and Dorsch, Fabian (eds.), *Perceptual Imagination and Perceptual Memory*. Oxford University Press.

Barnes, Elizabeth, and Cameron, Ross. 2009. The open future: bivalence, determinism and ontology. *Philosophical Studies*, **146**, 291–309.

2011. Back to the open future. *Philosophical Perspectives*, **25**(1), 1–26.

Barnes, Elizabeth, and Williams, J. R. G. 2011. A theory of metaphysical indeterminacy. *Oxford Studies in Metaphysics*, **6**, 103–148.

Barnes, Eric Christian. 2018. Prediction versus accommodation. In Zalta, Edward N. (ed.), *The Stanford Encyclopedia of Philosophy*, fall 2018 ed. Metaphysics Research Lab, Stanford University. https://plato.stanford.edu/archives/fall2018/entries/prediction-accommodation

Battaglia, Peter W., Hamrick, Jessica B., and Tenenbaum, Joshua B. 2013. Simulation as an engine of physical scene understanding. *Proceedings of the National Academy of Sciences*, **110**(45), 18327–18332.

Beck, Sigrid, and von Stechow, Arnim. 2015. Events, times and worlds: an LF architecture. Pages 13–47 in Fortmann, C., Lübbe, A., and Rapp, I. (eds.), *Situationsargumente im Nominalbereich*. De Gruyter.

Belnap, Nuel. 1992. Branching space–time. *Synthese*, **92**(3), 385–434.

2007. *From Newtonian Determinism to Branching Space–Time Indeterminism*. Unpublished manuscript, University of Pittsburgh.

2012. Newtonian determinism to branching space–times indeterminism in two moves. *Synthese*, **188**(1), 5–21.

Belnap, Nuel, and Green, Mitchell. 1994. Indeterminism and the thin red line. *Philosophical Perspectives*, **3**, 365–388.

Belnap, Nuel, Perloff, Michael, and Xu, Ming. 2001. *Facing the Future*. Oxford University Press.

Bennett, Jonathan. 2003. *A Philosophical Guide to Conditionals*. Oxford University Press.

Bennett, Michael, and Partee, Barbara H. 1972. *Toward the Logic of Tense and Aspect in English*. Indiana University Linguistics Club, Bloomington, IN. Reprinted in Partee (2008), pp. 59–109.

Benton, Matthew. 2012. Assertion, knowledge and predictions. *Analysis*, **72**, 102–105.

Benton, Matthew A., and Turri, John. 2014. Iffy predictions and proper expectations. *Synthese*, **191**(8), 1857–1866.

Benton, Matthew A., and Van Elswyk, Peter. 2018. Hedged assertion. Pages 245–264 in Goldberg, Sanford (ed.), *The Oxford Handbook of Assertion*. Oxford University Press.

Besson, Corine, and Hattiangadi, Anandi. 2014. The open future, bivalence and assertion. *Philosophical Studies*, **167**(2), 251–271.

Bittner, Maria. 2014. *Temporality: Universals and Variation*. Routledge.

Bonomi, Andrea, and Del Prete, Fabio. *Evaluating Future-Tensed Sentences in Changing Contexts*. Unpublished manuscript, University of Milan.

Borghini, Andrea, and Torrengo, Giuliano. 2013. The metaphysics of the thin red line. Pages 105–125 in: Correia, Fabrice, and Iacona, Andrea (eds.), *Around the Tree*. Springer.

Bourne, Craig. 2006. *A Future for Presentism*. Oxford University Press.

Boylan, David. In press a. Does success entail ability? *Noûs*.

In press b. What the future "might" brings. *Mind*.

Boylan, David, and Schultheis, Ginger. In press. The Qualitative Thesis. *The Journal of Philosophy*.

Brandom, Robert. 1994. *Making It Explicit: Reasoning, Representing, and Discursive Commitment*. Harvard University Press.

Briggs, R. A., and Forbes, Graeme A. 2012. The real truth about the unreal future. Pages 257–304 in Bennett, Karen, and Zimmerman, Dean (eds.), *Oxford Studies in Metaphysics, Vol. 7*. Oxford University Press.

Broad, C. D. 1923. *Scientific Thought*. Kegan Paul.

Burgess, John P. 1979. Logic and time. *Journal of Symbolic Logic*, **44**(4), 566–582.

Byrne, Ruth MJ. 2007. *The Rational Imagination: How People Create Alternatives to Reality*. MIT Press.

Caie, Michael. 2011. *Paradox and Belief*. PhD thesis, UC Berkeley.

Cameron, Ross. 2015. *The Moving Spotlight*. Oxford University Press.

Camp, Elisabeth. 2018. Insinuation, common ground and the conversational record. Pages 40–66 in Fogal, D., Harris, D., and Moss, M. (eds.), *New Work on Speech Acts*. Oxford University Press.

Cariani, Fabrizio. 2019. Conditionals in selection semantics. Pages 1–10 in *Proceedings of the 22nd Amsterdam Colloquium*.

2020. On predicting. *Ergo*, **7**(11), 339–361.

In press. Human Foreknowledge. *Philosophical Perspectives*.

Cariani, Fabrizio, and Goldstein, Simon. In press. Conditional heresies. *Philosophy and Phenomenological Research*.

Cariani, Fabrizio, and Santorio, Paolo. 2017. Selection semantics for *will*. Pages 80–89 in *Proceedings of the 19th Amsterdam Colloquium*.

2018. *Will* done better: selection semantics, future credence, and indeterminacy. *Mind*, **127**(505), 129–165.

Carruthers, Peter. 1990. What is empiricism? *Proceedings of the Aristotelian Society, Supplementary Volume*, 63–79.

Ciardelli, Ivano. In press. Restriction without quantification: embedding and probability for indicative conditionals. *Ergo*.

Comrie, Bernard. 1989. On identifying future tenses. Pages 51–63 in Abraham, Werner, and Janssen, Theo (eds.), *Tempus-Aspekt-Modus: die lexicalischen und grammatischen Formen in den germanischen Sprache*. Max Niemeyer Verlag.

Condoravdi, Cleo. 2002. Temporal interpretation of modals: modals for the present and for the past. Pages 59–88 in Beaver, D., Casillas, L., Clark, B., and Kaufmann, S. (eds.), *The Construction of Meaning*. CSLI Publications.

2003. *Moods and Modalities for* Will *and* Would. Handout from the 14th Amsterdam Colloquium.

Condoravdi, Cleo, and Lauer, Sven. 2011. Performative verbs and performative acts. *Proceedings of Sinn und Bedeutung*, **15**, 149–164.

Copley, Bridget. 2009. *The Semantics of the Future*. Routledge.

Crisp, Thomas. 2007. Presentism and the grounding objection. *Noûs*, **41**(1), 90–109.

De Brigard, Felipe. 2014. Is memory for remembering? Recollection as a form of episodic hypothetical thinking. *Synthese*, **191**(2), 155–185.

DeRose, Keith. 1994. Lewis on "might" and "would" counterfactual conditions. *Canadian Journal of Philosophy*, **24**(3), 413–418.

2002. Assertion, knowledge, and context. *Philosophical Review*, **111**(2), 167–203.

Dorr, Cian. 2003. Vagueness without ignorance. *Philosophical Perspectives*, **17**(1), 83–113.

Dorr, Cian, Goodman, Jeremy, and Hawthorne, John. 2014. Knowing against the odds. *Philosophical Studies*, **170**(2), 277–287.

Dorr, Cian, and Hawthorne, John. 2013. Embedding epistemic modals. *Mind*, **122**(488), 867–913.

Dorst, Kevin, and Mandelkern, Matt. *Good Guesses*. Unpublished manuscript, Oxford University.

Douven, Igor. 2006. Assertion, knowledge, and rational credibility. *Philosophical Review*, **115**(4), 449–485.

2009. Assertion, Moore, and Bayes. *Philosophical Studies*, **144**(3), 361–375.

Dowty, David R. 1982. Tenses, time adverbs, compositional semantic theory. *Linguistics and Philosophy*, **5**(1), 23–55.

Dowty, David, Peters, Stanley, and Wall, Robert. 1981. *Introduction to Montague Semantics*. Springer (Synthese Language Library).

Dummett, Michael. 1959. Truth. *Proceedings of the Aristotelian Society*, **59**(1), 141–62.

Eagle, Anthony. *"Might" Counterfactuals*. Unpublished manuscript, University of Adelaide.

2019. Chance versus randomness. In Zalta, Edward N. (ed.), *The Stanford Encyclopedia of Philosophy*, spring 2019 ed. Metaphysics Research Lab, Stanford University. https://plato.stanford.edu/entries/chance-randomness/

Edgington, Dorothy. 1986. Do conditionals have truth-conditions? *Critica*, **18**(52), 3–39.

Egan, Andy, Hawthorne, John, and Weatherson, Brian. 2005. Epistemic modals in context. Pages 131–169 in Preyer, G., and Peter, P. (eds.), *Contextualism in Philosophy*. Oxford University Press.

Enç, Mürvet. 1996. Tense and modality. Pages 345–358 in Lappin, Shalom (ed.), *The Handbook of Contemporary Semantic Theory*. Blackwell.

Etchemendy, John. 1990. *The Concept of Logical Consequence*. Harvard University Press.

Evans, Gareth. 1978. Can there be vague objects. *Analysis*, **38**(4), 208.

Feeney, Aidan, and Heit, Evan. 2007. *Inductive Reasoning: Experimental, Developmental, and Computational Approaches*. Cambridge University Press.

von Fintel, Kai. 1994. *Restrictions on Quantifier Domains*. PhD thesis, University of Massachusetts, Amherst.

1997. Bare plurals, bare conditionals and *only*. *Journal of Semantics*, **14**(1), 1–56.

1999. NPI licensing, Strawson entailment, and context dependency. *Journal of Semantics*, **16**(2), 97–148.

von Fintel, Kai, and Gillies, Anthony. 2010. Must … stay … strong! *Natural Language Semantics*, **18**(4), 351–383.

von Fintel, Kai, and Heim, Irene. 2011. *Notes on Intensional Semantics*. MIT.

von Fintel, Kai, and Iatridou, Sabine. *If and when "if"-clauses can restrict quantifiers*. Unpublished manuscript.

Forbus, Kenneth D. 1983. *Qualitative Reasoning about Space and Motion*. LEA Associates, Inc.

Frana, Ilaria, and Menéndez-Benito, Paula. 2019. Evidence and bias: the case of the evidential future in Italian. Pages 727–747 in Blake, Katherine, Davis, Forrest, Lamp, Kaelyn, and Rhyne, Joseph (eds.), *Semantics and Linguistic Theory*, vol. 29.

Frank, Annette. 1997. *Context Dependence in Modal Constructions*. PhD thesis, University of Stuttgart.

Friedman, Jane. 2019. Inquiry and belief. *Noûs*, **53**(2), 296–315.

Garber, Daniel. 1983. Old evidence and logical omniscience in Bayesian confirmation theory. Pages 99–131 in Earman, John (ed.), *Testing Scientific Theories*. University of Minnesota, Minneapolis.

Gerstenberg, Tobias, Goodman, Noah D., Lagnado, David A., and Tenenbaum, Joshua B. 2015. How, whether, why: causal judgments as counterfactual contrasts. *CogSci*, 1132–1137.

Giannakidou, Anastasia, and Mari, Alda. 2013. The future of Greek and Italian: An evidential analysis. Page 255–270 in *Proceedings of* Sinn und Bedeutung, vol. 17.

   2015. *Predicting the future in Greek and Italian: objective and subjective dimensions*. Unpublished manuscript, University of Chicago and Institut Jean Nicod, CNRS.

   2017. A unified analysis of the future as epistemic modality. *Language and Linguistic Theory*, **36**, 85–129.

Gibbard, Allan. 1981. Two recent theories of conditionals. Pages 211–247 in Harper, William, Stalnaker, Robert C., and Pearce, Glenn (eds.), *Ifs*. Reidel.

Goldberg, Sanford C. 2015. *Assertion: On the Philosophical Significance of Assertoric Speech*. Oxford University Press.

Goldblatt, Robert. 2006. Mathematical modal logic: a view of its evolution. Pages 1–98 in *Handbook of the History of Logic*, vol. 7. Elsevier.

Goldman, Alvin I. 1967. A causal theory of knowing. *Journal of Philosophy*, **64**(12), 357–372.

   1992. In defense of the simulation theory. *Mind and Language*, **7**(1-2), 104–119.

Goldstein, Simon. In press a. *Modal Credence*. Philosophers' Imprint.

   In press b. The theory of conditional assertion. *Journal of Philosophy*.

Green, Mitchell. 1995. Quantity, volubility and some varieties of discourse. *Linguistics and Philosophy*, **18**(1), 83–112.

   2014. *On Saying What Will Be*. Kluwer.

   2017. Speech acts. In Zalta, Edward N. (ed.), *The Stanford Encyclopedia of Philosophy*, winter 2017 ed. Metaphysics Research Lab, Stanford University. https://plato.stanford.edu/archives/win2020/entries/speech-acts/

Grice, H. Paul. 1975. Logic and conversation. Pages 22–40 in *Studies in the Ways of Words (1989)*. Harvard University Press.

Grönn, Atle, and von Stechow, Arnim. 2016. Tense. Pages 313–341 in Aloni, M., and Dekker, S. (eds.), *The Cambridge Handbook of Formal Semantics, Part III: Temporal and Aspectual Ontology and Other Semantic Structures*. Cambridge University Press.

Hall, Ned. 1994. Correcting the guide to objective chance. *Mind*, **103**(412), 505–518.

Hawthorne, John. 2005. Chance and counterfactuals. *Philosophy and Phenomenological Research*, **70**(2), 396–405.

Hawthorne, John, and Lasonen-Aarnio, Maria. 2008. Knowledge and objective chance. In Greenough, Patrick, and Pritchard, Duncan (eds.), *Williamson on Knowledge*. Oxford University Press.

Hawthorne, John, and Lepore, Ernest. 2011. On words. *Journal of Philosophy*, **108**(9), 447–485.

Higginbotham, James. 1986. Linguistic theory and Davidson's program in semantics. Pages 29–48 in Lepore, Ernie (ed.), *Truth and Interpretation: Perspectives on the Philosophy of Donald Davidson*. Blackwell.

Hirsch, Eli. 2006. Rashi's view of the open future: indeterminateness and bivalence. *Oxford Studies in Metaphysics*, **2**, 111–135.

Hockett, Charles D., et al. 1960. The origin of speech. *Scientific American*, **203**, 89–97.

Holguin, Ben. *Thinking, Guessing, and Believing*. Unpublished manuscript, New York University.

Huddleston, Rodney, and Pullum, Geoff. 2002. *Cambridge Grammar of the English Language*. Cambridge University Press.

Iacona, Andrea. 2013. Timeless truth. Pages 29–45 In Correia, Fabrice, and Iacona, Andrea (eds.), *Around the Tree*. Springer.

    Knowledge of Future Contingents. Unpublished manuscript, Universitá degli Studi di Torino.

Iaquinto, Samuele, and Torrengo, Giuliano. 2018. *Filosofia Del Futuro*. Raffaello Cortina.

Icard, Thomas F., Kominsky, Jonathan F., and Knobe, Joshua. 2017. Normality and actual causal strength. *Cognition*, **161**, 80–93.

Ippolito, Michela, and Farkas, Donka. 2019. Epistemic stance without epistemic modals: the case of the presumptive future. Pages 459–476 in Blake, Katherine, Davis, Forrest, Lamp, Kaelyn, , and Rhyne, Joseph (eds.), *Proceedings of Semantics and Linguistic Theory*, **29**. Linguistic Society of America.

Jerzak, Ethan. 2019. Non-classical knowledge. *Philosophy and Phenomenological Research*, **98**(1), 190–220.

Johnson-Laird, Philip Nicholas. 1983. *Mental Models: Towards a Cognitive Science of Language, Inference, and Consciousness*. Harvard University Press.

Jones, Russell E. 2010. Truth and contradiction in Aristotle *De Interpretatione* 6–9. *Phronesis*, **55**(1), 26–67.

Kahneman, Daniel, and Tversky, Amos. 1982. The simulation heuristic. Pages 201–208 in Kahneman, Daniel, Slovic, Stewart Paul, and Tversky, Amos (eds.), *Judgment under Uncertainty: Heuristics and Biases*. Cambridge University Press.

Kaplan, David. 1989a. Afterthoughts. Pages 565–614 in Almog, J., Perry, J., and Wettstein, H. (eds.), *Themes from Kaplan*. Oxford University Press.

    1989b. Demonstratives. Pages 481–563 in Almog, J., Perry, J., and Wettstein, H. (eds.), *Themes from Kaplan*. Oxford University Press.

Karttunen, Lauri, and Peters, Stanley. 1979. Conventional implicature. Pages 1–56 in Oh, Choon-Kyu, and Dinneen, David A. (eds.), *Syntax and Semantics, Volume 11: Presupposition*. Academic Press.

Kaufmann, Magdalena, and Kaufmann, Stefan. 2015. Conditionals and modality. Pages 274–312 in Lappin, S. (ed.), *The handbook of Contemporary Semantic Theory*. Wiley.

Kaufmann, Stefan. 2005. Conditional truth and future reference. *Journal of Semantics*, **22**(3), 231–280.

Kelp, Christoph, and Simion, Mona. 2018. The C account of assertion: a negative result. *Synthese*, 1–13.

Kennedy, Christopher, and Willer, Malte. 2016. Subjective attitudes and counterstance contingency. Pages 913–933 in Moroney, Mary, Little, Carol-Rose, Collard, Jacob, and Burgdorf, Dan (eds.), *Proceedings of Semantics and Linguistic Theory*, **26**. Linguistics Society of America.

Khoo, Justin. 2013. A note on Gibbard's proof. *Philosophical Studies*, **166**(1), 153–164.

2015. On indicative and subjunctive conditionals. *Philosophers Imprint*, **15**(32), 1–40.

King, Jeffrey. 2003. Tense, modality, and semantic values. *Philosophical Perspectives*, **17**(1), 195–246.

Kissine, Mikhail. 2008. Why will is not a modal. *Natural Language Semantics*, **16**(2), 129–155.

2014. *Will*, scope and modality: a response to Broekhuis and Verkuyl. *Natural Language Semantics*, **32**(4), 1427–1431.

Klecha, Peter. 2014. Diagnosing modality in predictive expressions. *Journal of Semantics*, **31**(3), 443–455.

2016. Modality and embedded temporal operators. *Semantics and Pragmatics*, **9**(9), 1–55.

Klinedinst, Nathan. 2011. Quantified conditionals and conditional excluded middle. *Journal of Semantics*, **28**(1), 149–170.

Knuuttila, Simo. 2015. Medieval theories of future contingents. In Zalta, Edward N. (ed.), *The Stanford Encyclopedia of Philosophy*, winter 2015 ed. https://plato.stanford.edu/archives/sum2020/entries/medieval-futcont/.

Kratzer, Angelika. 1977. What "must" and "can" must and can mean. *Linguistics and Philosophy*, **1**(3), 337–355. Reprinted with modifications as chapter 1 of Kratzer, Angelika. 2012. *Modals and Conditionals*. Oxford University Press.

1981. The notional category of modality. Pages 289–323 in Partee, B., and Portner, P. (eds.), *Formal Semantics: The Essential Readings*. Blackwell. Reprinted with modifications as chapter 2 of Kratzer, Angelika. 2012. *Modals and Conditionals*. Oxford University Press.

1991a. Conditionals. Pages 639–650 in von Stechow, D., & Wunderlich, A. (eds.), *Semantics: An International Handbook of Contemporary Research*. De Gruyter. from the *Semantics Archive*.

1991b. Modality. Pages 651–657 in von Stechow, D., & Wunderlich, A. (eds.), *Semantics: An International Handbook of Contemporary Research*. De Gruyter. Reprinted with modifications as chapter 4 of Kratzer, Angelika. 2012. *Modals and Conditionals*. Oxford University Press.

2012. *Modals and Conditionals*. Oxford University Press.

2021. Chasing Hook Quantified indicative conditionals. In Walters, Lee, and Hawthorne, John (eds.), *Conditionals, Probability, and Paradox: Themes from the Philosophy of Dorothy Edgington*. Oxford University Press.

Kripke, Saul. 1958. Letter to A. N. Prior. Dated Sept. 3, 1958. In *The Prior Collection, Bodleian Library, Oxford*. Reprinted in Ploug, Thomas, and Øhrstrøm, Peter. 2012. Branching time, indeterminism and tense logic. Unveiling the Kripke–Prior letters. *Synthese*, **188**, 372–375.

Križ, Manuel. 2015. *Aspects of Homogeneity in the Semantics of Natural Language.* Ph.D. thesis, University of Vienna.

Kroedel, Thomas. 2012. Counterfactuals and the epistemology of modality. *Philosophers' Imprint*, **12**.

Kvanvig, Jonathan. 2009. Assertion, knowledge, and lotteries. Pages 140–160 in Pritchard, Duncan, and Greenough, Patrick (eds.), *Williamson on Knowledge*. Oxford University Press.

Lackey, Jennifer. 1999. Testimonial knowledge and transmission. *Philosophical Quarterly*, **49**(197), 471–490.

2007. Norms of assertion. *Noûs*, **41**(4), 594–626.

2008. *Learning from Words: Testimony as a Source of Knowledge*. Oxford University Press on Demand.

Lassiter, Daniel. 2011. *Measurement and Modality: The Scalar Basis of Modal Semantics.* Ph.D. thesis, New York University.

2017. *Graded Modality*. Oxford University Press.

Leslie, Sarah Jane. 2009. *If, unless* and quantification. Pages 3–30 in Stainton, R. J., and Viger, C. (eds.), *Compositionality, Context and Semantic Values: Essays in Honour of Ernie Lepore*. Studies in Linguistics and Philosophy, vol. 85. Springer, Netherlands.

Levi, Isaac. 2007. Deliberation does crowd out prediction. In Ronnow-Rasmussen, T., Petersson, F., Joseffson, J., and Egonsson, D. (eds.), *Homage à Wlodek. Philosophical Papers Dedicated to Wlodek Rabinowicz.* https://www.fil.lu.se/hommageawlodek/site/papper/LeviIsaac.pdf

Levin, Janet. 2008. Assertion, practical reason and pragmatic theories of knowledge. *Philosophy and Phenomenological Research*, **76**(2), 359–384.

Lewis, David. 1973. *Counterfactuals*. Blackwell.

1979. Counterfactual dependence and time's arrow. *Noûs*, **13**(4), 455–476.

1980. Index, context, and content. Pages 79–100 in Stig Kanger and Sven Ōhman (eds.) *Philosophy and Grammar*. Springer, Dordrecht.

1986a. *On the Plurality of Worlds*. Blackwell.

1986b. A subjectivist's guide to objective chance. Pages 263–293 in *Philosophical Papers*, vol. II. Oxford University Press.

1994. Humean supervenience debugged. *Mind*, **103**(412), 473–490.

1996. Elusive knowledge. *Australasian Journal of Philosophy*, **74**(4), 549–567.

Łukasiewicz, Jan. 1970. On determinism. Pages 110–128 in Borkowski, Ł. (ed.), *Jan Łukasiewicz: Selected Works*. North Holland, Amsterdam.

MacFarlane, John. 2003. Future contingents and relative truth. *Philosophical Quarterly*, **53**, 321–336.

2005. Making sense of relative truth. *Proceedings of the Aristotelian Society*, **105**, 321–339.

2008. Truth in the garden of forking paths. Pages 81–102 in Kölbel, M., and Garcia-Carpintero, M. (eds.), *Relative Truth*. Oxford University Press.

2014. *Assessment Sensitivity*. Oxford University Press.

Maher, Patrick. 1988. Prediction, accommodation, and the logic of discovery. *PSA: Proceedings of the Biennial Meeting of the Philosophy of Science Association*, **1988**, 273–285.

Maitra, Ishani. 2011. Assertion, norms, and games. Pages 277–296 in Brown, Jessica, and Cappelen, Herman (eds.), *Assertion: New Philosophical Essays*. Oxford University Press.

Malpass, Alex, and Wawer, Jacek. 2012. A future for the thin red line. *Synthese*, **188**, 117–142.

Mandelkern, Matthew. 2018. Talking about worlds. *Philosophical Perspectives*, **32**(1), 298–325.

2019a. Bounded modality. *Philosophical Review*, **128**(1), 1–61.

2019b. Crises of identity. Pages 279–288 in *Proceedings of the 22nd Amsterdam Colloquium*.

2019c. Modality and expressibility. *Review of Symbolic Logic*, 1–38.

2019d. What "must" adds. *Linguistics and Philosophy*, **42**(3), 225–266.

In press. If *p*, Then *p*! *Journal of Philosophy*.

Mandelkern, Matthew, Schultheis, Ginger, and Boylan, David. 2017. Agentive modals. *Philosophical Review*, **126**(3), 301–343.

Markosian, Ned. 1995. The open past. *Philosophical Studies*, **79**(1), 95–105.

Matthewson, Lisa. 2015. Evidential restrictions on epistemic modals. Pages 141–160 in Alonso-Ovalle, Luis, and Menendez-Benito, Paula (eds.), *Epistemic Indefinites*. Oxford University Press.

McGee, Vann, and McLaughlin, Brian. 1995. Distinctions without a difference. *Southern Journal of Philosophy*, **33**(S1), 203–251.

Meacham, Christopher J. G. 2010. Two mistakes regarding the Principal Principle. *British Journal for the Philosophy of Science*, **61**(2), 407–431.

Montague, Richard. 1974. *Formal Philosophy*. Yale University Press.

Moss, Sarah. 2013. Epistemology formalized. *Philosophical Review*, **122**(1), 1–43.

2015. On the semantics and pragmatics of epistemic vocabulary. *Semantics & Pragmatics*, **8**.

2018. *Probabilistic Knowledge*. Oxford University Press.

Murray, Sarah E. 2014. Varieties of update. *Semantics and Pragmatics*, **7**, 2–1.

Ninan, Dilip. 2014. Taste predicates and the acquaintance inference. In *Proceedings of the SALT 24*.

2018. Relational semantics and domain semantics for epistemic modals. *Journal of Philosophical Logic*, **47**(1), 1–16.

Assertion, Evidence, and the Future. Unpublished manuscript, Tufts University.

Normore, Calvin. 1982. Future contingents. Pages 358–381 in Kretzmann, Norman, Kenny, Anthony, and Pinborg, Jan (eds.), *Cambridge History of Later Medieval Philosophy*. Cambridge University Press.

Ogihara, Toshiyuki. 2007. Tense and aspect in truth-conditional semantics. *Lingua*, **117**(2), 392–418.

Øhrstrøm, Peter. 2009. In defence of the thin red line: a case for Ockhamism. *Humana. Mente*, **8**, 17–32.

Øhrstrøm, Peter, and Hasle, Per. 2015. Future contingents. In Zalta, Edward N. (ed.), *The Stanford Encyclopedia of Philosophy*, winter 2015 ed. https://plato .stanford.edu/archives/sum2020/entries/future-contingents

Palmer, F. R. 1987. *Mood and Modality*. Cambridge University Press.

Partee, Barbara H. 1973. Some structural analogies between tenses and pronouns in English. *Journal of Philosophy*, 601–609.

    2008. *Compositionality in Formal Semantics: Selected Papers*. John Wiley & Sons.

Pearl, Judea. 2000. *Causality: Models, Reasoning and Inference*. Cambridge University Press.

Pearson, Hazel. 2013. A judge-free semantics for predicates of personal taste. *Journal of Semantics*, **30**(1), 103–154.

Ploug, Thomas, and Øhrstrøm, Peter. 2012. Branching time, indeterminism and tense logic. Unveiling the Kripke–Prior letters. *Synthese*, **188**, 367–379.

Portner, Paul. 2007. Imperatives and modals. *Natural Language Semantics*, **15**(4), 351–383.

    2009. *Modality*. Oxford University Press.

Prior, Arthur N. 1957. *Time and Modality*. Clarendon Press.

    1967. *Past, Present and Future*. Clarendon Press.

    1969. *Papers on Time and Tense*. Clarendon Press. New edition, P. Hasle et al. (eds.), Oxford University Press, 2003.

    1976. It was to be. Pages 97–108 in Geach, Peter, and Kenny, Anthony (eds.), *Papers in Semantics and Ethics*. Duckworth.

Rescher, Nicholas, and Urquhart, Alasdair. 1971. *Temporal Logic*, Vol. 3. Springer Science & Business Media.

Rett, Jessica. 2016. On a shared property of deontic and epistemic modals. Pages 200–229 in Charlow, Nate, and Chrisman, Matthew (eds.), *Deontic Modality*. Oxford University Press.

Rips, Lance. 1986. Mental muddles. Pages 258–286 in Brand, Myles, and Harnish, Robert M. (eds.), *The Representation of Knowledge and Belief*. The University of Arizona Press.

Roberts, Craige. 1989. Modal subordination and pronominal anaphora in discourse. *Linguistics and Philosophy*, **12**(6), 683–721.

Rosenkranz, Sven. 2012. In defence of Ockhamism. *Philosophia*, **40**(3), 617–631.

Santelli, Alessio. In press. Future contingents, branching time, and assertion. *Philosophia*.

Santorio, Paolo. 2017. Conditional excluded middle in informational semantics. Pages 385–394 in *Proceedings of the 21st Amsterdam Colloquium*.

    Trivializing Informational Consequence. In press, University of Maryland, College Park. In press. *Philosophy and Phenomenological Research*.

Saunders, Simon, and Wallace, D. 2008. Branching and uncertainty. *British Journal for the Philosophy of Science*, **59**(3), 293–305.

Schacter, Daniel L., Addis, Donna Rose, and Buckner, Randy L. 2007. Remembering the past to imagine the future: the prospective brain. *Nature Reviews Neuroscience*, **8**(9), 657–661.

Schlenker, Philippe. 2009. Local contexts. *Semantics and Pragmatics*, **2**, 3–1.

Schoubye, Anders J., and Rabern, Brian. 2017. Against the Russellian open future. *Mind*, **126**(504), 1217–1237.

Schulz, Katrin. 2010. Troubles at the semantics/syntax interface: some thoughts about the modal approach to conditionals. Pages 388–404 In *Proceedings of Sinn und Bedeutung*, vol. 14.

Schulz, Moritz. 2014. Counterfactuals and arbitrariness. *Mind*, **123**(492), 1021–1055.

2017. *Counterfactuals and Probability*. Oxford University Press.

Schwartz, Daniel L., and Black, Tamara. 1999. Inferences through imagined actions: knowing by simulated doing. *Journal of Experimental Psychology: Learning, Memory, and Cognition*, **25**(1), 116.

Searle, John R. 1969. *Speech Acts: An Essay in the Philosophy of Language*. Cambridge University Press.

1985. *Expression and Meaning: Studies in the Theory of Speech Acts*. Cambridge University Press.

Searle, John R., and Vanderveken, Daniel. 1985. *Foundations of Illocutionary Logic*. Cambridge University Press.

Sennet, Adam. 2016. Polysemy. In Goldberg, Sandy (ed.), *Oxford Handbooks Online: Philosophy*.

Simion, Mona, and Kelp, Christoph. 2020. Pages 59–74 in constitutive norm view of assertion. In Goldberg, Sandy (ed.), *The Oxford Handbook of Assertion*. Oxford University Press.

Skow, Brad. 2010. Deep metaphysical indeterminacy. *Philosophical Quarterly*, **60**(241), 851–858.

Sloman, Steven. 2005. *Causal Models: How People Think about the World and Its Alternatives*. Oxford University Press.

Spaulding, Shannon. 2016. Simulation theory. Pages 262–273 in Kind, Amy (ed.), *The Routledge Handbook of Philosophy of Imagination*. Routledge.

Sperber, Dan, and Wilson, Deirdre. 1986. *Relevance: Communication and Cognition*. Harvard University Press.

Spirtes, Peter, Glymour, Clark, and Scheines, Richard. 2000. *Causation, Prediction, and Search*. MIT Press.

Stalnaker, Robert. 1968. A theory of conditionals. *Studies in Logical Theory, American Philosophical Quarterly*, **Monograph Series 2**, 98–112.

1976. Indicative conditionals. *Philosophia*, **5**(3), 269–286.

1978. Assertion. Pages 78–95 in *Context and Content*. Oxford University Press.

1981. A defense of conditional excluded middle. Pages 87–104 in Harper, W. L., Pearce, G. A., and Stalnaker, R. (eds.), *Ifs*. Springer.

1984. *Inquiry*. MIT Press (Bradford Books).

1998. *Journal of Logic, Language, and Information (Special Issue on Context in Linguistics and Artificial Intelligence)*, **7**(1). Reprinted in Stalnaker, Robert. 1999. *Context and Content*. Oxford University Press.

1999. *Context and Content*. Oxford University Press.

2002. Common ground. *Linguistics and Philosophy*, **25**(5), 701–721.

Stephenson, Tamina. 2007. Judge dependence, epistemic modals, and predicates of personal taste. *Linguistics and Philosophy*, **30**(4), 487–525.

Stojanovic, Isidora. 2014. Talking about the future: unsettled truth and assertion. Pages 26–43 in De Brabanter, Philippe, Kissine, Mikhail, and Sharifzadeh, Saghie (eds.), *Future Times, Future Tenses*. Oxford University Press.

Stojnić, Una. In press. Content in a dynamic context. *Noûs*.

Strawson, P. F. 1952. *Introduction to Logical Theory*. Methuen.

Strohminger, Margot, and Yli-Vakkuri, Juhani. 2019. Knowledge of objective modality. *Philosophical Studies*, **176**(5), 1155–1175.

Sudo, Yasutada. 2012. *On the Semantics of* Phi *Features on Pronouns*. Ph.D. thesis, Massachusetts Institute of Technology.

Swanson, Eric. 2011. How not to theorize about the language of subjective uncertainty. Pages 249–269 in Egan, Andy, and Weatherson, Brian (eds.), *Epistemic Modality*. Oxford University Press.

Sweeney, Paula. 2015. Future contingents, indeterminacy and context. *Pacific Philosophical Quarterly*, **96**(3), 408–422.

Szpunar, Karl K. 2010. Episodic future thought: an emerging concept. *Perspectives on Psychological Science*, **5**(2), 142–162.

Szpunar, Karl K., and McDermott, Kathleen B. 2008. Episodic future thought and its relation to remembering: evidence from ratings of subjective experience. *Consciousness and Cognition*, **17**(1), 330–334.

Thomason, Richmond H. 1970. Indeterminist time and truth-value gaps. *Theoria*, **18**(3), 264–281.

1984. Combinations of tense and modality. Pages 135–165 in Gabbay, D., and Guenthner, F. (eds.), *Handbook of Philosophical Logic (Volume II: Extensions of Classical Logic)*. Springer.

Todd, Patrick. 2016. Future contingents are all false! On behalf of a Russellian open future. *Mind*, **125**(499), 775–798.

2020. The problem of future contingents: scoping out a solution. *Synthese* **197**, 5051–5072.

Todd, Patrick and Rabern, Brian. In press. Future contingents and the logic of temporal omniscience. *Noûs*.

Tooley, Michael. 1997. *Time, Tense and Causation*. Oxford University Press.

Torre, Stephan. 2011. The open future. *Philosophy Compass*, **6**(5), 360–373.

Torza, Alessandro. 2017. Quantum metaphysical indeterminacy and worldly incompleteness. *Synthese*, **197**, 4251–4264.

Tulenheimo, Tero. 2015. Cross-world identity, temporal quantifiers and the question of tensed contents. Pages 409–461 in Torza, Alessandro (ed.), *Quantifiers, Quantifiers, and Quantifiers: Themes in Logic, Metaphysics, and Language*. Springer.

Unger, Peter K. 1975. *Ignorance: A Case for Scepticism*. Oxford University Press.

Veltman, Frank. 1996. Defaults in update semantics. *Journal of Philosophical Logic*, **25**, 221–261.

Viebahn, Emanuel. 2018. Ambiguity and zeugma. *Pacific Philosophical Quarterly*, **99**(4), 749–762.

Von Stechow, Arnim. 1995. On the proper treatment of tense. In *Proceedings of Semantics and Linguistic Theory 5*.

Weiner, Matthew. 2005. Must we know what we say? *The Philosophical Review*, **114**, 227–251.

Weiner, Matthew, and Belnap, Nuel. 2006. How causal probabilities might fit into our objectively indeterministic world. *Synthese*, **149**(1), 1–36.

Wilensky, Uri, and Rand, William. 2015. *An Introduction to Agent-Based Modeling: Modeling Natural, Social, and Engineered Complex Systems with NetLogo*. MIT Press.

Willer, Malte, and Kennedy, Chris. 2016 Evidence, Attitudes and Counterstance Contingency. *Proceedings of Semantics and Linguistic Theory XXVI*, 913–933.

In press. *Assertion, Expression, Experience. Inquiry*.

Williams, John N. 1994. Moorean absurdity and the intentional "structure" of assertion. *Analysis*, **54**(3), 160.

Williams, Robert J. 2008a. *Aristotelian Indeterminacy and the Open Future*. University of Leeds.

2008b. Multiple actualities and ontically vague identity. *Philosophical Quarterly*, **58**(230), 134–154.

2010. Defending conditional excluded middle. *Noûs*, **44**(4), 650–668.

2000. *Knowledge and Its Limits*. Oxford University Press.

2008. *The Philosophy of Philosophy*. John Wiley & Sons.

Wilson, Alastair. 2011. Macroscopic ontology in Everettian quantum mechanics. *Philosophical Quarterly*, **61**(243), 363–382.

2014. Everettian quantum mechanics without branching time. *Synthese*, **188**, 67–84.

Wilson, Jessica M. 2013. A determinable-based account of metaphysical indeterminacy. *Inquiry*, **56**(4), 359–385.

Winans, Lauren. 2016. *Inferences of* Will. Ph.D. thesis, University of California at Los Angeles.

Yalcin, Seth. 2007. Epistemic modals. *Mind*, **116**(4), 983–1027.

2010. Probability operators. *Philosophy Compass*, 916–937.

2015. Actually, actually. *Analysis*, **75**(2), 185–191.

Zalta, Edward N. 1987. On the structural similarities between worlds and times. *Philosophical Studies*, **51**(2), 213–239.

Index

For EU product safety concerns, contact us at Calle de José Abascal, 56–1°, 28003 Madrid, Spain or eugpsr@cambridge.org.